Speaking Up and Spelling It Out

Speaking Up and Spelling It Out

Personal Essays on Augmentative and Alternative Communication

edited by

Melanie Fried-Oken, Ph.D., CCC-SLP
Oregon Health Sciences University
Portland

and

Hank A. Bersani, Jr., Ph.D.
Western Oregon University
Monmouth

·P A U L·H·
BROOKES
PUBLISHING Cº

Baltimore • London • Toronto • Sydney

Paul H. Brookes Publishing Co.
Post Office Box 10624
Baltimore, Maryland 21285-0624

www.brookespublishing.com

Typeset by Integrated Publishing Solutions, Grand Rapids, Michigan.
Manufactured in the United States of America by
The Maple Press Co., York, Pennsylvania.

Library of Congress Cataloging-in-Publication Data

Speaking up and spelling it out : personal essays on augmentative and alter-
native communication / edited by Melanie Fried-Oken and Hank A. Bersani.
    p. cm.
  Includes bibliographical references and index.
  ISBN 1-55766-447-1
  1. Communicative disorders.   2. Communication devices for the disabled.
I. Fried-Oken, Melanie. II. Bersani, Hank A.

RC423 .S6347 2000
616.85'5—dc21

                                   99-088696

British Library Cataloguing in Publication data are available from the British
Library.

Contents

About the Editors. vii
Contributors ix
Foreword   *Pat Mirenda*. xi
Acknowledgments. xv
Chapters Cross-Referenced by Topic xvii

Prologue: The Communication Dance
   Janice Staehely 1

  1 Fishes, Kayaks, Dances, and Funnels:
    An Introduction to *Speaking Up and Spelling It Out*
    Melanie Fried-Oken and Hank A. Bersani, Jr.. 13

  2 Sand and Sea
    Gregory M. Haslett 29

  3 Confessions of a Blabber Finger
    Gus Estrella 31

  4 If I Do Say So Myself!
    Peg L. Johnson 47

  5 Nobody Knows Me but Me, Myself, and I—
    the Three of Us
    A.J. Brown. 57

  6 Communication My Way
    Tara M. McMillen 77

  7 A Fish Story
    Mick Joyce 87

  8 One Life, Two Countries
    Solomon Vulf Rakhman. 97

  9 My Early Life and Education
    Sharon P. Price 105

 10 To Play Music
    Gregory M. Haslett 115

 11 Reflections on a Kayak Expedition in Scotland
    Spencer Houston 117

12 The AAC Manufacturer's Tale
   Toby Churchill 127

13 Partners with a View
   Laurence C. Thompson and M. Terry Thompson 135

14 Liberating Myself
   William L. Rush 147

15 Empowerment
   David Chapple 153

16 Reaching for the Stars and Almost Touching Them
   Arthur Honeyman 161

17 Others Say So, Too
   Peg L. Johnson 165

18 butt look: a different perspective
   Arthur Honeyman 171

19 How I Communicate
   Gail M. Grandy 173

20 Our Lives, Our Community, Our Caregivers
   Sharon Jodock-King and Alan R. King 181

21 Life with Cerebral Palsy
   Chris Featherly 189

22 Down Memory Lane
   Thomas J. Boumans 195

23 How I Got Here
   Mike Ward 201

24 With Communication, Anything Is Possible
   Jim Prentice 207

25 Making People Laugh and Cry
   Rick Hohn 215

26 I Almost Died, but Somehow I Lived
   Alan R. King 221

27 Just an Independent Guy Who Leads a Busy Life
   Michael B. Williams 231

28 Spaghetti Talk
   Gordon W. Cardona 237

29 More than an Exception to the Rule
   Bob Williams 245

30 Father Warrior of a CP Warrior
   Arthur Honeyman 255

31 AAC: Past Lessons and Future Issues
   Hank A. Bersani, Jr., and Melanie Fried-Oken 259

About the Editors

Melanie Fried-Oken, Ph.D., CCC-SLP, is Associate Professor of Neurology and Pediatrics at Oregon Health Sciences University (3181 Southwest Sam Jackson Park Road, L226, Portland, Oregon 97201). A speech-language pathologist at work, Melanie wears three hats: Director of the Assistive Technology Program at the Child Development and  Rehabilitation Center; Principal Investigator on a University Affiliated Program training grant entitled OTTR (Oregon Technology Training and Resources); and Clinician and Director of the Augmentative Communication Clinic in the Department of Neurology. She has been involved in the field of augmentative and alternative communication since 1979 (when it was still called nonvocal or argumentative communication!). Outside of the office, Melanie wears more than three hats: She is mother of Kiva, Adam, and Corey; partner to Barry; and organizer for all of the hiking, camping, traveling, and adventures that the family takes together.

Hank A. Bersani, Jr., Ph.D., is Associate Professor of Special Education in the School of Education at Western Oregon University (345 North Monmouth Avenue, Monmouth, Oregon 97361). Trained as a special educator, Hank "fell into" AAC in the early 1970s as a first-year teacher working with students with multiple and severe disabilities  who did not speak. These days he trains teachers on ways to integrate children who use AAC into the full range of school activities, from classroom to playground. His favorite piece of personal augmentative communication equipment is a computer with a good word processor and an excellent spell checker to accommodate for his poor penmanship and horrible spelling.

Contributors

Thomas J. Boumans
Broussard, Louisiana

A.J. Brown
West Vancouver, British Columbia
CANADA

Gordon W. Cardona
Alhambra, California

David Chapple
Garfield Heights, Ohio

Toby Churchill
Cambridge
ENGLAND

Gus Estrella
Silver Spring, Maryland

Chris Featherly
Justice, Illinois

Gail M. Grandy
Portland, Oregon

Gregory M. Haslett
Portland, Oregon

Rick Hohn
Vista, California

Arthur Honeyman
Portland, Oregon

Spencer Houston
Fortrose, Rossshire
SCOTLAND

Peg L. Johnson
Minneapolis, Minnesota

Mick Joyce
Madison, Wisconsin

Sharon Jodock-King &
Alan R. King
Seattle, Washington

Tara M. McMillen
Arlington, Texas

Jim Prentice
Monroeville, Pennsylvania

Sharon P. Price
Corvallis, Oregon

Solomon Vulf Rakhman
Philadelphia, Pennsylvania

William L. Rush
Lincoln, Nebraska

Janice Staehely
Portland, Oregon

Laurence C. Thompson &
M. Terry Thompson
Portland, Oregon
Honolulu, Hawaii

Mike Ward
Forest Grove, Oregon

Bob Williams
Silver Spring, Maryland

Michael B. Williams
Berkeley, California

Foreword

This is a book of stories, so I will start by telling one, too:

The phone rang: "Hello?"

"Hi, Pat, it's Jacqui. I'm calling to give you some bad news."

"Oh, yeah, what's that?"

"Rick died yesterday morning. His morning support person arrived at 7:30 and found him, and they think he must have died in his sleep. The funeral is on Thursday, and I thought you'd want to know...."

The funeral was amazing. Literally hundreds of people showed up—family members, friends, support staff from long ago and more recently, self-advocates, social workers, neighbors—everyone, it seemed, who had ever had the good fortune to meet and interact with this funny, affable, independent, committed young man with profound physical disabilities. As person after person stood to tell his or her favorite Rick story, I reflected on Rick's long journey to live in his own apartment and communicate freely.

I first met Rick somewhere in the middle of that journey when I provided augmentative and alternative communication (AAC) supports to young adults with severe and multiple disabilities through a community college in British Columbia in 1990–1991. Shortly before I met him, Rick had received a computer and some software that he was going to operate with a head switch. His staff had contacted me to ask for help programming messages into the device. I went to Rick's home, a house where he lived with three other guys, all of whom were AAC users in one way or another. It didn't take long before I realized that Rick's primary mode of communication was unaided—he was truly one of the most skilled individuals I had ever met in his use of facial expressions, gestures, eye gaze, and vocalizations to get messages across. He also used an old, beat-up Blissymbolics board with numbered symbols on it, combined with a plexiglas eye gaze display with the numbers 0–9. With this system, he sent numerically encoded messages to his support staff, who used the Blissymbolics board as a translation "dictionary," as Rick had long ago memorized its hundreds of Blissymbols and their numeric codes.

"Funny," he responded in Bliss when I asked what types of messages he wanted programmed in his computer.

"Funny? Do you mean jokes?" I asked.

Big smile. I wrote *jokes* on my list.

"What else?"

"Help."

"Help? Things you can say to get other people to help you?"

"No."

"Things you need help with?"

"No."

"Ways of letting us know that one of your roommates needs help?" suggested one of his support staff.

Big smile. I wrote *get help for others* on the list.

And so it went, for more than 2 hours, until there was a long list of messages Rick wanted to be able to communicate. "Great," I said. "Now all we have to do is pick out letter codes for the messages. I guess we should look for easy-to-remember first letter codes, eh?"

Rick gives me a blank, confused look.

"You know, like if you're going to tell a knock, knock joke, we might use the code 'KK' for <u>k</u>nock, <u>k</u>nock."

I get a blank look, again.

"Oh, well, maybe that's not a good example since you might not know that knock begins with a K. Maybe we could code that NN—nock, nock...."

He shakes his head. Stares at me with big eyes. I take a deep breath.

"Rick? You do know how to spell, right?"

He shakes his head, emphatically: "No, no."

"You don't know how to spell? At all?"

"No."

"But this software is for people who know how to spell or at least know the first letters of words."

Shake, shake. "No, no."

"No spelling? Can you read?" I already know the answer.

"No, no."

"So, you can't spell and you can't read, but you have a device that requires you to do at least some of each. Is that right? Am I missing something?"

"No, no."

I'm not missing anything. Too bad.

"So, what do you think we should do about this?"

Big smile. "School."

"School? You figure you should go to school to learn how to read and spell so you can use the machine?"

"Yes. YES."

Fast forward, 1 year later. I hear from a friend that Rick is enrolled in a literacy program for people with disabilities at a local community college. So, I decided to drop by one day to visit him and find out how it was going. The answer: Not too well, actually. Very hard. Not fun. Not much progress. Still, he was excited: maybe someday soon, the letters would all make sense. Meanwhile, his staff had made a meaner, leaner Blissymbolics board for him; he had a part-time job that he shared with an able-bodied support person; he had a girlfriend; weren't the Canucks playing great hockey this season, and . . . so forth and so on.

I ran into Rick again just a few weeks before he died. He had quit the reading class long ago, had given back the computer that needed him to spell, and was still using the Blissymbolics board with eye gaze and partner support. He was also the head of the local advocacy group for AAC users, was active in various community activities, had another part-time job copying data onto a computer spreadsheet using his head switch, and had another girlfriend . . . and life was good, and let's have dinner, okay? Okay! And then, a few days later, the phone rang, and it was Jacqui telling me that he was gone.

Back at the funeral, I listened as person after person talked about how Rick had touched their lives, how he had contributed in important ways to their understanding of themselves and others, how he had COMMUNICATED and SPOKEN ON BEHALF OF himself and others so eloquently. Now, as I read the stories of the AAC users who wrote for this book, I am reminded of how I felt at his funeral—humbled. Humbled by the sheer tenacity of people who have always known they have something to say, even when others told them they didn't, even when they had no way to say it. Humbled by the enormous patience of people who, all their lives, have had to put up with the insensitive comments, the dismissive words, the sometimes-inane "therapeutic" remedies others have imposed upon them. Humbled by the talent reflected in their poems, their stories, and their speeches, and humbled again by the fact that none of these would have been written if they did not have access to AAC. And humbled by the zest for life reflected in all of their contributions, even those written in the face of impending death.

This is a book for people who use AAC and for those who live, work, recreate, or go to school with AAC users. It is a book that I hope will be read by every professional who provides AAC supports and will be used in college and university courses as a complement to traditional AAC texts and articles. It is a book for my friend John and for my Aunt Rose, neither of whom know anything about AAC but both of whom enjoy a good read as much as the next person. And it is a book that I hope will be read by or read to every person who should have—but does not currently have—access to adequate AAC supports. I suspect that those individuals especially need to periodically be reminded that their dream to communicate effectively is shared by many others and is one that can come true. As Rick would say if someone read this book to him: "Good. Good. Yes. YES!"

Pat Mirenda
University of British Columbia

Acknowledgments

We must give our dear thanks to Maxine Heard, who typed out all of the essays and managed the correspondences, e-mails, and emotions that surrounded this book. Thanks also to the members of the Oregon Health Sciences University Assistive Technology team—Tina Anctil, Susan Hanks, Jane Murphy, Janice Staehely, and Emily Smith—for their encouragement.

We also appreciate the augmented speakers who put up with us as we made this journey together. They not only shared their expertise and personal stories but also gave considerable amounts of time and energy to produce what seem like short essays.

Finally, we thank our families who listened over the years while we chattered on and on about the excitement and importance of this project.

CHAPTERS CROSS-REFERENCED BY TOPIC

Essay Topic

Chapter/Author → Essay Topic ↓	Prologue *Janice Staehely*	Chapters 2 and 10 *Gregory M. Haslett*	Chapter 3 *Gus Estrella*	Chapters 4 and 17 *Peg L. Johnson*	Chapter 5 *A.J. Brown*	Chapter 6 *Tara M. McMillen*	Chapter 7 *Mick Joyce*	Chapter 8 *Solomon Vulf Rakhman*	Chapter 9 *Sharon P. Price*
Professional AAC Training			×						
Multicultural Issues and AAC			×					×	
Public Policy and AAC			×				×		×
Self-Determination and AAC	×		×	×	×	×			
Family-Centered Issues	×		×		×	×		×	×
Personal Care Attendants				×		×	×		
AAC in Intensive and Acute Care Settings									
Employment and AAC			×	×		×	×		
AAC for Adults with Severe Aphasia									
AAC for Adults with Acquired Physical Disabilities		×							
Educational Inclusion of AAC Users	×			×		×		×	×
Language Learning and Literacy			×						×
AAC and Developmental Disabilities	×		×	×	×		×		×
AAC Intervention	×			×					
Principles of Assessment				×					
The Role of Technology and Alternative Access	×		×				×		
Vocabulary and Story-telling									
What is AAC?	×			×	×				×

Essay Topic	Chapter 11 Spencer Houston	Chapter 12 Toby Churchill	Chapter 13 Laurence C. and M. Terry Thompson	Chapter 14 William L. Rush	Chapter 15 David Chapple	Chapters 16, 18, and 30 Arthur Honeyman	Chapter 19 Gail M. Grandy	Chapters 20 and 26 Sharon Jodock-King and Alan R. King
Professional AAC Training	X		X					
Multicultural Issues and AAC								
Public Policy and AAC								
Self-Determination and AAC	X						X	X
Family-Centered Issues			X			X	X	X
Personal Care Attendants		X						X
AAC in Intensive and Acute Care Settings		X						X
Employment and AAC		X			X			X
AAC for Adults with Severe Aphasia	X		X					
AAC for Adults with Acquired Physical Disabilities	X	X						
Educational Inclusion of AAC Users								
Language Learning and Literacy								
AAC and Developmental Disabilities				X	X	X	X	X
AAC Intervention	X		X	X			X	
Principles of Assessment								
The Role of Technology and Alternative Access	X	X	X	X	X			X
Vocabulary and Story-telling		X	X		X	X		X
What is AAC?								X

Essay Topic	Chapter 21 Chris Featherly	Chapter 22 Thomas J. Boumans	Chapter 23 Mike Ward	Chapter 24 Jim Prentice	Chapter 25 Rick Hohn	Chapter 27 Michael B. Williams	Chapter 28 Gordon W. Cardona	Chapter 29 Bob Williams
Professional AAC Training			×					×
Multicultural Issues and AAC								
Public Policy and AAC								×
Self-Determination and AAC					×	×		×
Family-Centered Issues	×							×
Personal Care Attendants				×		×		
AAC in Intensive and Acute Care Settings								
Employment and AAC				×				×
AAC for Adults with Severe Aphasia								
AAC for Adults with Acquired Physical Disabilities			×					
Educational Inclusion of AAC Users	×	×		×	×		×	
Language Learning and Literacy	×							
AAC and Developmental Disabilities	×	×		×	×	×	×	×
AAC Intervention	×	×					×	×
Principles of Assessment	×		×					
The Role of Technology and Alternative Access			×		×		×	×
Vocabulary and Storytelling								
What is AAC?						×		

xix

Prologue

The Communication Dance

Janice Staehely

Just as a dance couldn't possibly be a dance unless people moved to it, so language doesn't become communication until people grow to understand and express it back. It has to be a two-way exchange. This is why communicating is an action word.

Janice Staehely is a self-advocate who knows how important it is to speak up not only for herself but for all people with disabilities. She works at Oregon Health Sciences University as a trainer in the Assistive Technology Program. Part of her job is communicating with the doctors through her communication device, to aid them in conversing with their patients who have speaking disabilities. The other part of Janice's job involves speaking to classes at various schools on subjects such as disabilities awareness and self-advocacy. Janice was on the team that helped create the Robert Wood-Johnson grant in Oregon, which is now known as Self Determination Resources, Inc. (SDRI). SDRI's mission is to support people with disabilities to determine and direct their lives with freedom, authority, support, and responsibility. Janice is also a spokesperson for SDRI, and she has recently joined SDRI as a board member. Another committee that she is excited about is It's My Right! Women In Charge, which develops policies and services that empower women with disabilities to take charge of their supports and to be safe from harm. In addition to the above-mentioned activities, Janice also serves on the State Advisory Council for Special Education and the Advisory Board for *The Clarion*, a newspaper that reports on disabilities issues around Oregon. Janice resides in Oregon City, Oregon, and in her spare time she likes to read, write, be with friends and family, and go for walks with her dog, Duke.

I am very honored to have been asked to write this prologue. Although one of my greatest passions in my life is writing, I'd never dreamed I'd write a prologue to a book. Being born with cerebral palsy and living with dysarthric speech has intensified the burning desire to write because it has been the surest way of communicating for most of my life. The subject of this book has always been the most baffling one to me—augmentative and alternative communication (AAC). The hardest and the scariest hurdle of my life to grasp, and I am still grasping for it, is communication! Nevertheless, here I am introducing this book on AAC and enlightening you about my own personal story toward becoming a successful AAC user! How unbelievably thrilling!

Speaking Up and Spelling It Out is unique. More than 25 people who are nonspeaking have contributed chapters expressing their versions of how they developed their own styles of communication. You will read about funny, frustrating, and inspiring stories of these people's struggles and triumphs to conquer communication barriers. Yes, AAC is funny—for instance, when the listener repeats what they think the person who is not a natural speaker has just said, and it's some totally off-the-wall statement. Yes, AAC is frustrating when hardly anyone understands you. And yes, AAC is inspiring when a person finds that perfect communicator and his or her life suddenly takes off. You will find all of these examples in this book, so sit back and let yourself focus on the message each chapter has for you. This book is for everyone who has ever thrown their arms up in sudden helplessness because they had something important to say and had no good way to get the point across and those who communicate with them.

THE COMMUNICATION DANCE

One day as I was listening to the radio, the song "Life is a dance; you'll learn as you go" played. The words sounded so profound to me. I instantly pictured my life as a series of dances. I have been dancing all my life trying to find the perfect song that my feet just couldn't help but kick up and dance too. Just as a dance couldn't possibly be a dance unless people moved to it, so language doesn't become communication until people grow to understand and express it back. It has to be a two-way exchange. This is why communicating is an action word. You have to communicate to get something in return. Going to a dance and wanting to dance are two different things. You can go and sit on the sideline and pose like a beautiful wallflower; however, you will always feel like you're missing something unless you make it out onto the dance floor. Asking someone to dance with you is an action—with some risks involved!

BODY LANGUAGE

If life was one big dance-a-thon, I would have been a very content wallflower. Being the fifth and last child in my family, everyone knew what my every want was just by looking at the way my body was moving. When I was thirsty I would ask for a drink by clicking my tongue against the roof of my mouth. I used a lot of arm, hand, head, and eye pointing to say some words I couldn't get out. For example, if I wanted a straw, I would stare at the cabinet they were in until someone would guess I wanted a straw. I used my feet to communicate urgent messages. I would stomp my feet to get people's attention and then stare outside toward the driveway to let my family know someone was arriving to visit us. I knew how to shed tears or scream bloody murder to let Mom know one of my siblings was picking on me again. My communication skills were always being developed and redeveloped as I noticed which techniques worked and didn't work.

As much as I didn't want to enter the dance floor of life, it soon became very critical for my welfare to learn how to communicate. Sometimes it would take Mom weeks to figure out something that I had been trying to tell her. One such incident occurred when Mom tried to give me some cough syrup. My left arm always stiffens up and tends to fly around when I am excited or when something unpleasant is about to happen. Needless to say, my arm always flew up bumping Mom's arm, only to spill half of the sticky syrup all over the place. Mom thought I was being a brat and not wanting to take my awful tasting medicine. I tried telling her that I didn't mean to spill the syrup, but she didn't understand me. Finally one day just as my left arm was flying up toward Mom's descending hand with the spoon in it, my right arm flew up to grab my left arm and pull it back to my body. Mom's eyes opened wide and she said, "You mean to tell me that you couldn't control your arm before today?!" I nodded, and I was instantly forgiven.

> *I felt locked inside myself, without any clear way of communicating. I couldn't go up to someone I wanted to know better because of the time it takes to talk to me. Communication can be so frustrating at times!*

I learned soon that I was different from my older sisters and brothers. However, at the same time, my siblings taught me the art of good communication skills. Without their constant stimuli of teasing and talking to me like a normal person, I don't think I would have developed into the person I am now. By the constant chatter in the house, I didn't see why I couldn't communicate, too.

Most of the time I felt like the dance

was spinning much too fast for me! I enjoyed listening to conversations. Sometimes I even surprised myself by wanting to add my own two cents, but most of the time nobody knew what I said, and the whole subject would be dropped. This would make me feel sad; I ruined another exciting discussion. So, I grew content to just listen until someone would ask me my view on a subject. Then I would struggle to untie my tongue.

I also felt like everyone knew me, but I didn't know anyone. My family was really good about telling people how I was and what I was doing. I, on the other hand, felt like I was chained to my family, school, and church. I felt locked inside myself, without any clear way of communicating. I couldn't go up to someone I wanted to know better because of the time it takes to talk to me. Communication can be so frustrating at times!

SPEECH THERAPY (HOURS AND HOURS OF IT!)

I traveled about 20 miles every day to a special school designed for children who were physically disabled. I shined like a bright penny at that school! While I went to school there, I felt free to talk my mind, and I always knew that my teachers and friends were patient and willing to listen to what I had to say. I felt very safe and welcomed there. However, there was one thing that I didn't much care for at that school; we always had to leave our homeroom classes where we learned our lessons on the three R's to attend regularly scheduled occupational, physical, and speech therapy sessions. I always felt like I was missing out on learning some important stuff when I went unwillingly to my therapies!

I remember speech therapy was the most challenging of the three. From my early two's, therapists taught me how I should hold my head and torso up so that my lung capacity for speaking could be used properly. It is amazing what a little positioning can do to affect a person's speech performance. If I am sitting all slumped and have my head bent down, people are 10 times more likely to ask me to repeat the words I've said than when sitting in an aligned position.

The typewriter played a significant role in shaping my life. It was the source that led me to discover that I love to write. At school, I had access to an electric typewriter. I think I memorized the keyboard within a couple of weeks of first touching the typewriter. I then started to do my schoolwork on it; there was no turning back from then on! I remember getting my own typewriter to use at home. My grandma felt she had to teach me how to spell my name and the rest of my family's names. I pretended not knowing how to spell my name, because I liked the fact that Grandma thought me capable of learning something. At first I believed that I didn't have much to write about. However, it only took me a little while to figure out that I had tons to write about, and it only took a fraction of a second for my family to figure out that through the typewriter my thoughts were finally being expressed. If I was excited or upset about something, my family fully understood how I felt. I no longer had to worry about getting around words that I couldn't say; I could spell them. My main form of communication soon became something as impersonal as a big, bulky typewriter. I couldn't type anything without feeling that a couple pairs of eyes were waiting for my words to be typed out; nearly nothing I wrote was considered off-limits by my family!

CONTINUING TO BUILD CONFIDENCE

Speech therapists tried to control my drooling habit. What does this have to do with communicating, you ask. A great deal. When I drool, it makes me look more disabled than I really am and it makes most people think twice before talking to me. It takes a lot of self-control for me to keep from drooling. Quite often when I'm concentrating on a task, like this writing project, I'll discover my chin is wet. When I tried to talk to a stranger, the minute I lost my concentration and became so busy trying to talk I would start drooling, and I could feel the stranger pulling away. I was always frustrated and embarrassed when I started drooling! In an attempt to help me stop drooling, I wore a silly looking piece of head gear that matted down my hair and had straps coming down under my chin. Under my chin there was a little cup that collected the drool; it was quite an unpleasant feeling to know that there was drool under my chin and I couldn't wipe it away. Needless to say, it didn't take me long to stop drooling as much. I say "as much" because there will always be some times when I'm going to drool; I'll drool when I'm concentrating on something, I'll drool when I'm tired, I'll drool when my mouth hurts, I'll drool when I get sick, and I'll drool when I see a piece of chocolate in front of me. It took me a while to accept that I drooled. Now it's okay because I know I can control my drooling most of the time.

I remember wanting to be able to say my name properly, because I couldn't pronounce my name, Janice Staehely. Finally one of my speech therapists suggested I try just saying Jan, and use a "d" to make the "ja" sound. It worked! People started understanding that I was saying "Jan." Impressed, my sister Carol asked me how I was able to say my name. I should have never told her, because she started to call me "Dan." When I was in my preteens I was mistaken for a boy a lot, and Carol knew how to irritate me by calling me "Dan" when the people were out of earshot. I would get so mad at her, but in reality I was laughing right along with her, because I too thought it was funny! At least, it was always our little private affair when she teased, and I pretended to be utmost put out by it. Today I laugh at this story because now I remember nobody ever once guessed I was saying "Dan!" I've never stopped using the "d" technique.

THE LANGUAGE BOARD

My speech therapists were always concerned about how I communicated out in public. They wanted there to be a way for me to easily communicate an immediate comment or need. For this reason, cheap labor-intensive handmade language boards were made for me and many of my classmates. The language board was made up of words. Each word group had its own section typed on bright pieces of colored paper. A few of the sections were family and friends, the alphabet, nouns, verbs, adverbs, and adjectives.

As a ploy to get us to use the language board, our speech therapist made up a quiz show type of game that made us race against each other to win prizes. The game was fun, but out in the community the game didn't really help that much. I used my right index finger to point out the words that I wanted to say. Getting my finger to work properly was a task in itself and one thing—finding a flat surface so that I could use the board properly was another. The board unfolded into three different, wide pages; it was impossible to keep the board from slipping off my lap if I didn't have a table to lay it on. Despite all the hard work at practicing to use my language board, I think I always left it at home. In my opinion, it was much easier to use my own voice or to rely on my mom, sisters, or close friends to say my words for me.

THE HANDIVOICE

When I was preparing for the transition to my regular neighborhood junior high school, my far-thinking speech therapist suggested that I needed a better way of communicating. She, of course, was right. I so wanted to be understood at my new school, I agreed to stay at the special school a year longer so that I could learn the Handivoice. The best communicator around in the year 1981 was mine! The Handivoice looked more like a calculator than a communicator. In fact, the key pad had all the numbers that a normal calculator has, plus a row of control buttons. There were 999 selections spoken out by the communicator; a lot of memorization was needed in order to operate the

Handivoice. Each selection had a three-digit code. For instance, "Hi!" would be something like 335. There also were a few key phrases, like, "How are you?" and "I need help!" For quick access, these phrases were one-number hits. For example, "I need help!" would be 100. I only had to hit number 1 and then hit enter; the zeros would automatically be added, and then the computer spoke the phrase. If there was a word that was not in the vocabulary that I needed to say, I had to phonetically sound it out. A name like Carol would be about 21 digits long. By being creative, I was able to cut Carol down to being only six digits long, by using the word "care" and then adding "l" to that word—"CARE-L". When the Handivoice was turned off, everything that I had said prior to turning it off was erased. I remember my speech therapist and I laboriously programming my graduation speech into the Handivoice at the last minute, because I had accidentally turned the Handivoice off and lost the whole speech an hour before graduation began. What a stressful moment in our lives.

My most favorite memory of the Handivoice was when I was 13 and at camp. On the second day, I received a new counselor at the end of rest hour. We were introduced and left alone in the cabin to fend for ourselves. The counselor attempted to put my shoes on. The slightest movement of my dangling feet caused the shoes to fall off. After a few times of her efforts being wasted, the counselor was frustrated and must have been thinking that I was a big, spoiled brat! I, on the other hand, believed that the counselor was hopeless if she couldn't tell that the sneakers couldn't possibly be mine! I started trying to communicate what the problem was. However, I was too excited for my words to come out clear. Finally, I pointed to my Handivoice. With the device I was able to convey a message to her. "Those are not my shoes!" came out in a DEEP electronic male voice. There was a moment of silence, and then laughter broke loose. Laughter was the music that started our friendship.

Despite all my hopes and dreams for the Handivoice to help me become a great communicator, it didn't turn out that way. I just couldn't relate to communicating in numbers; my mind doesn't translate numbers into words. The male voice was an embarrassment to my young 14-year-old, want-to-fit-in self. Plus there wasn't any way I could store my own unique phrases for quicker conversations. However, I found a way to meet my new classmates with the Handivoice by letting them say silly things with it. Feeling that I had let everyone down by turning the device into a toy, I returned the Handivoice to my old school in hopes that someone would find a use for it.

EXCUSES

The excuse that I didn't have much to say to people helped me get out of getting better communication systems. Maybe other people have the same excuse. In my experience, finding words that were clear to speak was very hard to do. Just about half of the letters in the alphabet are hard for me to pronounce correctly, like c, g, h, j, m, n, r, s, v, and z. I am always trying to say easy words that everyone should understand. It's so frustrating to say things over and over again, and just when I think the person might be getting it, she or he will forget the train of thought. What I am trying to say here is that when a person becomes tired of struggling for words that no one can understand, after a little while a person may want to stop talking. You may be thinking here that getting somebody a communication device at this point would be a perfect time. However, I firmly believe that a nonspeaking person has to want a more efficient way of communicating before anyone can wholeheartedly help the person to find a new device. I had become used to not being able to say something in depth to a person that I started to believe that I was a person who didn't have much to tell people. Therefore, for the longest time, I didn't need a communication device that had some kind of mechanical voice that was almost as hard to understand as I was. I fooled myself into thinking that I didn't have anything to say. Today, I still have times where I'm at a party or meeting someone I haven't seen for years and words just won't come to me. It's a part of my character to get all tongue-tied when I'm in these types of situations, but this does not mean that I don't have lots to tell people when I'm in the right humor.

> *I had become so used to not being able to say something in depth to a person that I started to believe that I was a person who didn't have much to tell people. I fooled myself into thinking that I didn't have anything to say.*

It wasn't that getting my first communicator didn't give me some joys while I had the device. One time I had a conversation with a man at a shopping mall while I was waiting for Mom. Through that experience, I saw a small glimpse of what a user-friendly communicator could do for me. Another time when I got the feeling that a communicator could be beneficial to me was the time I talked my dad into building a ramp to get my big wheelchair up in the house. The only problem about my succeeding in getting Dad to build that ramp was that I'm afraid I drove the man crazy in doing so. Since the communicator was so complex to use, I told my dad I would call him a "turkey" until he had that ramp built. He heard the word at least a thousand times. I kept to my promise though—the day the ramp was built, I ceased calling him a turkey!

THE CANON COMMUNICATOR

Knowing that I couldn't very well quit communicating in high school, I clung to the Canon Communicator like it was the best device ever created. The Canon was a small box with keys that held the alphabet on it. As I typed words, a ticker tape would emerge from the side of the box, thus forming my very own paper trail. I believed the Canon was the perfect solution for me. Because I was determined to rely on my voice, I would just use it when I couldn't be understood. The problem was, too many of my words were misunderstood, and I would end up typing yards of ticker tape each day. However, I felt it was easier to express myself through writing, so I didn't mind all the work. The Canon Communicator is light, portable and for all the abuse I put it through, it never broke down.

I feel one of the biggest obstacles I had to overcome as I thought about getting a new communication system is the fear of the unknown. In the past, I was approached lots of times with the question, "Is there a better way for you to communicate?" Many times I just wanted to say something flippant like, "I'm communicating just fine. I like to type out every single word on my Canon Communicator. Seeing yards and yards of ticker type coming out of the Canon gives me a real sense of accomplishment. Don't even suggest I try to learn a new communication device, because I don't have the time or the patience to learn a new system of talking to people!" Nevertheless, once the question was asked, it spun out of control in my mind until I answered it.

THE LIBERATOR

Life is so ironic. No matter how I tried to break free from the square dance, the caller finally grabbed my hand and whirled me back into the familiar pattern of the dance step. In this case, the caller was a speech pathologist who, without a doubt, knew a communication device would enhance my life. My dance pattern turns out to be a form of AAC. In a square dance the group of dancers need to understand the dance pattern the caller has given. I have dropped hands with my dance partner many times, only to do my own jig. Now I realize I was spinning out of control and was messing up the dance for everyone I've wanted to communicate with. After years of being a wallflower, I grabbed hold of an outstretched hand and found many hands to take me into the dance. The Liberator was one of the instruments that played the right music for the steps!

With my new voice, my world began to open up. Cautiously at first, I went to work learning the Liberator; I didn't want another costly communication device collecting dust. However, my positive outlook of finally connecting with people by spoken words gave me the extra push I needed. Soon even my family's skepticism toward the Liberator vanished as they saw my communication with people increase. I will never forget the time when my sister was so pleased that she could keep a conversation with me going while tending her garden.

I can't tell you how much the Liberator has helped me! I can only give you a few scenes. I was able to ask a neighbor to unlock and open my door. Riding the bus with my friend Rosella, I noticed that her wheelchair was not properly fastened down, and I told the bus driver. I can now hold talks with many of my drivers as we drive to work and back. I can tell drivers how to find my apartment. I gave my job proposal almost totally using the Liberator. I can meet new people with confidence. I can give my input to the classes I attend. I can now write wherever I want, because I can open an endless amount of notebooks on the Liberator! And, it's starting to really bother me when people talk for me, or simply misunderstand the Liberator, because they think they know what I'm trying to say.

At times I am just amazed by the Liberator, by the simple fact that people seem to understand it so well, and by my willingness to use it. I thought I would be embarrassed by the voice, but I'm not anymore. Yet I am fully aware that it is a machine, and that at any time it could break down. I haven't given up using my own voice, and the Canon is on standby, waiting for words to be misspelled. Ah yes, they say they will ship a loaner Liberator to me until mine is fixed. And I have many steps that I use for dancing now. The electrifying steps are the Liberator and Canon; the natural steps are my body language and gestures; the quick steps are my computer for

> *I feel complete out in the community when I'm in my power chair and my communicator is in place. Having these two tools combined, I feel the power to do just about anything!*

writing and emailing; the slow steps are my voice, and I'm willing to waltz through any other step to get my message across!

I have come to a full circle on the dance floor! Discovering that I'm not any less of a person for needing a communication device has made all the difference in the world. In fact, I feel complete out in the community when I'm in my power chair and my communicator is in place. Having these two tools combined, I feel the power to do just about anything! I am actually living out a dream. Thanks to the power of a voice, I'm helping people understand how important it is to communicate.

CLOSING COMMENTS

If you are labeled as a nonspeaking person, or know someone who is, and have wanted to communicate more than you could, read the next few lines carefully. You owe it to yourself to think about finding a communicator that is right for you. I used to think that I could just get by with my own voice and interpreters. However, I was missing so much by thinking that I didn't need a communicator. I truly didn't believe that a communicator would ever be created that fits my needs the way my present device does. To think that I almost passed up a chance to be shown the device sends icy chills up my back. Upon hearing the clarity of the female voice, I was hooked: bait, line, and sinker! A person has to keep looking. Technology is making people's lives easier all the time; soon the technology you need will be developed, too.

In closing, I need to make an observation to hopefully ease the minds of parents. It really doesn't matter what communication system I have. What matters is that the system works for me. All too often, a parent will see me speaking with my device and say, "I want my son, Max, to have that communicator." This is what the parent actually means, "I see how well you're communicating, and I would give anything if Max could communicate with me." My advice is, start EARLY! Talk to Max all the time, and make sure you give him time to speak any way he can. Let him know that what he thinks matters. Let him make his own decisions—little decisions at first so that he won't become overwhelmed. If he has practice doing all these things, he will be prepared for his first communication system, whatever that may be.

Each one of us has a different dance step, and that is the most beautiful thing about life! That is what makes everyone unique. Some of us may be slow to start dancing, but once we start, slowing back down is unthinkable!

1

Fishes, Kayaks, Dances, and Funnels

An Introduction to *Speaking Up and Spelling It Out*

Melanie Fried-Oken and Hank A. Bersani, Jr.

SHINING STARS

This book is written by stars. They are people with severe speech and/or physical impairments who have been able to rise above the clouds of negative attitudes, policies, and practices. They have become or remained contributing members of society and their local communities. They have written stories about their experiences that show their dreams, determination, and drive to master communication in the face of societal handicaps. Arthur Honeyman even shares a poem with us called "Reaching for the Stars and Almost Touching

---

The first-person comments in this chapter were written by the first author.

Them." Singers refer to their voices as their instruments. These authors have found their voices with augmentative and alternative communication (AAC) (whether through a sophisticated communication device or a language board), and, by extension, they are virtuosos. They use more techniques to communicate than the average student or reader uses, and they challenge all of us to expand the expressive repertoires of our own natural expression.

PERSONAL VIEWS

You might expect this book to be about clinical evaluations, computer access, or even message selection. Well, you're wrong! It's about fishes, kayaks, dances, and your interactions with a group of well-rounded essayists. The authors have favored us with a unique look into the most personal aspects of their lives. These chapters are reflections of their daily experiences. Each author provides us with some personal wisdom about barriers and opportunities that they have observed or felt because of their communication impairments. Their testimonials span half a century and show how courage and expectations can rise above medical, educational, and vocational predictions for failure. As one author, Gus Estrella, so poignantly states, "Who and what put the dream and desire for succeeding in me? That doctor, who didn't see any hope for me as a member of society. Proving him wrong has been delightful, and everyone should experience that pleasure at some point in his or her life!"

Traditionally, texts have made use of the "case study," where authors or editors select important facts (either *with* an augmented speaker or *for* an augmented speaker) and interpret the facts for the reader. This book is different. Our focus here is on personal stories told in the first person. They are much more vibrant (and, frankly, more interesting) than traditional case studies. True, we have tried to build a collection of essays that hangs together well. And we often provided authors with questions as scaffolds that they could consider or answer in their essays. Some authors chose to structure their essays around our questions, others chose their own issues to address. The authors themselves selected the facts of their lives, retold the facts in words of their choosing, and interpreted the facts so that readers could deduce AAC therapeutic principles. Make no mistake about it, when we say that these authors chose their own words, we mean they physically chose the words. Each author actually typed out their stories using a wide range of access methods and symbols available with AAC. Authors used traditional keyboards with letters and word prediction software, single switches with keyboard emulation software, multi-meaning icons on dedicated devices, pictures on dynamic display devices, sign language, and even traditional pen and paper! These stories were not dictated (though the use of a writing assistant could be an augmented writing technique). Each character was actually produced by the author using augmented writing techniques, creativity, and lots of sweat!

A CHRONICLE

This collection of essays chronicles different stages in the lives of the authors and the people who encouraged them to strive for their greatest potential. Their histories are chronicled using humorous anecdotes, metaphor, poetry, and autobiography. One writer uses a poem to describe his relationship with his father. Some people write about their childhoods; others discuss employment or lack of it. One author refers to himself as a fish! Some of the authors learned to read and write before laws were written to include students with disabilities in school; before laws for equal opportunity and equal access were mandated; and even before technologies were available for portable ventilators, magnetic resonance images (MRIs), electric wheelchairs with head array switches, or personal computers. Two women both have cerebral palsy and are deaf, but their contributions show the diversity of people with disabilities. One of the women, A.J. Brown, grew up at home, went to Gallaudet College, and had a number of jobs. She shares with us her musings about people and their reactions to her. Gail Grandy is a deaf woman who grew up in a state institution for people with severe mental retardation. She taught herself communication strategies and effectively advocated for herself to leave the institution, to live on her own, and eventually to marry. In her essay, Gail chronicles her communication experiences by answering questions with symbols on a language board and dynamic screen device, with body language, and incomplete sentences that conform to her own language rules. Gail and A.J. are authors with similar impairments, different developmental experiences, and diverse stories to share with readers.

Gail and A.J. show us that augmented speakers use different approaches for augmented writing as well. If we consider communication across a natural continuum of expression, then we all use augmentative communication. In a loud bar, we use gestures to augment our spoken messages. In a small seminar class, we scribble notes to our classmates so that we don't interrupt the speaker. We rely on computers and e-mail to converse with family and friends. Readers may think that AAC refers to speaking. In fact, writing is another form of expression that is within the realm of AAC. In this sense, these stories are presented to the readers by augmented authors.

I remember the first time I read an article written by an augmented speaker. It was 1981, and Jimmy Viggiano, my colleague at the Tufts Rehabilitation Engineering Center, had just written an essay for the journal of the American Speech and Hearing Association. Another article by Rick Creech appeared in the same issue. In general, up until the late 1980s, my learning from augmented speakers generally took place in spontaneous face-to-face conversations, with little reading. I read the book of essays written by augmented speakers called *Conversations with Nonspeaking People* (Canadian Rehabilitation Council for the Disabled, 1984) and I read *Annie's Coming Out* (McDonald & Crossley, 1980). But mostly I spoke to people. I met people who advocated for their own discharge from state institutions and had reentered their communities; I watched the film *My Left Foot*; I read newsletters and magazines that featured augmented speakers as subjects, but not as authors. And all along I was providing speech pathology services to children and adults who relied on AAC systems. I don't remember asking their opinions often; I didn't rely on their experiences for message selection or value their input for device customization. After all, *I* was the professional. The professional what? Certainly not the professional augmented communicator!

JUST A FEW FACTS

Augmented speakers are authors. We hope that some day this will not seem odd. The fact is that this is one of the first volumes of its kind. Before you is a collection of 29 essays and poems, written by 27 authors from across the United States and Canada, including authors born in the United Kingdom, Russia, and Mexico. Of these authors, 18 were born with developmental disabilities and diagnosed with cerebral palsy (2 women also have deafness). In fact, the AAC manufacturers tell us that most children and adults who purchase devices have cerebral palsy. The remaining 5 authors have disabilities that they acquired with neurological disease as adults. Their communication was changed forever by stroke, brain injury, encephalitis, or ALS (amyotrophic lateral sclerosis, or Lou Gehrig's disease).

WHY ANOTHER BOOK ON AAC?

New books are appearing at a fast rate in the field of augmentative and alternative communication. We greedily read textbooks (Beukelman & Mirenda, 1998), clinical "how to" books (Light & Binger, 1998), and research-based books (Romski & Sevcik, 1996), written *by* professionals *for* professionals. These books serve an important function. In fact, our respect for and frequent use of Beukelman and Mirenda's book led us to propose this volume. In the acknowledgments section of the second edition, Beukelman and Mirenda plainly state that they depended on AAC users and their families when writing their book. The text is an invaluable resource, written for preservice or continuing education, and it is founded on the perspectives of AAC users. *Speaking Up and Spelling It Out* takes that acknowledgment one step further. AAC users and their families, assistants, and communication partners are the authors and our best teachers. It is, indeed, presumptuous of us to call ourselves teachers when we are simply interpreting the histories, behavior, and expressions of others within the AAC framework.

Beukelman and Mirenda successfully structure information about the AAC field for professionals and students so that facts and training principles are presented. Instead of taking the principles to the next higher plane, with this book we are going in reverse. Simply, we are sharing with the reader the backgrounds, histories, trials, and knowledge of the augmented speakers that permitted Beukelman and Mirenda to define the field and describe its therapeutic principles. We are looking at AAC from a broader base for education, health, and employment. But, as augmented speakers quickly become more able to communicate, their opinions, experiences, and recommendations are not appearing as quickly in our literature. True, we can still read about the augmented speaker's opinion in our newsletters or as invited lecturers at meetings. Some augmented speakers have written articles for scholarly journals. But as AAC becomes a standard lecture topic or course within university syllabi in the disabilities fields, we should be hearing more from the users and consumers of these products.

Today, as augmented speakers are becoming members of advocacy groups and speaking up at family meetings or employment seminars, we should be reading about their experiences and changing our policies, treatment approaches, and device designs appropriately. With this in mind, we began collecting stories by augmented authors. As we collected more personal stories and books written by augmented speakers, we became aware of the lack of a collection of personal stories with multiple perspectives and a wide range of experiences and opinions that could be used by students in many fields. Finally, in our advocacy work, we were aware that advocacy groups throughout this country, as well as professionals in the fields of developmental disabilities, were not hearing from augmented speakers. This collection serves as the response to that void.

HOUSEKEEPING

We'd like to take a minute to discuss some operations of this book. We need to talk about our editing principles and some terminology before we let you dive into the pool of augmented words!

Editing

A few words about editing. We are the editors of the volume, and as such it has been our work to recruit authors, develop topics, suggest ideas, and then get out of the way. We have provided minimal editorial feedback because we wanted to preserve the different communication styles of the augmented speakers. When symbols or sign language was selected for communication, we used the International Notations that have been approved for *Augmentative and Alternative Communication,* the journal of the International Society for Augmentative and Alternative Communication. What you will read here is what people wrote for us. We respected person-first language in the editors' chapters and the language of the authors in the other chapters. We were in frequent communication with many authors to clarify content or ambiguities.

Length

We are both familiar with professional textbooks and the ubiquitous 20-page chapter. The readers among us who are not familiar with AAC will learn to appreciate the physical and motor hurdles that are jumped by these authors to simply put their thoughts into print. Even the shortest essays represent massive amounts of time and, for many, significant physical exertion. One of my earliest teachers, Dr. Rick Foulds, impressed on me how time-intensive it is for an augmented speaker to express him or herself. He told me these facts: The average natural speaker produces 150—300 words per minute. (Those who know us will agree that we are among the 300 words-per-minute speakers!) The average word has five letters in it. The average augmented speaker who is using a scanning keyboard emulator without rate enhancement techniques selects five letters each minute. They, then, are speaking at a one word per minute rate (Foulds, 1980). Successful augmented speakers have learned to use codes, word prediction, and other techniques to speed up their rate of expression. We urge you, however, to be sensitive to the slow production rates for every character printed by each and every author in this book. Experienced AAC readers will already appreciate this fact.

Terminology

We must deal with terminology for a moment. In this book, the person who relies on AAC will be referred to as *an augmented speaker;* and the person who relies primarily on speech or natural writing will be referred to as *a natural speaker.*

Many authors talk about specific devices and software programs that they have used (either successfully or with problems). We have chosen to leave the references to specific devices in the text. Please note we are not endorsing or selecting specific equipment or communication strategies. Rather, we are simply helping people retell their stories about the process of finding a system of communication that fits and keeping up with technological changes. We have tried to describe or demystify names or acronyms of equipment when necessary. For example, VOCA stands for voice output communication aid; MAP stands for Minspeak Application Program. Also, some old devices are criticized repeatedly by different authors. Here again our hindsight raises its ugly head. They are being critical, but the fact is that we need to have appreciation for advances made over time. We are old enough to have a history, one that led us to the technologies of our present state (which also need to be refined).

The Internal Organization of the Book

We discussed the order of presentation of the various chapters for quite awhile. A conscious effort has been made to connect this volume with the Beukelman and Mirenda (1998) textbook, *Augmentative and Alternative Communication: Management of Severe Communication Disorders in Children and Adults, Second Edition.* Although the scope of the volume is not limited to serving as an accompanying text, we believe that it represents a technical and philosophical complement to that work. It contains personal stories specifically selected to supplement chapters in the Beukelman and Mirenda textbook. Consequently, for a time we argued that the organization of the essays should fit the Beukelman and Mirenda text but concluded that each essay addressed so many concerns that a simple parallel to the chapters in the text was not possible. We argued that the practice of AAC can be categorized into three arenas according to funding priorities: education, vocation, and health care. But it became clear that authors addressed each of these concerns in every chapter. Then we argued that the essays should be organized by developmental or acquired disabilities as the authors have insights on communication competence based on their prior success or lack thereof with speech. But grouping by time of disability made us ignore so many important points that the authors emphasized. We finally decided to organize the selections using the *funnel approach:* The volume begins with the chapters that give use the broadest, most inclusive "big picture" of AAC and moves to more selective, single-topic essays. For the reader or educator who needs more organization, we include in the front matter pages a matrix of topics that are covered by each author.

In real lives, all the different topics covered by the chapters come into place. No experiences are about just evaluations or just diversity. Those boundaries don't show up. You can't squeeze someone's experiences into a category. We have resisted categorizing or pigeonholing experiences, opting instead to offer "big picture" insights. Taking the ecological perspective, each essay is a whole picture with all the intertwining parts. Within the field of special education, Lou Brown (1976) coined the phrase "criterion of ultimate functioning." This criterion explores how well communication techniques or approaches work for individuals in the settings where they really use them. The final measure is not their success rate in the special education classroom or in the quiet speech therapy room, but in daily communication with various partners—how it really happens, in real life, in the real world. For the AAC student, the task may seem overwhelming. New clinicians learn to separate each issue, attach measurable parameters to them, and (hopefully) fit the pieces together into one puzzle. That way the AAC specialist can offer specific strategies for intervention. But that's the clinical side of the coin for the augmented speaker. The more interesting "shiny" side for augmented speakers consists of the real-life, real-world experiences that they share in this book. The astute student can read the augmented essays and learn how to integrate the individual issues, measurable parameters, and strategies for creative communication.

SCIENTISTS AND SCHOOL KIDS

Communication impairments affect all kinds of people, so all kinds of people use AAC. We continue to be struck not by the different personal situations but by their overarching similarities. Regardless of whether the authors have developmental disabilities or acquired disabilities or are from the United States, England, or Canada, they all echo the same major concerns: the evolution of technology for people with disabilities and the "goodness of fit" of communication systems for different needs. The underlying issues are strikingly similar, but the people are different. The same issues are raised by scientists and school kids.

TOOLS

A considerable amount of this text addresses the use of tools. *Tool* refers to an instrument, the means whereby something is accomplished. We used to think of tools as objects, but in this technological era, tools also refer to software or development kits or strategies that assist in functioning. I remember when my 2-year-old twin sons learned how to use tools: I was out of the house; my husband was in the shower. Adam and Corey found two empty cups in the kitchen and ran to the bathroom. Giggling, they opened the toilet bowl cover and the drawers in our bathroom vanity and proceeded to pour toilet water into each drawer. Then they closed the drawers and returned the cups to the kitchen. What was all the water pouring out of my bathroom drawers? Ingenious! I also remember commenting to my husband when the twins used the kitchen chairs as tools. They could stand on the chairs and get all the hidden treats they wanted from the cabinets. Geniuses, curious monkeys, or monsters? They had learned to use chairs and cups as tools to increase their daily functioning and activities.

Many of our authors also discuss the use of tools. In fact, for most of our authors, the introduction of communication tools was the start of a new life, of independence, of credibility, of self-esteem, of growth and learning with their community, of better health, and of productivity. These tools were often communication devices that were provided by professionals. More often than not, the authors were not the active children who could discover tool use in bathrooms and kitchens. Often, they were aware of the power of the tools and the need for their use before they even knew they were available. All too often, they had to wait until someone presented a tool to them. And then again, many tools were not good matches but were tolerated until better tools came through.

Lloyd, Fuller, and Arvidson (1997) remind us that the assistive technology tools are but one piece of the augmentative communication system. AAC remains a *human communication process,* with the displays, the communication devices, the assistive technologies, and the symbols being just a few pieces of the puzzle. But the augmented authors here spend a considerable amount of time discussing their tools, the acquisition of the best-matched tools for them, and the frustration that they felt for years before finding the right tools. In fact, it is because of the well-fitted tools that each author can write his or her story here! So many of these stories have a similar theme: the uphill climb to the best tools for written and spoken communication. For some authors, the tools are now seen as a means to an end and viewed from the perspective of active adults.

We can smile and even laugh at some of the challenges they overcome with the tools.

From another perspective, this book serves as a tool for us. Its function is to present personal experiences to students and professionals who are learning about the power of AAC and the power of the determined people who use it.

The stories serve as tools for their authors, as well. Through this medium, the person of experience can teach the naive reader about values, ethics, and practices encountered by the augmented speaker. And the authors can critique the tools that the professionals have developed for assessment, evaluation, intervention, and development. They can share their experiences with our practice: the good, the bad, and the, sometimes, ugly.

Finally, the reader can be viewed as a tool and an agent of change whose responsibility it is to learn from these personal stories and improve the attitudes, policies, and practices affecting people with severe communication impairments.

There are two kinds of fit that are important with tools: The tool has to fit the job (you don't hammer with a saw and you don't cut with a hammer), and the tool has to fit the worker (the size of the handle must match the size of the user's hand). In the same vein, the AAC tools have to fit the communication task and the communicator. A lot of the messages from the authors are about good or bad fits. What we would call technology abandonment is really either the case of a tool not fitting the task or not fitting the speaker. Our role here is not to tell readers how to conduct an environmental inventory, an ecological inventory, or a multidisciplinary assessment. They can locate that information in Beukelman and Mirenda's (1998) textbook. Rather, you will read about the results of good and bad assessments and about the evolution of the AAC assessment process by folks who experienced it. As readers, you are privileged to get first-hand views of AAC history unfolding before its consumers.

HISTORY

The field of AAC, as told by many authors here, started the same way that people invent tools in their backyards and garages to meet their needs. Alan R. King describes the ingenious rolling pins that were covered with symbols he accessed with his feet! Those of us trying to develop AAC tools began as tinkerers and consumers. As the field became more "professionalized," we somehow lost that primary input and opinion from the consumer and families. We designed some tools that were too cumbersome to use. But the consumer still tackled the odds and worked with the therapists. The authors in this book will mention over and over again how they accepted anything that the professional said for a period of time when choices were limited and the the consumer's input was limited. Gordon Cordona and Thomas Boumans take us through their personal chronology with VOCAs. Gordon admits that he thought it was fun and an honor to be evaluated for equipment and to play with many communication devices. But, he said, most devices were either too simple, had strange sounding voices, or were too big. His personal device trials mirror the chronology of communication device development and technology transfer. In Beukelman and Mirenda, we can read about the intelligibility of synthetic speech by communication partners, and then we can read Janice Staehely's personal description of how she used a deep male voice that was an embarrassment to her at age 14. The authors, indeed, *augment* the data presented in the various related textbooks. With changes in advocacy, in the role of disability in society, in legislation, and in the power of augmented writing, consumers are now more active, and the choices are greater. What we analyze in policy debates and eduational reform is creatively chronicled by augmented authors with personal stories. We have grown from the tinkerer-driven position to the engineer-driven position and now work somewhere between those two poles. The bar has been raised.

The same history is reflected in the old clinical argument about the appearance of speech or absence of speech upon introduction of a communication system. Larry and Terry Thompson repeatedly discuss the value of even a single word for the perceptions of communication competence. The authors who give us their device histories often start with statements about how their speech-language pathologists (SLPs) had them work very hard to control their athetoid mouths or to speak more clearly. Then the same SLP told them to abandon all speech attempts for devices with limited functions that could never provide enough language for their abilities. Now professionals suggest using speech for specific functions, including speech as one mode of communication in a complete augmentative communication system, and looking at other approaches that meet the user's needs in a participatory environment. Tara McMillen tells us how she, indeed, uses her personal assistant as one of her communication modes. The complexity of the communication system and its many approaches is discussed repeatedly by Beukelman and Mirenda (1998). The pendulum has swung from all speech to no speech to a middle position of accepting speech along with other approaches. AAC has a history now, and it parallels the swings in the clinical history as well.

SPECIAL INTERESTS

One of the pleasures of the editor's job is directing readers to some of the gems in the book. We know that you will get hooked on this volume as we did. You'll laugh aloud, tell your friends and colleagues some intriguing stories, and have a greater appreciation for people who live with communication disabilities. There are so many interesting stories recounted by our authors in this short volume that it is difficult to point to just a few highlights. Readers with questions about alternative access should read Mike Ward and A.J. Brown. Readers with a special interest in cultural issues will want to read Gus Estrella and Solomon Rakhman. The rocky road of employment is discussed by Mick Joyce, David Chapple, and Jim Prentice. If you are partial to poetry, then read the contributions by Gregory Haslett and Arthur Honeyman. Policies and the result of their enactment are discussed by Mick Joyce, Gus Estrella, and Sharon Price. The reader repeatedly will come upon some version of the message, "My parents were told that I would be as good as a vegetable." This is true whether the author was born in Russia, Mexico, Canada, or the United States. The travels of these "vegetables" is what led us to this "salad."

This book is, indeed, composed by those limited by the low expectations of naysayers, who outsmarted even their own bodies and became contributing members of society. A number of essayists discuss their early language learning skills, horrific speech therapy lessons, and the expectations of their teachers, parents, and therapists when they were young. Janice Staehely tells us about the cup she wore at the end of her chin to collect drool. It immediately improved her saliva control despite her therapists! She describes the hours of speech therapy that went nowhere. For many augmented writers, the attitudes and perceptions of their teachers and therapists were greater obstacles to communication than were their parents or even their physical impairments. A number of authors address evaluations, assessments, and testing. Peg Johnson remembers a critical moment from her young adulthood: "My IQ needed to be rechecked to attend high school. Being put in a room with a spooky, scary man whom I had never seen before was a horrific experience. My athetosis took over. Every muscle in my body froze!" That physical reaction is reiterated by other authors, including Alan King when he describes his ordeal in the hospital and David Chapple when he was so excited about getting that special call from his prospective employer that he lost control of his wheelchair and hung up on his future boss! It is a wake-up call for professionals who expect assessments to be completed in a timely fashion and clients to "try their hardest" when they are being assessed. We have all heard parents say that their children perform so much better at home than in school or in a clinical setting. The authors give us some reasons why. We should all listen carefully and adjust our expectations, protocols, and procedures, as Beukelman and Mirenda (1998) suggest.

The reader will be surprised by the medical community's lack of understanding of cerebral palsy and communication disabilities. Both Alan King and A.J. Brown discuss searches for diagnoses while working with physicians who really don't have a full picture of what they are confronting. A.J. remembers being a "hot potato" and going from neurologist to neurologist, with no eventual diagnosis. Because they cannot arrive at a diagnosis, she feels as if she is just a common weed instead of a rare breed of flower, but she boasts of being a hardy dandelion notwithstanding!

Some of the biggest issues for the new students of AAC are givens for the veteran users. Alan King, instead of spending a lot of time talking about how the foot was chosen as the access site, doesn't even address this as an issue. It is a given, not an important point, that he uses his foot for direct selection. Toby Churchill doesn't discuss his struggle to find the best device. He begins his narrative with the invention of the LightWRITER and minimizes his disability while bragging about his creativity.

A number of essays address personal care assistants and tell horror stories about experiences when one person is dependent on another. The authors describe good staff, bad staff, and needing to fire staff who could not be trusted. Sharon King tells us about the staff member who contemplated committing suicide with her stash of pills. Most authors report that mutual respect is needed if the personal assistant relationship is going to work. Tara McMillen raises the issue of whether a personal assistant is more than an employee as the job entails more than just helping a client. Michael Williams conducts rigorous interviews with candidates. He admits that hiring good assistants is just as important to his living independently as is getting the right communication systems and keeping his wheelchair in good working order.

Both of us lecture around the country and use personal experiences and clinical examples to highlight lecture points. We share amusing stories, like Jim Prentice's hotel room experience when the police were called in because he slept in; powerful stories, like that of Chris Featherly, who, because his grandmother knew he was doing more than the school saw and believed in him, is now independent with an electric wheelchair and communication device; and sad stories, like Rick Hohn's memories of his eighth-grade graduation ceremony when he needed "idiot cards" so that the audience could understand his speech. Rick remembers what it was like to hear his voice magnified for the first time, and how he would have given anything for his audience to understand him verbally. Who would have ever predicted that this same person would be a motivational speaker as an adult? Like a lot of teachers, we know the value of the personal story for illustrating critical points. But the years of collecting essays and working with the essays have changed the way we teach, what we teach, and our research agenda more than we could have expected. The personal power of the augmented speaker has also moved us into uncharted waters of self-determination and augmentative communication. Now when we meet eager students, we have them read personal stories and books written by augmented speakers before they start a research project. We share the podium with augmented speakers as much as possible. I remember being invited to lecture at the statewide amyotrophic lateral sclerosis (ALS) fair. When I asked if I could include an augmented speaker in the program, the conference organizer was shocked. Why, there were no patients sharing information at this meeting! This was a place for the *professionals* to give new information to consumers. Needless to say, I invited the spouse of a recently deceased patient to share my presentation time. Everyone at the meeting agreed that she was the star of the show. Although consumer participation is still a novel idea to the medical community, patients and/or their families are now invited to speak at the ALS fair.

RATE OF COMMUNICATION

Mike Ward talks about how his employment could continue as long as he could maintain a productive rate of communication. As his access changed and his rate deteriorated, his job effectively ended. Beukelman and Mirenda (1998) have a whole chapter addressing rate enhancement. But what does that mean for real lives? It can mean the loss of employment, as Mike Ward experienced when his motor function decreased with ALS, or the challenge of catching someone's attention long enough to show that you are an intelligent person despite physical disabilities, as other authors discuss. Michael Williams shares a story along these same lines when he describes how he uses a simple alphabet board to interview new personal assistants and judges them on their reactions to him. I once completed a survey of employed ALS patients who used AAC on their jobs. All the augmented speakers agreed that their job responsibilities and schedules certainly changed when they used augmentation instead of speech. They also noted that they could remain employed as long as they had text-based jobs that did not have time demands (Fried-Oken, 1993).

As you read this collection of essays, focus your attention on different perspectives based on whether the authors have acquired or developmental disabilities. Mike Ward has been using a ventilator for breathing for the past 6 years while remaining employed. Spencer Houston reports on having a stroke after being diagnosed with motor neuron disease. Larry and Terry Thompson discuss their relationships with friends after Larry's stroke and since the introduction of his VOCA.

MODES OF COMMUNICATION

The authors challenge us to expand our natural speaking repertoires by showing us the different ways they communicate. Mick Joyce and A.J. Brown, for example, use different types of communication for feelings, for faster or slower rates of conversation, or for showing the importance of a topic. From a different perspective, Mike Ward discusses various modes of communication that were dictated by his motor neuron disease and how his deteriorating motor function demanded new modes. Some augmented speakers give us their device histories. Jan Staehely describes her evolution through technologies and through different synthetic voices and access methods. Bill Rush talks about upgrading devices to expand his communication performance. Other authors give us their life histories and incidentally include their AAC techniques.

NEW AUDIENCES

As you can see from our discussion here, AAC specialists are no longer our restricted readership. Parents, educators, direct support staff, and individuals who use AAC themselves are interested in this discussion. People who live in the same town, city, or country should be interested in these chronicles. This volume makes new content accessible to the broadest possible audience. These essays are shorter and less technical than traditional textbook chapters, more personal than most research papers, and funnier than current newsletters. They invite the reader to enter the lives of people who experience barriers and unusual opportunities for communication. Janice Staehely tells us that communicating is an action word. Bob Williams reminds us that learning is not a passive act. He goes on to say that learning requires a great deal of communication and feedback. Communication is more than a basic human right, it is a basic human power. Essentially that is the message from all of the augmented authors. Indeed, the reader will learn about the power of communication through the actions (and antics) of the authors as they share their insights.

REFERENCES

Beukelman, D.R., & Mirenda, P. (1998). *Augmentative and alternative communication: Management of severe communication disorders in children and adults* (2nd ed.). Baltimore: Paul H. Brookes Publishing Co.

Brown, C. (1954). *My left foot.* London: Secker & Warburg.

Brown, L. (1976). The criterion of ultimate functioning. In M.T. Angele (Ed.), *Hey don't forget about me: Education's investment in the severely, profoundly, and multiply handicapped* (pp. 142–167). Reston, VA: Council for Exceptional Children.

Canadian Rehabilitation Council for the Disabled. (1984). *Conversations with nonspeaking people.* Toronto, Ontario: Canadian Rehabilitation Council for the Disabled.

Creech, R. (1981). Attitude as a misfortune. *Asha, 23,* 550–551.

Foulds, R. (1980). Communication rates of nonspeech expression as a function of manual tasks and linguistic constraints. *Proceedings of the International Conference on Rehabilitation Engineering* (pp. 83–87). Washington, DC: RESNA, Association for the Advancement of Rehabilitation Technology.

Fried-Oken, M. (1993). Do AAC users with degenerative neurological disease remain or return to the work force? *Proceedings of the Pittsburgh Employment Conference* (pp. 63–72). Pittsburgh: SHOUT.

Light, J.C., & Binger, C. (1998). *Building communicative competence with individuals who use augmentative and alternative communication.* Baltimore: Paul H. Brookes Publishing Co.

Lloyd, L.L., Fuller, D.R., & Arvidson, H.H. (1997). *Augmentative and alternative communication: A handbook of principles and practices.* Needham Heights, MA: Allyn & Bacon.

McDonald, A., & Crossley, R. (1980). *Annie's coming out.* London: Penguin Books Ltd.

Romski, M.A., & Sevcik, R.A. (1996). *Breaking the speech barrier: Language development through augmented means.* Baltimore: Paul H. Brookes Publishing Co.

Viggiano, J. (1981). Ignorance as handicap. *Asha, 23,* 551–552.

2

Sand and Sea

Gregory M. Haslett

Gregory M. Haslett is a physical therapy assistant and father of two teenage daughters. Greg was diagnosed with amyotrophic lateral sclerosis (ALS, or Lou Gehrig's disease) about 2 years ago. He now lives at home with his family in Portland, Oregon. Greg has been using a keyboard emulator and single switch on a personal computer for speaking, writing, and Internet access for about 6 months. Greg was a musician who enjoyed expressing himself without words. His contribution here is as lyrical as any musical composition that he has ever written or played.

Sand and Sea

How I long to be by the seashore

Walk in the sand, each step

Cradling my feet in a myriad of varied

Sensations as wisps of sea and wind

Intermix and relocate as they may

My family by my side warming my

Heart, my precious family.

3

Confessions of a
Blabber Finger

Gus Estrella

*Augmented communicators can have a
dream life just like mine—a job, competent
and timely communication with family and
friends, and a chance to make a difference.
In my opinion, these should be major goals
in our field.*

Gus Estrella is a Policy Analyst working on telecommunications and assistive technology in Washington, D.C., with the United Cerebral Palsy Associations (UCPA). He is also the project director for PAS-A System Change. Gus graduated from the University of Arizona, and after college he started substitute teaching. He worked in special education, which led to his previous job as an augmentative communication assistant. He also worked for the Department of Developmental Disabilities as a consultant and with children who were using AAC devices. He started working at the UCPA in May of 1995 as the first recipient of the Prentke-Romich Company/Semantic Compaction UCPA Leadership Fellowship Award.

MI FAMILIA

I can remember growing up; I would watch people moving their mouths and funny noises coming out of them. They would do this in front of others. At times they would laugh, other times they would just talk without any emotions, and still other times they would start to cry. I often wondered what was going on. Why were they acting so absurd? Then I would try doing the same absurdity and would wonder why I wasn't getting the same reaction from people around me, as others did. All I would get from the people around me was a pinch on my cheeks and then they would say, "Ah, isn't he just adorable?" It was so frustrating growing up. I wanted to tell my family and friends what I wanted and what I was thinking, and yet, I couldn't. I have to admit something, though. They did become pretty good at guessing what I wanted and needed. I often wished there could be something that would help me convey my desires. But there wasn't! I felt trapped. I had so much to say to people and so many questions to ask, and yet, how could I? They knew I had something to say but couldn't figure out how to get it out of me. I was like a time bomb ready to explode. To add to my dilemma, I was brought up, for the most part, in a bilingual family and Spanish was spoken most of the time.

Prior to starting preschool, my family and friends all spoke to me in Spanish. That was all I knew. So you can imagine my reaction when I started going to preschool. I was entering uncharted territories. I was about to be left with total strangers, foreigners! It was doubtful that anybody would know any Spanish, so what was the likelihood of somebody understanding my little signs for when I needed something, like lunch! What if I need to go to the little boys' room, and they think I'm having a seizure! These were the concerns that a little boy had to deal with and figure out how to cope with his new surroundings. So to whom could I turn for help and support? Basically, no one as there wasn't anybody who could relate to my situation. There wasn't an adult with a similar disability whom I could go to and seek advice from. I felt isolated since I couldn't tell anybody what I was thinking or feeling. I wanted to go home, to my safe haven, where everybody knew me, like in *Cheers!*

The reality was I had to learn how to communicate with people other than my family and friends. At the same time, a communication system had to be developed in order for me to be able to communicate. I needed a communication system that would allow me to communicate with whomever I wanted and say whatever was on my mind at the time.

In the late 1960s and early 1970s, every person with a severe speech disability and every special education teacher had a fantasy. It was for someone to develop a magical system that would just spit out a person's thoughts, in the language of their choice, and let the whole world know what they were thinking. Unfortunately, this was and still is only a fantasy! Even after the initial shock of being left with total strangers wore off a little, there was still some confusion about what language I was supposed to be using. For one thing, my day would start by talking to my parents in Spanish, then in school everyone would talk to me in English, and of course, when I got home it was back to speaking Spanish again. And some people wonder why I'm totally nuts? Now, I'm not saying that this was a disadvantage, because it wasn't, in my own personal opinion. Even though Spanish was spoken primarily when I was growing up, it didn't hinder the learning process.

I think I should talk a little about my family's background. When I was born, my parents were living in Nogales, Mexico, but I was born in Nogales, Arizona. It gives new meaning to the term *wetback* don't you think? And yes, I do have a green card! So as you can imagine, in the early 1960s, the last place you would want to be if you had any type of disability was somewhere in Mexico. Don't get me wrong; I love the place! In fact, I hear they make the best relief for constipation, called salsa! When I was growing up, for the most part, I was surrounded with family members who knew me and my unique way of communicating. They knew the meaning of every grunt and moan that I made. So they knew if I made a short grunting noise, it meant that I wanted something to drink, a long grunt meant I wanted some food and I wanted it that very moment. We even had grunts for when I needed to go to the little boys' room. A grunt and a moan meant I needed to tinkle. And of course, two grunts and a long moan meant that they should get a massive amount of toilet paper. But my question remained, in what language was I speaking? And, how did they know what I was trying to say? Even now, we can still communicate the same way, but because my vocabulary has gotten a little complicated, my grunts and moans have become a little un-

> But my question remained, in what language was I speaking? And, how did they know what I was trying to say? Even now, we can still communicate the same way, but because my vocabulary has gotten a little complicated, my grunts and moans have become a little unbearable!

bearable! So now I'm hearing, "Use your damn Liberator, that's what it is for!" Most of the time, my sisters and I just blow people's minds when we talk and I don't use an assistive device.

I think the one family member who had the most difficult time communicating with me was my father. I know when I was born the last thing on his mind was having a son with a disability, which was pretty normal since nobody really thinks they are going to have a child with a disability. I'm putting it pretty mildly when I say it threw him and my mother for a loop when they realized their son wasn't "normal." Now, keep in mind that I'm talking about the early 1960s and I was his first son, and the first-born son in a Mexican family should be "normal." So as you can imagine, realizing that you have a son who will never lead a "normal" life, even though you don't really know what that might be, is one of the hardest things you can ask a new father to accept, no matter what race he might be.

> *When I was growing up, for the most part, I was surrounded with family members who knew me and my unique way of communicating. They knew the meaning of every grunt and moan that I made.*

It took my father several years before he could accept my disability, but he finally did. I'm not saying that he woke one morning and everything was peachy keen, because it wasn't that simple. Basically, my mother's strong will, determination, and constant praying helped my father come to terms with my disability. For the first several years of my life, it was my mother who did everything for me from morning until bedtime. I wish I knew what exactly or could pinpoint the exact time in my life when my father came to terms with having a son with a disability, but I can't. I can remember, though, when we started to do things together like a father and son team and how great it felt knowing I had a father that saw nothing wrong with his only son. Unfortunately, this great man passed away September of 1996. In trying to find the words that best describe my father, the following are just a few of many words that come to mind: compassionate, loyal, trustworthy, and caring. The relationship I had with my father could be considered to be unique and a little on the wacky side. I don't think there was a time when I asked him for something, and I heard the word "no"! And of course, there are things we did together that my mother doesn't know about, and for some reason, I don't think she would have approved of them! But our relationship wasn't really complete. Even though my father could read and understood English fairly well, he wasn't able to write it, and this was causing a breakdown in communication between us. Because my father and I had a difficult time communicating with each other at the beginning, talking to him using my own voice was always an adventure. I can remember trying to say a certain phrase or word that was related to our conversation, but what he thought I had said was usually off in left field or somewhere out there. For example, we could have been talking about what I did on the computer and I would be trying to say, "the apple" in Spanish, and for some odd reason he thought I had said some number, like twelve. Don't ask how he got twelve from apple, since even in Spanish the two don't sound similar! And of course, I had a smartass response! I would say, "No, thirteen"! He would respond with, "Fourteen," and just look at me thinking, "Smartass!"

Now at the same time, there are advantages of using my grunts, I mean my own voice and body gestures, since nobody knows what the hell I'm saying! Whenever my father and I would start talking without the use of an assistive device, the people around us would start to wonder about my father. Wouldn't you? I mean if you saw a person carrying on a conversation with someone and all you could hear were grunts and moans and then the person would laugh like a madman, wouldn't you want to call the nearest psychiatric hospital?

COMMUNICATION EVOLUTION

Prior to getting the voice output communication aids, I was using a crusty old word board which meant that I had to spell some words out individually, making talking to my father a little difficult. This crusty old word board evolved in elementary school when my teachers and I experimented with different techniques. One technique was seeing my teachers walking back and forth in front of the blackboard pointing at the alphabet. I started pointing to the alphabet, as well. The fun part about this technique occurred when I didn't know how to spell a word. Then people would wonder if they were practicing for the DUI test that they might have to pass in the very near future! Eventually, one teacher got tired of this technique and took out this old word board to see if I would be able to use something like that. And a few days later, she started to regret taking that board out since I wouldn't shut up. I think it gave new meaning to the term *nonverbal student*. Nevertheless, this word board became my link to telling people what I was thinking and, yes, even gave me the freedom of telling a few

> I guess nobody informed me that a high school student with cerebral palsy shouldn't take physics.

choice individuals where to go. Not that I would do something like that, mind you. Basically, this word board was responsible for getting me through all my high school courses, including physics. I think you might be thinking, "Did I read physics?" Well, doesn't everyone take physics in high school? You mean, I didn't follow the norm, again? What was wrong with me? I guess nobody informed me that a high school student with cerebral palsy shouldn't take physics. But can you imagine trying to explain to someone where to put all those obscure wiggly-do-hickeys and those numbers to the umpteenth power with a word board and hoping they will understand what you're talking about and not think you're an obscure individual and need help?

GOING ELECTRONIC

It wasn't until my sixth year at the university that I got my first augmentative communication device. Prior to this, all I knew was my crusty old word board. So my transition from the word board to an electronic talking device wasn't the smoothest thing to happen in my life. In my mind, the word board was the best thing to come around since the happy hour! I figured I had been using a word board since the beginning of time and I was doing just fine with it. I could talk to people, provided they could read. I was making friends and making people laugh. I was communicating fine with the word board, so why would I need something new that might slow me down or might not work at all? Even after I had gotten my electronic device, I would still use the word board since it wasn't working as fast or like they said it would.

> *I finally had a more powerful VOCA, and I started to have real conversations with people whom I had always wanted to talk. My father was one person that I had always wanted to have a conversation with, but there was always a barrier. Finally that barrier was broken!*

Eventually, I saw that if I learned the software program and learned how to use the device, that in fact I could have a real conversation and people would respond differently. This became even clearer when I finally had a more powerful VOCA and I started to have real conversations with people whom I had always wanted to talk. My father was one person that I had always wanted to have a conversation with, but there was always a barrier. Finally that barrier was broken! Now we were able to carry on a real conversation without needing someone to translate my grunts into real words! We were able to talk about women, not that we would do something like that, mind you! Plus, we were able to talk about all the beers we had the night before at the football game, without my mother knowing what we really did! Now we could have our little secrets that would drive my mother nuts!

SPEECH PATHOLOGISTS

Some speech pathologists have, in my experience, some odd expectations. The first and perhaps the most poisonous is that we have to master and demonstrate the mastery of certain language concepts before we're allowed to try communication aids with the kind of power that might help us really talk. Umm, how can I master a language if I can't talk with my own voice, and you won't give me a communication aid? Even mastering a machine can be a complex task, as complex as learning how to dribble a basketball, especially when you have cerebral palsy! Now the question arises at school, how much more time is allotted an able-bodied student to master dribbling versus the time allotted to help the nonspeaking child with his communication aid? Clearly, it's not equal and very different, especially when the able-bodied student is able to pick up a ball at any given moment, and the nonspeaking student doesn't have equal access to a communication aid. We will need help, and by help, I don't mean repeated exercises in pointing to shapes and colors. Maybe pointing to hourglass-shaped figures? We need help, and by we, I mean the many, many of us, mastering the little words that make up language we hear around us. I think I had to learn to spell before I could use the word "it." And later I found out that if you put the letters "s" and "h" in front of it, it has a completely different meaning! And they say I don't have language skills! The words I was given were words that would produce pictures, not words that would make language. And they wanted me to master a language? I was also given piles of sentences and criticized for not using them. I don't know about you, but I don't think in terms of pre-formed sentences. Sometimes I even change my thought halfway through the sentence, and I have also been known to throw in a very descriptive word when the mood strikes me! I can think of few things more dehumanizing and even demeaning then selecting canned sentences from a list and seeing the subject matter that you want to talk about is nowhere to be found!

What gives communication joy is when you tell your partner something he or she doesn't already know, and perhaps you didn't know yourself what you were going to say until you were halfway through composing your sentences! The living waters of life are contained in the sparkling stream of language as it gushes forth from our tongues or, in my case, my fingers. Yes, I have become a blabber finger. I have even been known to talk with my middle finger! And during these times, you would think I was taxi cab driver! I am told by some clinicians that certain children can only talk about the here and now and objects they can see. This is raw bologna. I grew up with many other children with severe disabilities, and we communicated up a storm with each other through our eyes. I don't get what clinicians mean, because children with mild to moderate cognitive impairments really can understand a lot. However, when they are given a test in which they are supposed to follow complex instructions and use concepts they may not have experienced much of, they're going to clam up.

I sometimes get a wry smile on my face when I hear that a child needs to learn to communicate before he or she can attempt to learn language. Personally, I would like to see a clinician take the test that he or she can't explain to the child and ask, "So who's the cognitive impaired now?" Well, the big news here is that little kids with cognitive impairments are often communicating with each other and their caregivers all the time. And most of the time, they talk about the idiotic things that the clinician had them do! When this communication is measured, however, an entirely new social rubric sets in. The communication takes on an unreal quality. The natural communication already developed by the child is not useful in this context.

Kids don't tell people things that they're not interested in, especially when they know that the person asking the question already knows the answer. The kid is thinking, "Why are you wasting my time? You already know the answer!" Luckily, I was a bright little rugrat, and I caught onto the game and started using my middle finger at an early age! But not everybody does. Speech pathologists in my experience have been sincere and hardworking, given the limited taste of reality they received in their academic programs. But their best is often figuring what's wrong with us, rather than what we can do. And more often than not, they tend to forget to ask us what our needs are! Commissioner Bob Williams, from the Administration on Developmental Disabilities, uses the metaphor that "we become cloaked in a veil of incompetence." The tools science has developed to help find where to start with us have actually become perverted into barriers. An oft-repeated witticism is that

The living waters of life are contained in the sparkling stream of language as it gushes forth from our tongues or, in my case, my fingers. Yes, I have become a blabber finger.

"pre" anything can be used to mean "not." For example, pre-reading often means not reading. Well, let me tell you, what do you think pre-language means? Unfortunately, it usually means, not language. I thank God that my family and one very special therapist, a rarity I might add, saw a lot of potential in me and helped me escape the first barrier of the devastating barriers of assumed incompetence and low expectations.

HOW FAR IS THE ROAD TO SUCCESS?

So how important is an augmentative communication device to a person who has a severe speech disability? And when does the importance of an augmentative communication device become more evident to the person and to their family and friends? This may vary from person to person, and it could occur during different stages in a person's life. In my personal life, the importance became more evident at different points in my life. One was definitely when my father and I started talking and sharing things that we couldn't before. We would talk about baseball, the Los Angles Dodgers in particular. And who can forget basketball and the Arizona Wildcats? We were finally having father and son conversations, just like the other fathers and sons were having since the beginning of time. Prior to this, I had no idea what I was missing out on, not really talking to my father and sharing my deepest thoughts and desires with him. At the same time, I don't think either of us knew that something was missing in our relationship, since we used to do things together and communicated with each other in our special way. So in our minds nothing was wrong. Everything was peachy keen; we were a normal father and son team. I think the same thing can be said about the relationship between my mother and myself, but the difference was that she was able to understand me better than my father.

And yet, it's hard to convey the difference my VOCA has made in our lives. I would imagine it eliminated the frustration that my parents had since I was little. The Liberator eliminated the frustration of not knowing what their child was wanting, what his dreams and desires were—of not being sure if he wanted to go to school, or was it something that they just assumed that he wanted? Of course, they didn't force me into doing something that I didn't want to do; that's not what I'm saying. What I'm saying is, despite their frustration of not being able to really understand what I wanted to tell them, they had the patience to figure out what I wanted and what was best for me. I'm sure they had their times when they thought, "What are we doing?" And I wouldn't have blamed them if they had just quit!

Nobody in this world knows how glad I am that they didn't give up on me, otherwise who knows where I would be now!

Another point in my life where the importance of an augmentative communication device became more evident was when I started having nieces and nephews and they were growing up not knowing what their uncle was thinking. These days I find myself having meaningful conversations with my nieces, talking with them about school, life, what they're thinking, and, of course, joking and teasing them about boys! At the same time, I can also help correct them when they start going down the wrong path and start getting into trouble with their mother and grandmother. But most important, they respect me and value my opinion and even ask for my advice on occasion.

ROAD BLOCKS AND DETOURS

The road to my successful employment had its series of roadblocks and detours. I think it started when I graduated from high school and proceeded directly into college. After graduating from high school, I became terribly ill and started going to college right after high school. To this day I'm not sure what came over me when I made that decision to start college right away. Nonetheless, I found myself going to college at the University of Arizona with a word board. When I first met with a guidance counselor, he gave me some options. So I decided to go on the 10-year plan. I started drinking ten pots of coffee and five cases of Mountain Dew a day. And guess what happened? I graduated in 8 years! I started off majoring in computers, the way to the bank, but something happened, and I ended up in creative writing, the way to waiting tables, but something was telling me that wasn't an option for me. Maybe making tossed salads? It suddenly dawned on me why I received a funny look from my vocational rehabilitation (VR) counselor when I informed her about the change. I figured it was because I might be her waiter someday and she would hate it if I might find out she was a rotten tipper, plus I might drool in her food out of spite. Okay, I made it through the first roadblock; I had a college degree! What was next? My degree was in creative writing, and something was telling me that finding a job was almost impossible. It wasn't totally impossible, since my degree wasn't in history! So a friend suggested that I try substitute teaching. At first I thought she was crazy, and I was right; she was crazy, but I went ahead and got my substitute certificate. When I started to substitute teach, I starting getting funny looks. Gee, I wonder why? I figured it was a disability thing or something like that. Nevertheless, I actually did receive assignments. I remember one assignment in particular where

I was supposed to substitute at a high school in an economics class. When I arrived at the school, I reported to the assistant principal's office, which was an eye-opening experience on her part. As she was turning around, her jaw dropped—I was just glad it wasn't her dress! She then proceeded to ask, "May I help you?" "Yes, I'm here to sub for this teacher," I replied which threw her for a loop, to say the least. After she had composed herself from the news, she exclaimed, "But you're disabled!" I just sat there smiling, not wanting to risk losing the assignment but thinking, "Thank you! I'm so glad you noticed! I knew you were a woman well before I noticed those shoes you're wearing!" For the most part, I mainly worked in special education, which led to my previous job as an augmentative communication assistant. I was very much involved in creating the position and making sure I had all of the job's qualifications, ensuring that I would get the position that became a full-time position with the school district. I would work with students who used, or who were starting to use, augmentative communication devices. We noticed that there was a need for students who were starting to use AAC devices to have someone whom they could look up to and who could relate to their situation, in other words, a mentor.

This brings me to the position I currently proudly hold: I'm the first recipient of the Prentke-Romich Company Semantic Compaction /UCPA Leadership Fellowship Award. Now that is one hell of a Liberator mouthful, if you ask me! Now can anyone of you repeat that last sentence five times really fast without drooling? Anyway, back in December of 1994, I was sitting on my couch relaxing after a long day at work when I received the announcement about the fellowship. At first, I wasn't really sure if I wanted to apply. It sounded like it would be a good learning experience and it could broaden my horizons. Well, without boring you with the details, let's say I ended up submitting the application and you can fill in the blanks after that. So what made me apply for the fellowship? I mean, I'm from sunny and warm Arizona; I had a decent paying job, a comfortable living arrangement, a lot of friends (especially of the female persuasion) and I was willing to give all that up to move to the nation's capital? I must have brain damage! I mean, who wouldn't want to experience more politics than a person could ever imagine, or handle, for that matter. And one mustn't forget the nice winters that everyone brags about! And if you believed that line, you would also believe that I'm writing this in Hawaii! I guess, basically, I was looking for a change of jobs and surroundings. But the interesting thing about the description of the fellowship was that nothing was said about snow!

I realized this little fact during the blizzard of '96 as I sat stuck at home counting the little bumps on the ceiling in my apartment. Oh, by the way, there are 9,859,001 little bumps just on the living room ceiling. I think during the next blizzard, and God forbid there is a next, I'm going to see how many icon sequences it takes to run down the batteries on my Liberator. I figure that would make the developer very proud of me, don't you think?

Yes, it is devastating that individuals with severe speech and severe physical disabilities have that wall to hurdle in order to achieve meaningful employment. But in my humble opinion, what is more devastating is that individuals with severe speech and severe physical disabilities are not given the opportunity that I was given, nor are they encouraged to dream and reach for the ultimate goal, achieving meaningful employment!

Some might argue that luck had a lot to do with my success, and others might say that it was the people I knew. Personally, I think it's a combination of the two, but there are other factors that can be added to the equation. One is me, personally. It was me that had the dream and desire of making something out of myself. I mean I could have been given the top job in the country, but without that desire of succeeding, that job would have been meaningless! Now the second part of this is, who and what put the dream and desire of succeeding in me? One is that doctor, who didn't see any hope for me as a member of society. Proving him wrong has been delightful, and everyone should experience that pleasure at some point in his or her life! Second, I couldn't disappoint my very special speech pathologist who saw a future for me! And last but certainly not least, my parents. Personally, I can't explain what guided my parents in knowing what was best for their disabled son. They just did what they thought was natural, and it worked. I know sometimes they have wondered about the monster they created! And I have done my best to make them wonder about me and the things I have come up with, like moving crosscountry! The main thing that my parents did was to encourage me! They never said, "No you can't," unless it was something that went against their beliefs, like burning down a building! (I could never figure that one—I mean, it looks like so much fun!) What I'm trying to say is, they didn't limit me because of the disability, nor did they limit the family because of it either. As a family, we did everything that any family would do and went everywhere together. Sometimes there would be steps into a building where the owners hadn't thought of the concept called ramps. For the most part, these steps would stop someone who uses a wheelchair for mobility, but if you had a father like I did, you would hear, "Hold on," and the next thing you know, you're going up a flight of stairs. So were there any limitations in my parents' eyes? Hell, no! You wouldn't want to be the person that told my mother that her son couldn't attend a particular school. This did happen, and let's just say, two days later I was attending the school that I was supposed to attend! I don't think language became a barrier in this situation! Now in all this, there was a barrier and it was between my parents and I. The barrier I'm talking about is one that every family experiences, but ours was at a different level to some extent. I'm talking about the lack of communication between my parents and me. This lack of communication was due to the fact that I had no real means of communicating with my parents. Yes, I had a word board, but as you can see, that too became a communication barrier. The appearance of a VOCA, indeed, equalized communication between my parents and their only son.

These days I find myself in a shirt and tie talking to individuals who make decisions that affect the lives of people with disabilities. A lot of the time, these individuals have no clue whatsoever as to what assistive technology is and how it can help a person with a disability. Nor do they know how crucial personal assistance services are to a person who can't get out of bed by him- or herself. My job has been to make them see, in real life, the impact their decisions have on the lives of people with disabilities and how they can make a difference in the disability community. Again, this is another point in my life where I realized how crucial my Liberator had become in my daily life, not only when it came to my new job, but also with staying in touch with my family and friends over the telephone.

The importance of having an augmentative communication device became more evident with my moving to the Washington, D.C., area. My Liberator has enabled me to have real conversations over the telephone with my family, including my nieces. When I first got my Liberator, I came to the realization that I was able not only to talk to my nieces, but also to enlighten them when they didn't behave. And that is always fun! Another thing that I find so wonderful about being able to talk to my nieces is that now they can come to me for advice, and we can have our little secrets. I also get a kick out of them, because the youngest ones look at my Liberator as a toy or a dog and ask me to make it speak! The oldest ones try to remember a few icon sequences, like for their names. But it's hard to explain the joy my Liberator has brought me! Because now I can talk to my family, including my little nieces, my friends, and the general public, and know that I will be understood.

CONCLUSIONS

Please remember that pre-language does not mean no language. It means there's a mind in this individual that needs to be developed. We need to increase the expectations of augmented communicators' abilities and potentials. We need to rethink how one can learn to talk while at the same time mastering language. Remember, not every basketball player becomes a Michael Jordan. Many, many basketball players who never make it do it for the fun of playing and the exercise rather than for the money. Augmented communicators just want to talk like anyone else. They need the availability of hours of practice, the availability of their communication aid at all times, the proper language technology, and the supports put in place to achieve the goal of communication. It's not the shapes and colors or the sentences that need to be taught, it's the words that glue language together—the little words that build the sentences, not the picture words. Children with mild to moderate cognitive impairments really can understand a lot. Oftentimes this means they can actually communicate a lot. They just need the right tools, a push behind them, and proper language therapy to achieve this. The tests that are given offer just a starting point for these individuals, and these tests can sometimes become barriers. Please, use your own good common sense and look at the individual's assets and build on them rather than use tests which state difficulties about the person's abilities. Dig in, get the support of both the school and the social services agencies, get the devices funded, and make us work our little tails off until we master enough language to become competent communicators.

People who rely on augmented communication are very fortunate to live in a time when the language technology is available and the prosthetic speech is understandable. Thanks to all of the hard work in this field, augmented communicators now have the chance never before afforded them. Augmented communicators can have a dream life just like mine—a job, competent and timely communication with family and friends, and a chance to make a difference. In my opinion, these should be major goals in our field.

4

If I Do Say So Myself!

Peg L. Johnson

*Honest and effective communication is crucial
for any healthy relationship and even more
so when one of the partners is an augmented
communicator.*

Peg L. Johnson lives in Minneapolis, Minnesota. She has been employed by the Minneapolis Public Library since 1979. A college graduate, she is the author of a book entitled *Express Yourself* and the founder and coordinator of a support group for AAC users. She enjoys theater, travel, and college and professional basketball and football. Go Gophers and Vikings!

Living with a communication disability has always been a unique challenge. Having been born in . . . well, let's just say I'm an early baby boomer. I didn't grow up with computers, much less voice output communication aids (VOCAs). Throughout my entire life, I have had to develop my own system of expressing myself. It has only been recently that I have been able to take advantage of the new augmentative and alternative communication (AAC) technologies. AAC is now a big part of my life.

Though my life has been a series of challenges, I have had many successes. I developed a stubborn streak early on, which, I suspect, is one reason I've been able to overcome many obstacles in my path. As a result of severe athetoid cerebral palsy, my verbal communication skills evolved slowly and gradually. As a little tike, I used a multitude of unique sounds, facial expressions, gestures, and eye movements to make my wishes known. At the age of 2 I was required to take my first IQ test in order to be admitted to a nursery school for crippled children. My mom says the tester wasn't quite sure about my intellectual abilities until I glared at my mom with a certain contorted expression indicative of my need to visit the restroom *immediately!* After we returned, the psychologist had concluded that if I was able to nonverbally tell my mom of my need for a bathroom, I wasn't as intellectually delayed as she first believed.

My sounds eventually turned into single syllable words which served me quite well at the special crippled children's grade school. Little by little my words turned into incomplete sentences, which I still use today.

When it came time to attend high school, my IQ needed to be rechecked. Being put in a room with a spooky, scary man whom I had never seen before was a horrific experience. My athetosis took charge. Every muscle in my body froze. The environment and the people around me influence my ability to perform. Stress and tension really have a disastrous effect on my muscle control. There are certain times when it is vitally important to speak, and that is the time when my breathing is the worst. It does take air to speak!

> *The environment and the people around me influence my ability to perform. Stress and tension really have a disastrous effect on my muscle control. There are certain times when it is vitally important to speak and that is the time when my breathing is the worst. It does take air to speak!*

Needless to say, it took many advocates to convince "authorities" to permit me to enter junior high on a trial basis. I was taken off probation after making the "A" honor roll for three straight quarters.

Despite extensive speech and motor limitations, I graduated seventh in my high school class of 200 able-bodied students. "They" told me I couldn't do it, so I had to prove them wrong. "They" also told me I couldn't go to college. Wrong again! While in college, I became interested in augmentative and alternative communication. What began as a term paper for a computer course became a book and eventually led to the formation of a nonprofit corporation to assist AAC users. In 1988, I founded Express Yourself of Minneapolis, Inc., which provides support and advocacy to individuals with severe speech impairments. Presently, there are three part-time speech-language pathologists working with our two support groups. This is my current challenge.

Early on I was discouraged from trying to enter the workforce. Since 1979, I have been employed at the Minneapolis Public Library. I just hope nobody tells me that I can't play center for the Minnesota Timber Wolves basketball team. (Even though at this point they could use my help.)

My written communication also evolved through the years. In my younger days, much of my time was spent learning how to hold a pencil and how to form letters and numbers. My first exposure to sentence structure occurred when I enrolled in my seventh-grade English class. Subjects, verbs, and direct objects were foreign to me. Playing catch-up was not fun! Throughout junior and senior high, my class assignments were all dictated and then transcribed by my dedicated parents. One of my favorite high school teachers designed a specialized typing course to meet the needs of his orthopedically handicapped students. Boy, did that class ever change my life. The teacher accepted nothing but perfection. Writing has ended up to be my most effective means of communication. I type letters and notes to everyone: doctors, dentists, professors, business associates, and even friends and family at times.

I'm sure my life would be quite different if I had used a VOCA as a child. Finding effective and efficient ways to communicate has always been a challenge. Due to my fast-paced lifestyle and my desire to be independent, I have had to rely on personal assistants to interpret and clarify my speech. It's quick, it's efficient, and it has worked for me. My speech is intelligible to familiar listeners and allows me to interact with the individual. Eye contact and social closeness are important parts of human interaction

In the fall of 1991, I decided to apply to the Medical Assistance Fund for the purchase of a VOCA called the Liberator. The application process required the assistance of many professionals—doctor, occupational therapist, speech-language pathologist, assistive technology specialist, and a legal advocate. Medical Assistance paid for a short rental trial period before the purchase. I took the device out into the community and documented actual examples of situations where I needed it, such as making bank transactions, shopping in a mall, ordering my own food in restaurants, making my own telephone calls, and preprogramming short speeches used in group meetings or conferences. After 2 years of effort, including one denial, the purchase was approved.

Personal assistants are vitally important to a person with a severe disability. In Minnesota, personal care assistant (PCA) services are paid through the state's Medical Assistance Fund. Hours are allocated to an individual based on the severity of the individual's disability. The program is administered by qualified provider agencies that supervise and manage the payments to the PCA's. My agency provides a half-day seminar on the philosophy of independent living and the general do's and don'ts of being a PCA. I also give them a 35-page autobiography to help them know me better. I personally recruit, employ, train, and sometimes terminate them. However, if an individual is unable to perform these functions, the provider agency will do this for them.

During the last 25 years, more than 54 personal assistants have worked for me. Most have been college students with a vast range of interests and backgrounds. Help wanted ads in college and university newsletters have been a successful source of recruiting assistants. I prefer hiring people who have not had previous experience working with individuals with disabilities—in other words, people without any preconceived ideas as to the "right" way or the "wrong" way to perform a given task. I need and expect things to be done *my way*. After all, whose life is it anyway?

Interviewing potential applicants is always an extremely stressful endeavor. I assess their natural comfort level to interact with me because it is relatively easy to train them to do the individual tasks. Being somebody's hands and voice is extremely difficult. There is an inherent tendency for assistants to feel the need to take charge of my life. This does NOT work! I prefer having between two and six attendants work for me at a time, so not any one person can take charge. Some are definitely more suited for the job than others. There have been assistants that I've been able to clone to be an extension of me. When this happens, it has proven to be a relationship of quality.

Establishing a good working relationship is critical. It's true that assistants are employees and need to perform and act accordingly. I am, however, very sensitive and responsive to the needs of the people assisting me. I expect my assistants to be more than just robots that come to do their assigned tasks. The human interaction is extremely important to me. It is truly impossible to anticipate my wants and expectations from day to day without interacting with me. Some mornings I want strawberry yogurt for breakfast, other days a bowl of puffed wheat seems more palatable. It's not my style to be demanding—*Do this! Do that!* I would rather the assistant feel important and valued as a person, acknowledging that she or he has a meaningful purpose in my life. Consequently, I expect a high level of active involvement during their working hours. If this isn't possible, they are terminated.

Honest and effective communication is crucial for any healthy relationship and even more so when one of the partners is an augmented communicator. Excellent active listening skills are critical. Listening is an art. When I am speaking or using my VOCA, it is essential that my communication partner indicate in some manner that they are receiving and understanding the message. I am totally dependent on clarification, paraphrasing, and nonverbal gestures (a nod, a smile, a blank facial expression, etc.) throughout an entire conversation. Giving my communication partner the subject matter of the exchange oftentimes facilitates efficient interaction. It also speeds up the communication process.

To save time and energy, I prefer to allow my communication partner to finish my sentences, as long as she is in tune with what I am attempting to say. In order to speed up the process, I need to clarify, deny, or confirm the accuracy of their interpretation. Very receptive listening skills are real important. However, some augmentative communicators want to finish their own words or sentences whether their partner can predict the message or not. It's up to the individual.

Assistants should never attempt to answer questions for me. Most of us are hard to second guess so it is necessary that all communication interactions be channeled through me. There are times when I'm slow to respond. It isn't that I don't hear the question, it just takes me longer to communicate my thoughts and ideas. Often when I'm having a business conversation over the phone, my assistants may have to ask the caller to "wait a few seconds" while I formulate a response.

Particularly when I'm using my VOCA, I succinctly state my thoughts. I do expect my assistants to be involved with the interaction so they can readily expand or offer background information when necessary. Ideally, my assistants and I develop an understanding that there will be specific times when it's important to repeat after me, and other times I will need them to expound on what I'm saying. But when the interaction seems to be going well, it's probably best that they just let me continue. Some kind of signal or cue needs to be in place. There are assistants who pick up on this automatically, and some that never will.

There have been cases when my assistants are not interested enough in me as a person to take the necessary time and effort to actually listen to what I have to say. When this occurs, my anxiety level increases and ability decreases and the interaction stops. I don't need to be discounted by my assistants.

In public I encounter a wide variety of reactions to my disability. People frequently assume that a person's mental capability is directly related to their physical limitations or their physical appearance. There are a few people who are able to communicate with me on an adult basis. Some people attempt to communicate with me but retreat after not understanding my speech. There are others who are unable to deal with the situation at all and simply pat me on the head or say, "It's nice you could get out today." A big part of my assistant's responsibilities is not only to interpret and clarify my thoughts and needs, but also be a role model for others as how to interact with me. The unfamiliar third party will inevitably start relating to my assistant instead of me. When this occurs, it is important for my assistant to refocus the conversation back into my arena. She can simply turn her head and eyes my way and wait for me to generate a response.

It is very annoying to be treated like a child. When I order a cup of coffee, the waitress will invariably tell me that the coffee is hot! Some days a comment of this nature doesn't bother me at all. I write it off that they do not know any better, or maybe they say that to everyone. Other days I become exasperated wondering why they feel the necessity to inform me that the coffee is hot. Coffee should be hot!

Due to my poor speech, people automatically assume that I'm retarded and treat me accordingly. In order to help overcome this, I consider my appearance to be extremely important. Percy Ross once wrote, "Neatness scores points with most everybody.... Appearance may not make the person, but it makes a difference." This has proven to be true in my case. I have found that when I am dressed in my professional suits, it is easier for people to interact on an equal basis.

It is expected that the assistant that gets me dressed in the morning will do her best to make sure my hair is styled, my makeup is applied neatly, and that my clothes and jewelry are put on correctly. Other assistants that come throughout the day are expected to help me maintain this appearance. This is done by straightening my clothes, putting my jacket on right, and keeping my face clean while

I am eating. It goes without saying that my assistants are strongly encouraged to maintain their own appearances. When we are together they should also be dressed for the occasion and conduct themselves in an appropriate manner. My nonverbal message or statement opens doors which can turn into a verbal interchange. Motivational speakers say that what a person sees is five times more important than what one hears. It works for me!

As an individual with severe speech and motor limitations, I have always struggled to be an equal and contributing member of this society. From the first day of my life, I have been driven to succeed, driven to prove that a speech disability would never hold me back. That certainly has been quite a challenge!

Living with a communication disability is very stressful. Whenever feasible it is vital for me to use strategies that reduce my stress level as much as possible. My assistants are asked to perform tasks that theoretically I could do for myself. However, it is far more important for me to be involved and active in the community than it is for me to feed or dress myself. This also involves communication. At this stage in my life, there's no way that I can or need to handle ALL of my own communication needs. Therefore, I prefer my assistants handle the routine activities so I can focus on my various other responsibilities.

My independence is extremely important to me. Just 2 years ago, upon acquiring an accessible van, I began using my electric wheelchair for all activities. Now I am more inclined to seek out a conversation partner without relying on my assistant to make a judgement as to where to sit. This has already had a big impact on my communication style. I am more apt to initiate a conversation rather than just listen. Some studies have shown that powered mobility increases communication by 400%. I believe it! My VOCA is becoming more important to me now that I have independent mobility. I am in the process of unlearning some of my automatic communication behavior. One of my goals is to reduce my dependency on my assistant to interpret my speech. However, I don't foresee that the use of technology will ever replace the role of personal assistants in my life. I use an eclectic approach to communication. I utilize whatever method or combination of methods is the easiest and fastest in a particular situation to express myself. You could call me a multifaceted augmented communicator. My communication needs are met via my assistants, IBM computer, telecommunication device for the deaf

(TDD), electric typewriter, tiny memo writer, Liberator, and, of course, my computer terminal at work.

As an individual with severe speech and motor limitations, I have always struggled to be an equal and contributing member of this society. For some silly reason I believe that I must work harder when I work, study harder when I study, communicate harder when I communicate, and even play harder when I play. From the first day of my life, I have been driven to succeed, driven to prove that a speech disability would never hold me back. That certainly has been quite a challenge! The words of Daniel Webster sum it up best: "If all of my possessions were taken from me with one exception, I would choose to keep the power of communication, for by it I would soon gain all the rest."

5

Nobody Knows Me but Me, Myself, and I—the Three of Us

A.J. Brown

[When I was younger,] I felt this was agreeable, to have someone to do the talking for me. If I went back, knowing what I know now, I'd be livid if anyone dared speak for me.

A.J. Brown lives in Vancouver, British Columbia, Canada, with her beautiful black 3-year-old cat named Panther-Comedy. She is self-employed as a network marketer. When she isn't petting her purring cat, she enjoys walks and practices Tai Chi.

BLUE BABY, NOT BLUE BLOODED (DARN)

Just before I was born, my mother was given a drug called Pitocin. This drug made me come out into this big, wide world so fast I couldn't catch my breath. I became a blue baby. But I'm not blue anymore! Nor do I have blue-colored blood. This was how I became deaf. Also, this is how I suspect I got this neurological condition that still is yet to be named. Pitocin is still used to induce labor, but usually it is administered safely.

Now, this drug, Pitocin, I don't know if it had just been approved by the FDA or if it was still being experimented on back then. If it was still being experimented on, then was I part of this experiment, and it didn't do what it was supposed to do? I really wonder, because the doctor who delivered me has some secrets surrounding my birth. He pawed through my file and removed some pertinent information. So, I can't know what went wrong. I guess he was afraid of being sued. Maybe he was thinking mistakes or accidents happen. (My mother told me recently that she saw this doctor a few years after my arrival into this world. She noticed that he looked back at her, like he knew he made a mistake or something.)

I was late with milestones, like my first word, first independent step, and first independent bike ride. I must have been about 10 or 12 when I got the training wheels off. I always had sluggish movements. I was 3 when my mother was finally able to convince my pediatrician that I'm deaf. He actually thought I was mentally challenged. I could fool lots of people that I was an ordinary, happy, hearing baby. This was because I watched what was going on and picked up on what I thought was happening. I mimicked the surrounding environment. I can remember looking at baby books with pictures of various animals. I got to know the picture and then the word next to the picture. I even tried to eat these books. Most babies put everything in their mouths; I was no different. A moving "garborator," *c'est moi!* Another way I learned to read and write in school was by mimicking others, repeating, and copying.

One thing I didn't do very well was timed tests, especially those horrid standardized tests and their ilk. I knew from early on that these were discriminatory. There was one particularly awful one in elementary school—a timed IQ test. This was the one that got me on edge for life, that life isn't fair. I mean, the test was supposed to measure intelligence?! Compared to what or to whom?! I had to fill in those bubbles perfectly before moving on to the next question. I thought the idea of this test was to fill out those bubbles perfectly, in 10 minutes. I don't know the result of that test, and I don't care. From the gist of what they were saying about me, I felt I failed that test; I was to be the dunce forever. Because I was slow-moving, my school thought I was therefore slow-witted. Well! Thanks a lot!

I waited for the results of a standardized college test once. That was embarrassing beyond belief for me. The result was that I got into the bottom fifth percentile. The teacher who gave me the results said that percentile didn't mean percent and that it was actually very good. How "oxymoronish"! The bottom fifth percentile, and that's very good?! Sure didn't make any sense to me. I think she was trying to sugarcoat it for me. No wonder I was almost the last person to know the results. It's hard to forget that test, filling out those tiny bubbles. I intended to come back to a few questions at the end, when I had the time. I wanted to go back, but found that I had already filled in those bubbles! It was hard to recall to which question I wanted to go back. That must be why I got the low mark. That was absolutely awful.

> Because I was slow-moving, my school thought I was therefore slow-witted. Well! Thanks a lot!

A GARDEN VARIETY OF WEEDS—MY DIAGNOSIS? PART ONE

I was diagnosed at 13 as having cerebral palsy. This came about after we moved to Winnipeg. Just after we moved there, my sister came down with mononucleosis, of which I got a touch. The sleeping sickness is what they nicknamed mononucleosis. After 2 months I became more spastic. I blame the very cold weather, but my mother thinks it's because I caught mononucleosis. The doctor we saw, who I think was just a general practitioner, said, "Oh, you have cerebral palsy." I thought, "Oh, great, another disease." I thought this because I had lots of sickness when I was growing up, always coming down with something new and exciting. Oh sure, I had the usual chicken pox and measles, but at the same time. I took longer to get over them. I came down with whooping cough and missed a lot of the last part of fifth grade. I had lots of flus and colds.

I carry on with this thing called Life. We, my mother and I, moved back to Vancouver. I did twelfth grade. I came down with mononucleosis again. This time was worse than when I was 13. A few months later, my left leg was dragging, so it looked like I was limping along. I went off to Gallaudet University in Washington, D.C. It was called Gallaudet College then, in 1985. Gallaudet is currently the world's only liberal arts university for Deaf people.

In late 1985, I developed idiopathic scoliosis. What these fancy words mean is that I had an abnormal curvature of the spine for no known reason. It was excruciatingly painful. I was leaning over to the right. I sort of looked like a big banana, only less graceful. When I came home that Christmas, I did the first whirlwind of doctors. They were all baffled. They kept referring me to someone else. I just wanted the nightmare to stop. I was a hot potato; no one really seemed to want to take me on. I eventually saw two neurologists who diagnosed me as having idiopathic scoliosis and progressive spastic paraplegia. The term cerebral palsy had been relegated to a garden variety of weeds. Cerebral palsy is common and weeds are common, so cerebral palsy is a weed. This term refers to so many symptoms that they are grouped together. The name progressive spastic para-plegia is more rare than cerbral palsy.

My mother did the communicating for me when we saw these two neurologists. She felt the appointments would go faster if she answered their questions. This was in part because she is a nurse. She felt she could answer their questions as she was more familiar with medical jargon. At the time, I felt this was agreeable, to have someone do the talking for me, as if I was a helpless, flimsy, weak-minded, blond wimp—as if I had no brain for myself. If I went back, knowing what I know now, I'd be livid if anyone dared speak for me. This is because no one knows me but me, myself, and I, the three of us. I am in charge of this life. At the time, because I was suffering so much, I didn't have much energy to communicate anyway after traveling across the city to see this neurologist.

FLAT, BUT NOT FLAPPED

Immediately after the first surgery for the scoliosis, I think I was doing okay. I was turned over once every 12 hours. This was done two or three times. I was still reacting to the anesthetic. Having a neurological condition where spasticity is dominant, I was more spastic than usual immediately after the surgery. This was because the anesthetic made me relax like an able-bodied person—me, the human elastic! In order for the surgeon to be able to work on my back, I was sandwiched between two boards and wrapped in cloth to keep my spasticity down. I guess if I hadn't been tied up then my body would have wreaked havoc on itself, maybe even damaged the Herrington rods and caused paralysis. I don't know, but I believe anything's possible.

After a day or two of being turned over every 12 hours, maybe it was 6 hours, a student doctor decided to play professional doctor with me. He administered the wrong drug to me. I guess he thought this drug would help speed up my recovery. It sure as heck didn't! It changed my skin color to a deep purple, according to my mother. It sent me to the intensive care unit (ICU) for 2 or 3 weeks. I remember telling my mother I felt like I was dying. If I died, I told her that I wanted to be cremated and have my ashes poured from the Lions Gate Bridge. I passed out, and they took me to the ICU. A vivid dream I had was of moving down a long, rocky corridor. I came to a fork, and I went to the fork on the right side. It wasn't until much later that I realized this was called a near death experience. In total, I was in the hospital for 11 weeks. Then I was transferred to a rehabilitation center for a few months as an inpatient and then as an outpatient for another few months. While I was an outpatient, I didn't feel I was getting back to my old self. This revelation occurred in September when I realized I should have been back at the university.

A SURPRISE, A TRIP, AND SELF-CONSCIOUSNESS

That September my mother came home with a nice surprise. She said when she was shopping in the mall, she happened to stop in a book store when she saw the musician/performer Bryan Adams. She went up to him and noticed that his radar for potential fans was up. He was trying to hide behind a book, like that dinosaur with the long neck and long tail can hide behind a lamppost! She tapped his shoulder and said, "May I have your autograph?" There was a long pause, and he said, "What's the magic word?" "Oh, please." A piece of paper was signed. After that, she told him I had been in the hospital for 11 weeks. His rock star persona dropped immediately and he said something like, "I hope she gets better soon." That picked up my spirits, for a while. It meant a lot to me; I never realized that famous people could do that. I knew some would do a small thing like that for kids, but for a 20-year-old fogy like me? Wow!

I slumped into depression because I was not making any physical progress. It was becoming winter and dark most of my waking hours, which wasn't helping any either. I missed going back to the university for September. I had better get moving and feel better for January, then! My mother announced, "We will go to Hawaii for 2 or 3 weeks for Christmas and New Year's!" Her travel agent thought she was nuts, with such short notice, especially to find a hotel that was wheelchair accessible. There was ONE such hotel, on the island of Kauai.

This trip was definitely what the doctor ordered! I met lots of people who were interested in me as a person, which I thought to be liberating. I made friends fast there. Every morning in the hotel restaurant, I'd go by people and say hi. There were a few swimming

pools there, all outdoors. The pools were different sizes, tempera-
tures, and depths, even a hot tub next to a cave/grotto. One day it decided to rain, and my mother took a look out the window and wanted
a nap. Me, I wanted to go out and swim in the rain. I figured I'm gonna
get wet anyway! This is Hawaii, where the rain is warm! I thought it
would be romantic. I swam for a while, changed to a different pool.
Then I went off to the hot tub to relax and let the gentle rain cool me
off. After a while, a small group of people came into the grotto: a
Hawaiian religious man, a photographer, a man, and a woman. They
got married. The newlyweds presented me with a beautiful lei. Later,
I told my mother this and she said, "Oh yeah?" not sure whether to
believe me or not. We went to the hotel restaurant for dinner, and the
couple that was just married was there, too. We all sat together for
drinks beforehand. They told us they searched the globe for the perfect spot to be married for 7 months. Amazing! That grotto was it for
them. On the day of their wedding, they had no witnesses, just me in
a bathing suit looking like a happy clam.

On the second to last day of this trip, I was swimming in the pool
and met a musician who was in a band that was performing that
night in the hotel pub. I don't think he said he was the singer! I took
my chances and signed up my mother and myself for the evening. We
arrived expecting chopped liver, but he was a really excellent Elvis
Presley impersonator. He looked, moved, sounded, and behaved just
like Elvis. At about 11 P.M. my mother said good night. I stayed til
long after the bar was supposed to close. On their breaks, they came
to talk to me a bit. They did their thing. They offered me a push back
to my room, which I gratefully accepted. Methinks it was around 4
or 5 A.M. when Elvis and his band "crashed our room door," according to my mother. I bet they would have stayed to chat some more!
My mother wanted her sleep. She said, "Thank yew verra much!
Goodbye!" I think she was very self-conscious of her appearance with
only one breast and nothing to hide the fact that she had lost her
other one to cancer. Whenever she gets caught, she will try and grab
a towel. By the way, I too am self-conscious of my appearance. I try
to hide my terrible posture by wearing a sweater, at least over my
shoulders. The surgeon in 1986–1987 created this bad posture, saying it will make me "more attractive to men."

A BIG DAY

Graduation day from Gallaudet University was very special to me. I
was determined to walk across that stage without my wheelchair and
without my forearm crutches. I had been sneaking around, practicing my short walk across that stage and trying to build up my stam-

ina for this big event. On this beautiful May day, I gave my crutches to my mother and said something like, "Will you take these back to my dorm room, please?" She looked at me with tears in her eyes as she took them. I was ready to move on with life, come hell or high water. Nothing was going to ruin my day. When they called my name, the president of the university, I. King Jordan, greeted me with a hug. I was the only one who got this special treatment! I think this was because he knew of my surgery in 1986. I was on the dean's list that year. I felt I would need some extra time to recover from my surgery, so I got special permission from him to get the fall semester 1986 off. He was the dean at the time. I hadn't didn't realized it, but I had made a friend out of him that first meeting. I blundered! At that time, most people in authority at Gallaudet were hearing. I assumed he was also hearing. I sat down at this first meeting with him and started to blabber away. He signed in his humble, small way, PLEASE SIGN. Boy, was I embarrassed! That summer after the surgery I got a note from his office saying congratulations on making the dean's list again for the spring semester. A handwritten note said something like, "We have heard that you are having surgery this summer. Get well." How it was phrased was most inspiring and heartwarming! I think this arrived before my grades! I didn't get it until after I was in the ICU. The memory of that note still brings me to tears of how poignant it was.

MY VARIED MODES OF COMMUNICATION

During those five years, from 1985 to 1990, sign language was my main mode of communicating. I guess my mouth got weak from not speaking and using the various parts of it. Maybe it was an after-effect of mononucleosis, which I got for the third time earlier in 1990, just like when I was in high school. After twelfth grade, I dragged my left leg. After graduating from the university, communication became a problem. I would speak and hope they understood what I was saying, even trying to mime, even though I didn't know mime. If that didn't work, then I'd fall back on the old handwriting thing. I'd hope they could read my chicken scratch!

In 1994 or 1995, it was arranged for me to try out new technology. At the time, it was new! I tried out an SL30 LightWRITER, which I nicknamed my voice or my communication device. This was a godsend. It saved me an aching hand, and it saved me from frustration with meeting new people. On the other hand, I missed out on eye contact. It's sure lousy for people who are illiterate or impatient, though. Sign language is great because I can sign away and most people can understand me, but it's no good because so few know it. It would be nice if everyone could learn this creative language.

One reason why I don't specify which sign language I use is because there is a great big war between Sign Exact English, or SEE, and American Sign Language, or ASL. I understand both of these languages are American in origin. Me, myself, and I think this debate is madness. This so-called debate rages because no one is sure which is more beneficial to Deaf children learning English. I don't know because I didn't grow up with sign language. The languages I know are English, which is my native language; then French, which I don't use; then sign language. SEE is bulky and awkward. I was asked if ASL can become like spoken English. My answer was, "Can we do this to other spoken languages? I'm not sure. It's best to have a sign language interpreter. We can translate languages, but the meaning from the original language is always lost. We can come close with ASL, though."

At my job for the government, my socks were knocked off! Someone got the idea to learn sign language, and in 1998 my supervisor told me she was attempting this great feat, along with others as well. Wow, I felt spoiled!

The phone is something I can't use. (I was trained to use the phone as a kid, though. This was when I had a few more decibels of hearing. I learned how the phone works, but it didn't catch on with me. Now, I've lost a bit more of my hearing. If I must use the phone, then I panic if I hear something on the other end, and I can't make it out.) I have a TDD, or telecommunication device for the deaf, which I use instead. However, not everyone has a TDD. The reason is it's expensive. I've noticed some public phones have a TDD now. My reaction was, "It's about time! I won't have to carry mine with me everywhere I go." The TDD public phones are not everywhere, though. I guess it costs more. To reach hearing people who don't have a TDD, I use Message Relay. I've heard stories, though, of some of the operators on relay. Some don't say word for word what people say to each other, even though they are supposed to. I heard that once, an operator had phone sex while a deaf person was typing out a very long response. Like in every profession, there is the occasional bad apple. How do I know when the phone rings, as it often does? I have a flashing light system. When the phone rings for a call or for someone at the door, the lights flash. I have a television that has the caption decoder chip. This puts the dialogue on the screen. I'm still new with captions, so when a conversation goes by fast I have to decide what I want to do: get the dialogue or watch the actors. Hmm, big decision. I don't have much use for an alarm clock. I have one now named Panther, my beautiful black cat. He isn't always reliable, but that's fine. I'm sure he will become reliable as he gets older.

WHAT'S IT LIKE IN THERE, HONEYSUCKLE?

Some people have asked me what it's like being deaf. At first, I didn't know how to answer this question. My sister says I must be lucky, because everything is silent. Much later she suggested I answer, "Can you describe a sunset? No one can." This is because we all experience each unique situation from our own perspective. For me, being deaf is actually quite noisy because of tinnitus. Sometimes my tinnitus is more noticeable than other times, like when I'm sick. My tinnitus frequently sounds like a long, endless drone, changing pitch every now and then; at other times it's like Morse code. It's rare that I get angry. Being angry is such a waste of precious energy. If I know something can be changed, I can become angry. Otherwise, I stick to my usual happy-go-lucky self.

LONG WAY ROUND TO WORK

I graduated from the university in 1990. I tried to look for a job. I didn't find any that wanted me, with a degree in English literature. Ah, nuts! I headed back to school to take music. I did this for a year, then changed to take some business courses for the next year. By this time, I got fed up with school and wanted a change. I decided to have some fun, acting with a group called Theatre Terrific. With them, I got to travel throughout British Columbia. Theatre Terrific is a non-profit organization that trains people with disabilities to act for stage, television, film, and radio.

I told my mother I was sick of studying and wanted a change. I said I'd be acting; I got a part in a play. Her reaction was definitely NOT what I anticipated! I was expecting a response befitting every parent's worst nightmare, such as, "You can't do this! You won't survive! How will you eat, pay rent, and so on?" I guess her reaction was pure shock. She buried her face in her hands; no words were spoken.

The acting gig was a 2-year thing. The first year was a total blast. Lots of high school students were amazed with us. Some of the kids weren't sure if they could laugh at us or not, though. After we performed the play, we opened the floor for a question and answer period. In one high school, one of the kids asked us about teasing. This kid had witnessed a cruel teasing of someone who is mentally challenged. I was shocked! I assumed kids knew better than that with increased awareness and exposure nowadays. I told this audience if anyone teases you like that, then just try to ignore them by keeping busy and look for friends. To look for true friends is fundamentally difficult and downright hard on the patience. If you spend the time, then you're rewarded. I hope that kid is okay. If I go and act again, I'll say you should find something creative that you can do. That will earn people's respect.

Year 2 came along, with a new couple of able-bodied actors who we had to break in as well as a new sign language interpreter. The new guy was difficult to get along with, for me. The interpreter was complaining that the pay was not up to her standards—and this from a new sign language graduate! I didn't finish that year. The interpreter couldn't take traveling long distances, interpreting what was going on during transit, interpreting the play, then traveling again. She expected a lot more than she was doing. I suspect Theatre Terrific told her there was no money left to pay her high fees. Theatre Terrific told her to reduce her fees or she would be fired. She quit. I was left high and dry; they wouldn't say whether I was fired, de-hired, laid off, or what. My mother said they were patronizing me. I was humiliated by this. She was doing her part in getting me to stop acting. She was doing what I thought she would do at first. She also said, "The more educated a person is, the more subtle the patronizing is." I felt like I was forced into a blind alley with ferocious dogs nipping at my heels with no way out—at Christmas time, too! But, it was a fun thing to do while it lasted. If I do it again, I'll be sure and pay the interpreter myself. This will save them from going broke.

Now I have two jobs. Both are temporary and deciduous. For one, I do data entry for the government. This one lasts from March to June. My other temporary job is for the post office, sorting. This one is during the Christmas rush.

A GARDEN VARIETY OF WEEDS—MY DIAGNOSIS? PART TWO

While I was acting, I decided to look up progressive spastic paraplegia, the diagnosis I was handed in 1986. Little did I know what I was getting myself into! I intended just to go to the local public library and punch those three words into the computer and have it spit out a list of books or articles on this thing. No such luck! The librarian there tried to help by asking unrelated questions. I was stuck for a while. I asked the neurologists who diagnosed me with this for something to get me started. Dr. Number One had retired by then! I felt I had to hound the other one until I got something about progressive spastic paraplegia. This felt like talking to a brick wall. I had to know what this thing was. If it was a disease, then I could look for a possible cure. Or, if this was something that just happens, then I could sit back and sign off.

While I was hounding Dr. Number Two, I discovered a medical library at the University of British Columbia (UBC). I asked the librarian to help me look up progressive spastic paraplegia. I thought I had to be a medical student for this help. I guess anyone can ask for information, eh? I suppose my doing this put pressure on Dr. Number Two to find me something. Maybe they have these so-called spy cameras in the medical library as well! Hey, I don't know, but I finally got an article sent to me from Dr. Number Two's office. Whew, NOW I could find out what *progressive spastic paraplegia* meant!

When I first read this article, it felt like meaningless gobbledygook. I needed a medical or neurological dictionary. I borrowed my mother's nursing dictionary. She didn't think it would help much as there are newer terms than her dictionary would have. I took it anyway and used it first to break down words into smaller parts and then piece them together. I did this to every other word. This was actually fun for me, pretending to be a surgeon! When I was finally able to read what this article said, it didn't sound much like me at all.

With progressive spastic paraplegia, the complex form, I could develop other sicknesses as well. One of those named was adrenoleukodystrophy. According to the American Heritage Dictionary and my taking apart this word, it means a disease that affects the kidneys and blood and caused by "defective nutrition."

I decided to go back to the medical library to look up other articles that were listed in the bibliography of this first article. There were about 100 others. I wanted to get them all to see if there was something I missed, even though some were in foreign languages. By the time I got about 10 others, I noticed they all sounded like something other than what I had.

It was time to find a new neurologist. Dr. Number One had retired, and Dr. Number Two was a children's neurologist. Again, it was time to be a hot potato. I asked my general practitioner for a referral to get the ball going. She referred me to a neurologist in her building—I forget his name now. For this neurologist, I had my new talking device. I went to this appointment by myself. I was glad he was patient with me. I answered his questions as well as I could. He referred me to a neurologist from New Zealand at UBC. When I saw this one, it seemed like he was also patient with me. However, I asked for his assessment of me. In it, he said something like, "Thank you for your notes, they were a big help. This patient was slow to communicate." I was back and forth between these two for about a year.

I told them both to decide who was to be my neurologist, that I would stick to just that one and they could consult with each other as they pleased.

I was sent to do some tests. Dr. New Zealand sent me along to see a metabiologist. I recollect this one blood-taker who looked like she had YEARS of experience finding a good vein. Not so! This one, after putting the rubber band on and patting my arm waiting for a vein to appear put the needle in. No blood came. I guess being in the hospital for surgery made my body want to be stingy giving blood. I was going to suggest she try my other arm. Nope. She moved the needle around a few times under my skin. She had me whimpering! The pain was unbearable! I was very tempted to take my arm away, but I thought that would only make it worse. She just cut me with the needle. That caused me to have a black bruise for 2 or 3 months.

One blood test required a lot of red tape. It was one where they wanted to check for acanthocytes in my blood. Dr. New Zealand drew me a picture of an acanthocyte. Acanthocytes are cells that resemble holly with points going out from the cell. First, I needed approval from another doctor, then approval from the hospital. I was thinking, "What's all the fuss about? It's just a simple blood test!" Maybe this wasn't a simple blood test. Maybe they were going to expose my blood to some toxic stuff or radiation and voilà, acanthocytes appear! I don't know because it didn't get approved by the second doctor. I don't know if I have acanthocytes swimming around in my blood or not.

My paranoid imagination can get the best of me sometimes! I was thinking what if I have acanthocytes in my blood? Will I kick the bucket tomorrow? I recall a nurse at the infirmary at Gallaudet said there was something missing in my blood, but she wouldn't say what. Okay, so something's missing. (Looking back, I think what she meant was that my blood was missing some antibodies. I found out that my body can't fight off the family of diseases of which mononucleosis is a member. This is why I got this disease more than once.) What does this mean? Will I croak the next day? Am I a time bomb, just waiting for the right situation or the right ingredients??

A couple of times, I had extreme pain in my back. I felt it would be easier to go to the hospital to be taken care of. Each time, I felt they were much more interested in my blood than in helping me get over my pain. When I asked, they would just say it's standard procedure. Uh huh. They're feeding their pet vampires on my blood, I bet! The vampires only want MY blood and only when I'm in the hospital!

Anyway, Dr. New Zealand decided to send me off to have a magnetic resonance imaging (MRI) test. This was the one that caught my having extra iron in my basal ganglia and some pin size holes in there, too. Hey, so I have a leaky bucket! Oh, goody! This test, the MRI, concluded that I have Hallervorden-Spatz. Dr. New Zealand said these holes are in part what's causing me to have less energy.

Upon hearing that, I trudged off to the ol' medical library at UBC. I got about 20 or so articles, over a year. Using my previous researched definitions of neurological terms, at first this diagnosis sounded like me—the picture of my head, the spasticity associated with the possibility of the extra iron. While I was studying this with more interest and trying to be objective, I thought it was correct. I was heartbroken when I learned that this thing is progressive and that the last stages of the disease are devastating. The main things I could expect to happen would be that I would slowly lose control of my body with increased spasticity and end up mentally deteriorated. This destroyed me. At least now I knew what I had, so I could carry on as usual until I couldn't anymore.

One day I was rereading one of the articles and found that it didn't sound like me. I checked again with the others I got. I got some more, even getting the list from the med-line from the computer. There were 160 articles on Hallervorden-Spatz. There was even an article in German about the man after whom it is named. I wanted to know anything and everything about this disease, including a possible cure, no matter how remote or obscure. I was even willing to see if there were untried and unproven ways to beat it. I was disappointed there were only articles written by those in mainstream medicine. There were other articles in other languages, too. I wasn't sure how or if I would be able to get them translated.

It was about this time that I was back at G.F. Strong Rehabilitation Hospital for assistance in accommodating me at work. My occupational therapist was interested in my research; I wasn't sure why at first. One day, she told me to give her some of what I found. She told me she was from Germany. I should have said, "Oh, why didn't you say so?" I guess we are still in this culture of, "You don't ask; I don't tell." She translated the biography of Hallervorden, saying all the things he accomplished and what he discovered. She was going to do some of the others, but she had to go back home. Huh. Seems the professionals who try to help me, leave me.

It was from these articles that I started to question the diagnosis of Hallervorden-Spatz. The more information I had, the less I seemed to fit the prognosis. Most of the people who had this thing had noticeable changes in their childhood. These people died between ages 20 and 30. I would be 34 on my next birthday. This really didn't sound like me. Whew! That disease sure sounds miserable.

Okey dokey. Round number three! Maybe THIS time they'll get it right? Maybe they hurried before or weren't careful with looking at all of my symptoms? I got to see a brand new neurologist. Right off the bat, I told him I wanted him to stay here and work with me on naming whatever I have. My mother came along for this one, but just because this guy is famous. My reaction was, "Oh, he's famous, eh? How do you know?" But I didn't say that. I had become tired of people coming and going like they were on spectacle, just for me, in a parade. This new neurologist said he wanted three things done: another MRI, a specialized eye exam, and a throat exam.

The MRI was inconclusive because they say I moved too much! Nevertheless, it looked like a conference was happening in there. First there was one person; then this one motioned for a second person who got two others. They got me out, and I thought, "Oh good, this is all over. I can go!" No such luck. The second guy, who was cute, said to keep still. I was keeping still! I guess I shouldn't have been grimacing, breathing, or blinking? I asked for a copy of the results from the test. The eye exam stated that there was not enough evidence for a diagnosis of Hallervorden-Spatz. The throat exam said the same thing. Back again to Dr Number Five and he said he didn't know what I had. He was probably afraid that I'd head off to the library and research whatever name he came up with and find out THAT didn't fit me either.

If anyone asks me, I can probably say I don't know. Won't that sound intelligent? One person asked me if I was in a car accident. Maybe I should have said yes? Maybe I can just hope it's cerebral palsy and say that if anyone asks me what's wrong? Maybe I could say a synapse is out of alignment? I could say it's called "XYZ." Or, I could say it was an accident at birth. However, I DO know that something MIGHT be missing from my blood, and MAYBE I have holes in my basal ganglia. Maybe I could find out, one day, on my own. Cerebral palsy's the name now, BUT that's not definite. After all that, I'm not some exotic, rare breed of flower but a common weed. I'm a hardy dandelion, maybe?

HUH?! DISABLED? ME?!

I can trace back to elementary school; I was in the school library, trying to pick out a book. I heard this exquisite and delicious sound. I had believed the library was supposed to be a quiet place! This piece of music was "Fur Elise." It sounded sad and happy at the same time. I had to hear more of this magic voice. When I got to the piano, it was already surrounded by people. Everything about it engrossed and fascinated me. There was mystery in it.

I got an opportunity at high school. On my schedule, there was this choice: choir or homeroom. Homeroom would be so boring for me!

Just sitting there trying to keep quiet doing homework was mind boggling. I knew I would distract the others with how I concentrate on things, by talking to myself under my breath, breathing loudly, and laughing at the characters in the stories for homework. I decided to go into choir. This was a lot of fun, even though someone told me I was flat?! I thought this was a scare tactic to get me out, but I didn't give in and cry about it. I wanted to do this and so I did. I did this for the five years at that school from seventh to eleventh grade.

ME, MYSELF, AND I = DISabled

I can be made to feel like I'm disabled, though. Once, while I was working for a deaf organization, I was taking a break and I thought to say hello to another person who had cerebral palsy and was deaf as well. His friend was extremely patronizing, and he didn't even mind! She said, upon me approaching and saying hello to them all, that the guy had found his girlfriend at long last. The guy just blinked. She insulted me by calling me "a cripple." My God! I thought that kind of vocabulary went out of style when people were being de-institutionalized back in the fifties, sixties, or seventies! Yikes! I wanted to rip her hair out!

At times, I feel like I'm an outcast. I'm greeted either by being shown the door or with a sincere, warm welcome, and sometimes in between the two extremes. I went to a job interview and the interviewer had, on his face, the reaction of, "Oh my god! What do I do now? She's DISABLED!" I know I'm not alone, in having a disability, but this sure rubs it in. Even my own mother thrusts upon me the unwanted label of "role model." My reaction was "role model" for whom, those who are able-bodied or those who happen to have a disability? She also wanted me "to be a bridge between the disabled, the deaf, and the able-bodied." I can understand the actress Marlee Matlin's point of view of not wanting to be a role model. This is a tremendous weight to place on one's shoulders. I'm glad that the movie

> If you dare pat an adult on the head, like me, myself, and I, watch out! That is the most belittling, demeaning, and thoughtless thing anyone can do.

industry is finally seeing that there are some talented actors who happen to have disabilities. It's very strange to see able-bodied actors playing a role that a disabled person should be playing, though some of these actors can do an excellent job. Ah, I guess they want big glamorous names. Aha, and it's probably easier, faster, and more efficient to communicate with able-bodied people.

HOPES, DREAMS, AND DESIRES

I had images of becoming a ballerina, a model, and an actress while I was growing up. I never thought of myself as "disabled." It puzzles me when someone asks me what's wrong. I assume they mean that I look as if I'm upset about something, then that's why they ask me. But they ask me what's wrong to mean what's my disability. Huh? Whoa! I'm disabled?! Where did you get THAT idea from? Also, growing up, it never dawned on me that I was different from everyone else. Sure, I had physiotherapy, didn't everyone? That was how I thought during those tender years. Recently, the neurologist, Dr. Number Two, asked me, "Do you think of yourself as disabled?" "Ha ha, definitely not," was my shoot from the hips and lips answer. I wonder what makes people ask these questions. Sure, they're curious, but what does it really mean?

Lots of people tell me I could be and should be a model. This is always after I show a picture to them; they say I'm photogenic. They think that because I'm so photogenic, that I should be modeling in a snap of fingers. I'd like to. It's not that simple though. This industry is fickle—long hair, short hair, frizzy hair, and clothes and shoes to match. Blah. I gave up trying to keep up with these so-called trends long ago. However, I appear MUCH younger than my age. I don't understand why either of my so-called agents discourage me from trying to get in the movie and model industries.

BEING TEASED

This particular phrase bewilders me: "Sticks and stones may break my bones, but names will never hurt me." Yow! Whoever thought of that must have had elephant skin. I've never had a broken bone, but lots of scrapes. I don't intend to find out what it's like to have a broken bone! I have heard once a bone is broken that pain is always there. I have been called names, though. These names have stayed with me since the day I heard them and they still sting. I've tried to develop elephant skin.

I wonder who coined the phrase "deaf and dumb." At the time

when it was created, it meant deaf and mute. I guess they didn't think to change the words as times changed. Now, dumb means stupid. When I first heard this expression, I thought it was derogatory, insulting, and hurtful. I couldn't imagine anyone teasing me this way.

When I was going to high school, from seventh to eleventh grade, I was relentlessly and cruelly teased by another girl whose name was Mary. I didn't understand why I was a target for being picked on like this. My mother came up with this four-line poem that must have hurt her feelings. I learned it and said it to her. Actually, she was on the honor roll every year. I always had to study more just to keep my head above the water. Because of her superior ability to learn the material, I didn't understand why she was like she was. Maybe teasing me and seeing how I reacted gave her a euphoric feeling? Gee. Or, maybe she thought I was less of a person because I had disabilities? Or, maybe she thought like how I believe the Buddhists think, that at the beginning we are all disabled in a variety of ways, but after a few lifetimes, we reach perfection; therefore, by the end of these lifetimes, we should not be disabled. Ah, I don't feel any resentment toward her. She's now an anchor for a television morning news show.

EENY, MEENY, MINY, MOE

I don't know which disability I like or dislike more. Both have their advantages and disadvantages. Being deaf is great because I can sit up front in public places like a seminar. It's not terrific, though, because I can't hear the small inflections in people's speech that indicate one's true feelings. Having this neurological condition is nice, because some people offer up their warmed up seat on the bus! It's also not so good because someone once asked me if I was drunk. Both get me patronizing remarks, and some people have said to me, "Oh, I'm so sorry you have that awful disability!" Oh, really? Can you prove that you're sorry? Not that I care, but I'm tired of hearing people's pity stories, and I don't have time for these kind of people. Still, I like myself overall. I've gotten discounts at some touristy places here because of my disabilities—I don't mind being taken advantage of in THAT way!

Some people think I can hear. Ha! They go ahead and ask me, "How do I get to Capilano Suspension Bridge from here?" Well, I, of course, don't realize at first that they said something to me. Ya hafta get my attention FIRST, then fire away. I've noticed after two tries most people give up and move on the next person. I guess I look like I know where I am and where I'm going—a local person, someone who knows the area.

A SERIES OF IRRITATIONS

Some people can sure be irritating! I find this especially when I go out to buy things. Once, I went to buy a new vacuum. First, I looked up vacuums in Consumer Reports to see what a good value would be. I went with my homemaker to the store. We picked out one that I felt would be a good quality. We went to make the purchase and to ask about the warranty. The woman talked to my homemaker! "Hello, you nitwit! You talk to me; I'm the brain here!" was what I was tempted to say. She turned her head to face my homemaker so I couldn't see what exactly she was saying. Blah!

Another time, I got on the skytrain here in Vancouver. It was the very first stop. Some young uniformed guy told me to get off. He said it fast and quietly. I didn't hear what he said. I stayed right there. He came back after checking the other cars and told me again to get off. I asked him why and indicated the lighted sign said it was going the other way. He said he didn't understand me. Oh, good for you! At that time I didn't have my communication device, as I didn't anticipate a conversation, I asked again why I had to get off, slowly so maybe he would get it. I even used the sign for why. He was becoming agitated and I thought he was going to pass out from the strain of meeting me. I also thought maybe he might be sincerely worried for my safety; maybe there was a bomb on this train. He finally said, "Ma'am, it's not in service!" "Ah, NOW I gotcha!" I must have exasperated him. When the ordeal was over, I noticed some people were watching. Huh. I'm a ma'am now. Is that supposed to be a term of respect or an insult?

Another example of irritating people is when I took Panther to the groomer to be taken off for his own holiday from me. I wrote a letter to the owner of the cattery saying what else Panther had with him. Again, I went with my homemaker. The woman talked to my homemaker, not me. I was not impressed. This is SO frustrating when this happens. I guess it's easier for strangers to try and talk to someone WITH me rather than TO me. She was abrupt with me and told me that Panther couldn't have this or that with him. Even though the brochure said to include his brush, when she took it out, I made a handwritten note saying the brush was removed. She scratched over that. Eventually I made a trip to visit him and give him his brush there at the cattery.

Yet another story: I went to buy a new adapter for my Light-WRITER, my voice. I went alone. I was greeted by a shy man who was trying to help. He didn't know where the thing to measure electric output was located. His co-worker took over. This co-worker was obnoxious to me. He was carrying on a conversation with someone I suppose was a friend who looked like Bob Vila, that home repair guy. I didn't care who he was! Friend or not, famous or not, he should have finished his conversation before helping me. He informed me that the one I had was broken. Well, duh! I wanted to say, "I know that. I've been trying to tell you just that, that I need a new one." The guy then backed up, pushing the first guy into the wall, all the while having that conversation. He walked over to the other side of the store and probably picked out the most expensive adapter they had. When I left, I wanted to wring his neck.

A PUZZLE

There is one question that crops up when people are first getting to know me, to which my answer earns a reaction of astonishment. They ask me if I live on my own. Huh?? Of course I do. Who doesn't live on their own? I have since I left home for the university. "Home" for me is where I hang my hat. At least, I'd like it that way. Or they will ask me if I'm in my own apartment, ALL alone. I guess some people assume that all disabled people live at home with their parents. Ugh!

PARTING WORDS, BUT NOT GOODBYE

I went to a camp for the deaf in 1984. At the end of this fantastic experience, the director gave us a dramatic and powerful message. He dropped a stone into a slow moving river and ripples went out from it. While they were continuously expanding, he said that that was us. Each of us will go our separate ways, some getting where they want faster than others. He said it doesn't matter about speed, but how we get there. I didn't understand this until much, much later. Deep stuff!

You see, I'm no different from any average Jane Doe. I have hopes, dreams, and desires of my own. I may be a little slow at communicating, but methinks it's worth the time you spend. We don't need to rush about life. Even the three of us, me, myself and I, forget to take a break from the hecticness. We all go down this road of life, as individuals. Some have a map; others just wing it. How we do stuff is probably the goal, not necessarily always the speed. We all say things in our own unique way. Mine is—here we are!

6

Communication My Way

Tara M. McMillen

When time is not important, I use many ways to communicate. Most people develop their own style.

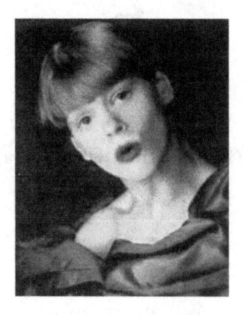

Tara M. McMillen lives in Austin, Texas. She sees herself first and foremost as a writer, writing about nondisability topics. She is a disability advocate and graduate of the Texas Partners in Policymaking program.

Hi. My name is Tara McMillen. I am a 22-year-old college student who has had cerebral palsy from birth. I am majoring in English for two reasons. First, I like to write stories and essays about real life. Mostly, I write about children. I don't just write about persons with disabilities; I write about all children. My second reason for being an English major (with the goal of becoming a published writer) is because I basically have been writing since I was born, so it comes naturally. You see, I am nonverbal. Writing stories helps me to relax. I am always searching for ideas. When I find something interesting or when something upsets me, I write about it.

As for the history of my communication, when I was growing up, my mom was responsible for getting me to communicate. It was very hard at first because I used to point at whatever I wanted and cry when I didn't get it. It was difficult because I knew what I wanted but just couldn't seem to get the message across. Mom encouraged me to verbalize what I was thinking. So, my first communicator was a homemade board. Mom made it out of illustrations cut from a Richard Scarry storybook. It was cute. The pictures of little animals doing everyday things made me want to talk. In preschool, the teachers tried to stimulate me to talk on my own. I did exercises to relax my muscles and even did humming. Then came the Blissymbol Board in grade school. It had more than my first board did and came in handy to carry around. This gave me the tools to develop vocabulary and make complete sentences. There were symbols above the words, so even if I couldn't read all the words, I could still communicate by pointing at the symbols.

When I was 7, I got my first talking machine. It was big and heavy! My speech teacher and I had to learn number codes in order to use it. We had to learn it together. That was neat because it wasn't like a teacher teaching me. Sometimes we just played and discovered things on our own, saying, "Cool, now let's see what happens when we push this button!" We spent hours trying to find the right codes for the words. I called it Ben, after my great-grandpa. The company who made it hooked me up to be voice-pals with Henry Winkler, but that is a story all on its own. For camp and everyday activities, I needed a lighter machine. Mom had to find the funding to get me a Cannon Communicator. It was a little typewriter that hooked onto my belt.

My last communicator, which has been with me for a long time, is my Epson HX-20 Communicator with a Real Voice SpeechPac. It is programmable for phrases and can also be in different modes or voices for different situations, like telling a joke. This is handy because in different modes the codes can mean different phrases. It speaks phonetically and can be programmed to say anything, and I mean anything. It has a tape drive which holds memory and is very durable, TRUST ME. There are two things I do not like about it, though. For one thing, it is way too heavy for me to carry around. Also, the reading window cannot be edited. If I make a mistake, I have to start from the beginning. But, for the first time, I can speak with a female voice, something important since I am a girl. What makes it even neater is the printer built into it. So, if I want to tell a secret, I can just print it out.

I got the Epson when I was entering junior high. Boy! That was scary! Not only was I the only person in the whole school that had a disability, I was the first person they had that didn't talk. Also, I didn't have an assistant. The teachers were afraid too. But after my mom and the speech teacher talked, they began to feel relaxed. I was afraid I wouldn't fit in. Sure I had been mainstreamed in grade school, but only in a few classes.

I had a hard time that year because I couldn't talk. When I saw people out in hall, there wasn't enough time to whip out my machine and talk. Lunch time was the worst because no one would sit by me, or if they did it would be because there was nowhere else to sit. I did have some friends though. Once, this one friend and I were walking in the hall, and I was trying to tell him something. After several tries I waved my hand, telling him to forget it, but as soon as we got into the classroom he opened my communicator and asked me what I was trying to say. From that day on I knew people really wanted to hear what I had to say and it didn't matter how I conveyed it.

When I had my back surgery during my eighth-grade year, I didn't have my machine. It was very hard to express what I wanted because I was lying on my back and couldn't move. Mom understood me but the doctors and nurses couldn't. They had me blink "yes" or "no." It was better when I was sitting up but still hard to communicate. I had to use my Blissymbol Board which made it frustrating at times because of my poor spelling. Nevertheless, I got my point across by finding another way to say it.

Although communication devices do work, I communicate in several different ways. Sometimes, I use my machine to talk with friends and family. But there are also times when I need to talk fast; that's when I use my assistant. My assistant spends more than 60 hours a week with me. Because of this, she knows how I feel about certain issues and knows most of my experiences. Therefore, she can express my feelings in a way that makes me feel comfortable and confident.

Sometimes, I communicate in different ways to express my feelings. I use facial expressions. I might feel really down and walk around in a draggy way. Other times when I am happy, I walk around proud and have a smile on my face. My assistant can see these feelings and express them to other people. Often, when we are in a meeting or just talking to friends, I can push one or two letters and she can predict what I am trying to say.

When time is not important, I use many ways to communicate. Most people develop their own style. I use my machine, finger spelling, body language, and my own version of sign language. My friends and family can understand what I am saying. For a quiet and relaxing lunch, I can be myself and have time to talk.

Once, after the evening activities at camp, my friends and I were sitting around just talking up a storm. Chirsti and Jean have difficulties like me. Chirsti can talk, somewhat. I can understand her most of the time. At other times, she has a board she uses by holding a straw in her mouth to point at words or letters. Jean, on the other hand, has to blink when she doesn't use her computer. Chirsti says the alphabet, and Jean stops blinking or moves her body to show it is the right letter. Then, I write the letters down until they make a word. It seems hard, I know, but once we got started it became easier. Chirsti and I guessed the next word. Sometimes we got it right. Sometimes we got it wrong. This technique was an improvement for Jean. She used to not let anyone guess what she was trying to say. As for me, I don't mind because it's less work for me.

It's funny. Most nonverbal people can understand each other, sometimes better than people who can talk. You will find this is often true because we use similar ways to communicate. It is easy to spot the signs. Over the years, I have trained my hearing. I now can understand other people with speech impediments if they talk slowly. Shocks people to death! They say, "You actually understood that?" I say, "Sure, didn't you?" An example was Jean's birthday party. It was after we had eaten and Jean had opened her presents. She was trying to tell Chirsti and me "Thank you." Chirsti and I said, "You're welcome." The others who couldn't understand just said, "Fine, leave us out of your conversation."

When I am out in public where people are concerned with time, I use my assistant. Some people think I shouldn't because they think people should wait and listen to me. Heck, if I wanted to do that I could go home and write them a 10-page essay. The fact is, I don't want to make them wait and I don't want to wait, not when I have an assistant. Why should I? This is a free country last time I checked!

Let me give you an example where I came across this problem. My assistant and I went to a meeting to give input for this program I am in called Community Living Assistance and Support Services (CLASS). (CLASS is how I got my assistant. Thanks to this Medicaid Waiver Program I can go to college and do the things I need to do every day.) During the meeting, I raised my hand to talk. When my assistant started talking for me—I was nodding my head to reassure everyone that the words were coming from me—the person in charge shut my assistant down. Interrupting, she abruptly said, "This is not a meeting for attendants (a word I do not like), only for participants." I didn't like that at all! I felt like I couldn't talk since she shut my assistant down. My assistant tried to explain but the person would not listen. I thought it was very unprofessional of her. It also made other clients who couldn't talk feel like they didn't count.

My assistant said, "Tara would like to say ... " before she started talking. She always does this. It's a good rule of thumb. Otherwise the client might feel left out. As assistants, you should teach others this. While I am at it, also teach people to talk to the client instead of you. In addition, people often talk too loudly to a nonverbal person. They must think we cannot hear because we cannot talk, so they talk loudly and very s-l-o-w-l-y. Boy, sometimes I just want to pop them upside the head and say, "THINK!" Just because one thing isn't working the way you expect doesn't mean the rest of it will be different. This happens frequently, so be prepared.

Anyway, as I was saying, my assistant and I had spent hours to make sure she knew what I had to say. We were prepared. She was going to talk, and I was going to nod my head showing them they were my words. After that frustrating incident, I made a note saying that although it might seem she's talking for herself, she's really talking for me. I carry it when there's a meeting we have to attend.

This brings up another issue about communicators. One thing an assistant can do that a machine cannot do is show emotions. A machine can do only so much; you can turn the volume up or down but that's about it. When I am really happy or concerned with something, my assistant can show that emotion because she is with me most of the time. I grab her attention to show I want her to interject on an issue. She reads me and knows how to act to show what I am feeling. This only comes from forming a close relationship.

Another example of the types of things that can happen to a nonverbal person is an experience I had as a participant of a disability training program. This came before I made my card. The program is called Partners in Policymaking, a program that is supposed to be on the cutting edge to empower persons with disabilities with independence. Now, this is a program that helps people with disabilities to be involved in the disability world. They are supposed to honor the way you choose to do things.

I brought my assistant and wanted her assistance during ongoing discussions. The people who ran the program were opposed to how I chose to communicate in group discussion. I couldn't understand why. I did it to save them time. Also, my communicator is hard to understand. You have to be around it for a while. The staff and I went around and around on this issue until practically the end of the program. I wrote them letters to try to express my feelings and even used my communicator to discuss it privately with them. It still bugs me a little that they did that.

Sometimes, I even get criticism from other people with disabilities. During that training program, I got grief from a guy who was in a wheelchair and *could* talk. He was saying all this stuff that didn't make sense to me; for example, they wanted to hear from me in my own words. I argued that what I had to say was more important than the vehicle I used to say it. To me, my assistant was just functioning as a higher-level communication device. She was communicating my exact ideas, only faster than I can type. What I should have told him was this. If he saw a little girl bleeding to death, would he go himself in his chair or send his assistant to get help? (I know it is an extreme case, but it does get my point across.) He was entitled to his opinion, I guess. I just wish people would respect the way I want to communicate. It would make it easier on everyone.

Another time when my assistant comes in handy is at the doctor's office. He is usually in a hurry to see his other patients. I use my assistant to tell him what's wrong. Even when I am not sick, I have her do it to save time. It's more comfortable for me because that way I don't have to try to spell. (I know it's not good to speak for others, but it seems many people have difficulty with spelling.) By using my assistant in this way, the doctor can see what he needs to do for me quickly and easily.

My assistant also sets up my meetings. She does this because it is almost impossible for me to do it. Sometimes, I will try by going back and forth holding the phone up to my ear then holding the phone over the speaker of the machine. Whenever I do it, it is hard to keep it up for a long time because my hand gets tired. I used to call up the radio station and request a song this way. The DJ got a kick out of it. When my assistant calls to set up my appointments, we go over what to say. She tells me everything they say. Sometimes I am right there while she's on the phone. She tells me what's going on. Often when the person isn't concerned with time, I can interject by finger spelling, writing my thoughts on paper, or using my machine. Other times, I get on the other line and just listen. I make a sound when I want my assistant to know something important to say and she watches me.

As I already mentioned, my assistant helps me in meetings. She interprets what I want to say. She also interprets what they are saying to me. Sometimes I cannot understand what they are saying; you know how it can be. She also directs people to listen to me. In my meetings for the CLASS program, that is an important point because the program is supposed to be client driven. I am the one who is supposed to have the say about my services.

My friend Anita who is nonverbal (that's not her real name, by the way) had me come to one of her meetings with CLASS. Man! It was awful. I wanted to get out of there as fast as I could. If it wasn't for Anita's wanting my support, I would have left in protest. One of the program people just ran the whole meeting. Anita and her assistant were trying to interject Anita's desires, but it wasn't working. The person was telling Anita what to do and how it was going to be. After the meeting, Anita broke down and cried. I felt really bad for her. I know if it had happened to me I wouldn't have faith in the program either. My assistant and I tried to comfort her. That's why talking things over before a meeting and being strong on your position is very important. If you are going to use your assistant to help during meetings, be sure to let her know how important it is to hold your position. It is easy to be bullied.

I use my assistant in college too. She sits in class and takes notes, since I cannot very easily. She asks questions for me when I have them. This is one place where the teachers know that when my assistant talks, she is talking for me at my request. My assistant still starts every question with, "Tara would like to . . . " That's important.

College goes a lot easier with an assistant. When I don't understand something, she interprets it. When I have a test, she helps me to set it up in the college office designed to help students with various disabilities. On tests, when I don't understand something, she doesn't give me the answers. She puts it in a different way where I can understand what is being asked. When I write a paper, she reads it back to me to see if I think I need to make changes. It really helps for me to hear my own mistakes. She helps me to tell the cooks what I want for lunch and helps me pay for it. In the book store, she helps to ask where to find things and helps me pay. If someone comes up to me, she helps me to communicate, if I request it. Without my assistant, college would feel like an impossibility.

Okay, one more paragraph before I leave. Assistants have a challenging job, and having an assistant is a challenge at first. You have to get to know each other. Being an assistant takes a special person who can handle responsibility. It takes time and effort to do the job. It takes more than just helping a client. It takes patience, especially on a bad day. Once you two establish a relationship, you will develop a feel for working together. My assistant calls it good symbiosis: a relationship between two different organisms (in this case two different people) in close association that is of benefit to each. It all comes with time. Some day you won't even have to ask; your assistant will just know what to do. You can even make up your own sign language to make it easier for you to communicate together. If you make the right mix there will be learning, teaching, and leaning on, and two lives will be enriched. For the assistant, a usually low-paying job will become worth far more than the money paid. For you, the client, all of the experience of another person's life is there for you to glean from, and . . . you may find a lifelong friend.

7

A Fish Story

Mick Joyce

If I am a fish out of water, then what kind of water do I need to do my thing, to live up to my full potential, to swim up stream, mate, and die like the salmon? Good question! I have been searching for the answer to this question for many years myself.

Mick Joyce is a private research consultant. He does consumer education and research on health care, social issues, and employment among other things. Mr. Joyce holds two masters' degrees; one in Urban and Regional Planning and another in Health Policy Administration. He was awarded the Words+ ISAAC Outstanding Consumer Lectureship Award in 1992 and was the 1996 recipient of the United Cerebral Palsy Association–Prentke-Romich Company (UCPA–PRC) Communication Technology Employment Award. Mick is an active AT user, employing AAC devices, special wheelchair seating, a lift-equipped van, and various special computer software to do his work and remain connected to the community.

INTRODUCTION: A FISH OUT OF WATER

I am a fish out of water. Like Forrest Gump, the Rainman, and Edward Scissorhands, I operate more effectively by creating my own world than by trying to live in other people's reality. Of course, sometimes I, like Gump, stumble into others' tangibilities, and it works fairly well. Unlike Forrest, however, I seem to be two standard deviations away from the mean instead of one. This departure is due mainly to my muddled speech and my need for a personal care worker.

What type of fish am I? I'd like to say I am a multicolored rainbow trout, a swift and speedy musky, or a graceful marlin that can leap high in the air. But I'm not. I feel more like a bullhead spending most days in a muddy, squalid river in South Dakota. I am not too pleasing to the human eye: I have projectiles on my face that sting on contact, and my meat is only tolerated after much beer batter. Regardless, I am one of God's creations and am needed in the vast scheme of checks and balances, the ecosystem of the river of life.

If I am a fish out of water, then what kind of water do I need to do my thing, to live up to my full potential, to swim up stream, mate, and die like the salmon? Good question! I have been searching for the answer to this question for many years myself. In the remaining pages of this essay, I will continue this searching. I invite you to come along for the ride. We won't come up with the flawless flow, the immaculate reservoir, or the saltless sea, but in this exercise, our search will bring us closer to the pure pool that exists only in virtual reality.

ABOUT ME: A REALLY FISHY FISH

I feel like a fish out of water because I have cerebral palsy. My speech and mobility are involved. I need help with the so-called activities of daily living: eating, dressing, grooming. The people that help me are called personal care workers (PCWs). Back in college, we used to call them attendants, if not something worse. At the present time, my main PCW is my sister. A guy I've known for years helps me out on weekends doing, among other things, duties that my sister may find morally wicked, like purchasing beer. Once in a while I have others help me, depending on my needs. Sometimes my sister goes away for a weekend, and I may call a back-up person or may "rough it," making my way through pizza after pizza.

Being a fish out of water, I can hardly stand living with myself, much less another person. This is why I live by myself in a small condo that I own in Madison, Wisconsin. I am blessed with the capability of getting in and out of bed, munching on pretzel sticks, and getting beer from the refrigerator if needed. This comes in handy on those long Wisconsin winter nights when the snow is piled high and it's cold enough to freeze the hair off a brass monkey. What does a fish out of water do when it's five below on Saturday night? Fish do a slimy polka step.

Another thing that makes me sort of a fishy guy is my education. I have two masters' degrees in fields related to government. People don't expect fish to obtain advanced degrees, especially in something like policy analysis and political wrangling. I am a little dubious about mentioning that I have this earthly knowledge. I use it when I need it for self-advocacy purposes. It helps, for example, to understand that the American health care system is, for the most part, not understandable.

In my 10 years in Madison, I have not been able to obtain steady employment. I have worked part time for various state agencies, but this is the exception rather than the rule, a trend that's due to change. Employers, especially in government, do not warm up to fish that quickly, especially when the saltwater fish are in power and you're a freshwater fish. Right now, I am engaged in doing some consulting and writing and in starting my own business, while looking for the ultimate state job.

MY COMMUNICATION STYLE: THE FISH CONNECTION

It's not easy for fish to communicate out of water. In water, they use sound waves and other devices to facilitate spoken language. Outside of water, these techniques are useless for the most part, putting these creatures at a disadvantage. I am not that different in my home. I have an IBM-based AAC device called EZ Keys with a MultiVoice speech synthesizer, fax, modem, speaker phone, e-mail, voice mail, and other technologies that are helpful. Outside, I just have my MultiVoice AAC device and me.

I didn't obtain my communication device with a voice synthesizer until about 10 years ago. By this time, I had hacked my way through college, four jobs, and one graduate program. Because of these experiences, I know my speech is understandable to some people if they take the time to listen. But the fact is, most people don't take the time and don't know how to listen. This I find increasingly true as time goes on. I call it the, "I talk too slow; you listen too fast" phenomenon. That passes some of the responsibility to the other party.

Having this as my general bias, I like to make people sweat a bit before I unveil my computer and MultiVoice. Some people, to my surprise, don't sweat at all and are quite comfortable with my speech and understand me most of the time. I have tried to draw a composite picture of these people. Some are bilingual, some have prior contact with people with disabilities, and some are like me, damned determined. Others are highly motivated, like a computer salesperson.

> *I know my speech is understandable to some people if they take the time to listen. But the fact is, most people don't take the time and don't know how to listen.*

In talking to people with whom I am close—PCWs, work associates, family and friends—I mostly use my real voice. Sometimes, however, even these people need help. I am usually by a computer, which I use without voice output, typing words they don't understand. Sometimes, they had a rough night on the town and aren't as willing to listen. In these situations, I am forced to use the computer, hand signals, or some more profane modes of communication. Usually something works. If not, this may be a time to reverse roles, to keep one's mouth shut and ears open.

PERSONAL CARE WORKERS: FISH OF DIFFERENT COLORS

The Good Book said that God in his infinite wisdom filled the sea with great sea monsters and other living creatures that swarm the waters (Gen. 1: 20–24). No one knows this more than people with disabilities who hire PCWs. Even one's own sister can be a great sea monster if she stays up all night fighting those demons of darkness.

Much good, however, outweighs bad, as my sister has been my primary helper for 12 years. Before that, for 8 years I had a retired dairy farmer. He had a mixed bag of vices and virtues as well, but as with my sister, good points overrode bad points. Before that, it was an engineering student for 3 years, and before that, a janitor, a medical student, and a student who had no vocational goal.

There were many more—too many for this writing or any writing. PCWs usually stay with me a long time, mainly because I attend to them while they attend to me. Through the years, I've played the role of psychologist, legal consultant, financial advisor, doctor, and whatever else was needed. PCW relationships are like any other human endeavor, a two-way street.

As I have run the gamut of types of PCWs, so too I have had to figure out different ways of paying for them. When you are a fish out of water, fishing for cash to pay the fish in water is usually not an easy task. At first, when I was in college, vocational rehabilitation picked up the tab, a cash payment to me of $250 per month. I would then pay the PCW a flat rate of $4 per hour, about a dollar over minimum wage. This would buy me about 80 hours per month or about 3 or 4 hours a day. They didn't get paid for school breaks. This freed up funds for the next month when I might need more hours than the prior one.

Life went on, and I was soon out of college and on the job. Vocational rehabilitation was no longer a source for PCW funds. At that time, there were no employment incentive programs for people with disabilities designed to ease the financial crunch of PCW payments. I paid workers out of my own pocket. Not making a lot, I lived in low-income housing, which allowed me to deduct my PCW expense from my income. This lowered my rent considerably and made living affordable from my perspective. Again, I paid my PCW $4 and $5 per hour. My accountant and I did battle with the IRS yearly to get a clear ruling on whether this was a business or medical expense. We finally gave up on this effort and continued to claim it as a business expense.

When moving to Wisconsin, I had to learn a new system. In graduate school I obtained some funding from the Community Development Block grant. This money was relatively free of strings and consisted of a flat sum, but I no longer had control of the money; the county did. This lessened the flexibility of the funds. I couldn't, for example, hold off in low work months and increase cash flow in high work months.

In 1990, Wisconsin adopted a Personal Care Program, mainly to divert money from the Block grant. Because it was funded by Medicaid, and some work incentive programs were in place, I was able to work and make a wage that I could live on without low-income housing. Work had no effect on my personal care under this system. In fact, with all the work incentives in place, one is still, in my opinion, discouraged from working. This is because of the uncertainty many programs have regarding when to cut off benefits. Unfortunately, most of these programs use much of the funds on program administration and "quality control" instead of funneling direct cash payments to the consumers. This further erodes consumer empowerment.

Putting payment and policy issues aside, most of my PCWs I had known before they became workers. They understood me before I employed them. On a few occasions, I did interview people. In the interviews I asked for a detailed list of experiences with people with disabilities. If they had trouble understanding me, I would write it out using longhand, a typewriter, or a computer; I'd try to detect if they were willing to listen to me. If they weren't, they were not acceptable.

Today, if I needed a PCW, I'd most likely use my voice output communication aid, then slowly remove it from the scene, except on monster mornings. It would be understood before employment that computers and voice synthesizers were there for back-up purposes, but within a month or two, the individual would be expected to understand my normal speech. None of my workers were formally trained in communications. I suppose it would help to a certain extent. But since everyone has an individual communication style and unique speech patterns and lifelong experiences, formal training would not help beyond the basic, "this is a computer; it doesn't bite" type of awareness. In my view, informal, on-the-job training is much more effective ("This is Mick, and he does bite if people don't understand and do what he says").

THE TWO FISH: SCALY EXPERIENCES

We have clearly established we are dealing with the two fish, one out of water, the other in water, or at least partly submerged. The challenge is to get these two creatures to communicate with each other. As I said, I am a fishy fish, using not one, but many modes of communication. These include fax, modem, e-mail, and my regular voice, along with my MultiVoice voice output communication aid and a computer.

Much of the time I use my regular voice to talk with my PCWs. This, however, is not without error. Many times this has led to misunderstanding, such as the times I was saying "yes" when my sister thought I was saying "no." Of course, as she will gleefully point out, my "yes" sounds more like "yeah" and my "no" sounds more like "na." This could be critical in downtown Washington, D.C., traffic when the question is, "Do I turn right at the next stop light?" In these and other highly pressured situations, we resort to hand signals; I can do the "yes" signal fairly well. The "no" signal is harder for me, and I have to improvise a bit.

My weekend PCW and I like to talk politics. This is a fishy topic no matter what kind of fish are talking about it. Because of my training, I happened to know a lot of heavy-handed words that he doesn't understand. This calls for a creative substitution process. Because I am supposed to be a writer, I should be fairly good at this. I anticipate words that are not easily understood before I say them and fill in the appropriate substitution almost automatically. For example, words starting with "v" or "f" are usually difficult for me. The word "fish" usually comes out "pish" and the word "various" will come out "berries." When I see these words coming, I usually substitute them before they leave my mouth. Some words just can't be substituted. That's when I need my computer or voice synthesizer. Just knowing I have these systems on hand makes me more relaxed and puts the PCW at ease.

Does one ever see a fish use a telephone? Not usually! I have trouble with this wonderful trinket of technology. I try getting around it by e-mail, fax, or anything. I tried my MultiVoice voice output communication aid with many preprogrammed phrases, but nothing seems to do the job. For me, a telephone is a constricting device. Sometimes the person I want to talk to understands me fairly well, but the secretary is something else. Most fuss and fume, put you on hold several times, and then expect you to say who you want, why, and where you can be reached all in five seconds.

In these situations, when possible, I prefer my PCW to stand by to repeat what I say, at least in the initial stages of the conversation. Then I phase them out after I get the person I want or the topic of the conversation is established. This has its drawbacks as well. Sometimes, the caller prefers talking to the PCW and not me. It doesn't have to be all one-sided.

Many times I use my voice output device, as well. This sometimes works. But all too often the three voice combo confuses listeners ("Will the real Mick Joyce stand up?"). The basic thing to remember is to do whatever works for the individual caller. What works for one may not work for another. Communication, especially for fish on the phone, is definitely an art, not a science. Sometimes it's just faster to have my sister or weekend PCW make calls for me themselves, like for ordering a computer part. Although this runs against the basic independent living paragon, when it works, ideals sometimes have to go by the wayside.

> *Sometimes it's just faster to have my sister or weekend PCW make calls for me themselves, like for ordering a computer part. Although this runs against the basic independent living paragon, when it works, ideals sometimes have to go by the wayside.*

Being somewhat of a technology freak, I am always trying new stuff. I have heard about the MultiPhone, the IBM Phone Communicator, and similar devices. I think they serve the purpose: one purpose. Because they are made for a relatively small group of consumers, their cost is high relative to their function. Because of this and other difficulties (service and technical support), when selecting technology items, I always look to the mainstream market equipment first. In my search, I found a sound card with a fax/modem and speaker phone with voice mail capability. I intend to try it out next week. In the future, there will be similar and more eccentric configurations on the market.

In regular conversation, my sister and I work very well together compared to on the telephone. She automatically deletes most profanities I utter which I usually agree, afterwards, are too strong. In ideal situations, I like to have my real voice, my MultiVoice voice output communication aid, and my PCW all available at the same time for my use. Because I am not King of the Fish World, this ideal state rarely exists. Instead, I usually have one or two of these entities available to me at once.

If it happens to be a PCW, I use him or her to the extent necessary to get my message across. For example, I do not mind them finishing sentences, repeating and summarizing comments, or interceding when communication breaks down. Sometimes they do too much or too little, and sometimes it's difficult to tell. I try to inject appropriate feedback when needed.

For me there are no strict rules. It's whatever works. What may work in one situation may not work in others. The same configurations of resources, listeners, and technical support that is available in one place may not be available in another. Equipment breaks down, PCWs become sea monsters, and I have good and bad days.

I am a fish out of water working with other fish. This is a fishy world we live in, and communication is a fishy business. Given this circumstance, I ride the political waves, tackle the tide of public opinion, and try to stay away from the hook and sinker of self-fulfilling prophesy. And, I am always looking for that ultimate mammoth pool in the sky where I can swim and jump and not ever have to look for food.

8

One Life, Two Countries

Solomon Vulf Rakhman

I never thought that my speech could be corrected . . . Then the doctor told me about computers that can talk. . . . And the hope was planted in me that I could become even more INDEPENDENT.

Since migrating to the United States in 1988, Solomon Vulf Rakhman is proud to call Philadelphia, Pennsylvania, his hometown. For the past 5 years, he has been working as a consultant for the Institute on Disabilities/University Affiliated Program at Temple University while pursuing his bachelor's degree in economics there. His career plans are centered on working to reshape government policies to enable people with disabilities to achieve economic and personal independence to the best of their abilities. His favorite book is *Conscience of a Conservative* by Barry M. Goldwater.

THE BEST MEDICINE?

I have spent most of my life in the former Soviet Union where I, like all individuals with disabilities there, led a very unhappy and frustrated sort of life. My disability is the result of criminal malpractice that is very common in Soviet medicine, which proclaimed itself "the best and the most humane medicine in the world." I was born in the best hospital of the city. But at the moment of my birth nobody was near my mother. The doctor and the nurses, believing that I wouldn't be born until morning, left my mother alone and went to sleep. When they woke up it was too late. I was already without breath. They revived me after 1½ hours. They lied to my parents telling them that I was going to be okay. Only when I was 6 months old, my mom, noticing that something was wrong, went to the doctor who revealed the truth. And it was that I have cerebral palsy, and that those vital months of treatment were lost.

At that point, the treatment began. My mom and I were put in the hospital for children with cerebral palsy. The building in which this hospital was located used to be (you would never guess) a barn for horses that belonged to some landowner before the Revolution! In one room, there were 15–20 beds on which the mothers and their kids lay. There was no question: If the child couldn't take care of himself, the mother had to stay in the hospital with him. One time there was a fire across the street, and only by the grace of God did it not reach our building. If it had, this barn would have burned like a paper house with everybody in it.

As you probably know, medical treatment is free in Russia. Some people think, "Free treatment?! Oh, everybody can get it!" Well, like my father always says: "Free medicine is free of medicine." If you want to get something done, you have to pay. From the time my disability became apparent, my parents went to some great sacrifices to make my life as normal as possible. My mom left her job to be with me at home and at the numerous hospitals. My father quit his job as an engineer, which paid barely enough to support a normal family provided both parents worked, which was impossible in our case because my mom had to stay with me. For the next 15 years (until we came to the U.S.), he worked hard on half-legal jobs, many times risking going to jail, in order to earn the money needed for my treatment and for our living.

From the very beginning my parents, as well as the other members of our family, had hope in me. Never once did they pity me or treat me like somebody inferior. Instead, they made sure that I grew up like a normal kid and developed both physically and mentally to the fullest.

Before I learned to walk, through a lot of hurt and pain that was not only mine, my parents used a baby carriage, modified by my dad. He made a lot of things for me: my first walker, standers, parallel bars, and mats. All of this he had to make himself because none of these devices were produced anywhere in the U.S.S.R. Parents had to make pretty much all such devices by themselves. However, some devices made for people with disabilities usually did not fit well, so that those who wore them always had blood sores.

But, how about wheelchairs? I'll tell you later what kind of wheelchair I received when I really needed one. You can also ask my dad, who grew up right after World War II, what "wheelchairs" the disabled war veterans used.

"SPECIAL" SCHOOL

Now to get back to my life story. At the age of 7, I went to "boarding school for crippled children." It was a common three-story building, with a lot of stairs, so that only children who could somehow move by themselves could attend. Imagine going on crutches from the first floor of one wing of one building to the third floor of the other, up six sets of stairs, and making it in 10 minutes between periods?! After my first year, during which I was sick three fourths of the time, it was recommended I be taught at home. And for the next 3 years teachers came to my home.

My "disability package" also includes a speech disability. As I look back on my childhood, I can remember how frustrating it was when even your own parents don't understand you. I know how much anguish it was for them. Over the years we have developed some strategies that made it easier for us to communicate. But the circle of people who understood me was very small and was restricted to my family and a few close family friends who knew me well and took the time to listen to me one on one. And when I wanted to talk to an unfamiliar person or some kids on the playground, I couldn't do it. I either had to let it go (which I often did) or ask somebody in my family to come and "translate" for me. Most of the time I had to pass a chance of making a joke or a remark or asking a question around the table because it meant that people either had to stop talking, and wait until somebody would get what I was saying and interpret my speech or go on and then my response would be out of place, so people would need to remember back to what they were talking about. All this made me feel like a pest.

In fourth grade I begged my parents to let me try to go to school again. It was some experience. Thank God we lived only 500 yards from school. And though it was the height of my walking career, this trip took me about an hour each way. Plus, somebody had to be with me all day to walk me from room to room. It was really a hard time for my family, and I thank them for giving me this experience.

THINKING AHEAD

After that year, my mobility, because of the wrong kind of therapy, had gotten worse and worse to the point that I couldn't walk anymore. Since I couldn't walk I could not even go out of the house. I had to sit at home all day. Though my school provided teaching at home, it was a very depressing time. It got me wondering what I would do 10–20 years from then. I heard many stories from graduates of my school about how people with even mild disabilities, no matter how smart they were, weren't admitted to colleges but forced to go to trade schools. And even after that, they were mocked at and pushed from job to job, until they were forced to quit and live on a pension that was so small that it wasn't enough to pay for an apartment, let alone anything else. Note: The cost of an apartment in the Soviet Union is (or was) the cheapest in the world.

And what about people who can't take care of themselves? I once saw a program featuring a man with a Ph.D. who suffered a spine fracture. He was put in the hospital where he could never get out of bed. And when he asked for some job, he was given the task of putting together parts of fake Christmas trees—a bright man with a college degree doing a job like that only because he is disabled.

Not long before we left the Soviet Union, after many hours on the phone with different agencies, my parents got me a "wheelchair." It had levers that were meant for the individual to move it. But it was so heavy and bulky that even my dad and my brother together couldn't push it.

On April 28, 1988, we left "the land of the mutual equality" and made a 2-hour flight to "the world of the Raging Giant of Capitalism," as it was called by Soviet propaganda—just 2 hours from Moscow to Vienna. Oh, Vienna, the pearl of my heart!

We spent 17 days in Vienna while our immigration papers were being processed. This was the most luxurious time of our lives. I had access to a wheelchair for the first time, so we went everywhere, and now I could go along with my family and see everything.

After Vienna, we went to Italy, the second destination of the immigration process. There we spent 2 months in a small town on the shore of the Tyrrhenian Sea. In Italy I was examined by a psychiatrist who said that I have the potential to finish high school, go to college, and become whoever I want to be, except president of the United States. But, he said I needed a way to communicate. That is also an area affected by my disability. But I never thought that my speech could be corrected. And I accepted this as a fact, that only people who were familiar with me could understand my speech. Then the doctor told me about computers that can talk. That's how for the first time I heard about augmentative communication. And the hope was planted in me that I could become even more INDEPENDENT. If I wanted to talk to somebody, I would no more have to wait for my mom or my brother to come to "translate" for me or to try to talk myself and wonder whether the other person really understands me or just pretends to.

AMERICA

The moment we got out from the plane somebody appeared, like from nowhere, with—guess what—A WHEELCHAIR! Then, soon after we settled in our new homeland, another miracle happened. One morning a yellow bus came and loaded me on my wheelchair and took me to Widener Memorial School. And there to my utmost amazement I was shown, and then given, a COMPUTER THAT CAN TALK! From that moment on, I knew that I had left my misfortune behind me. I knew that in this world, I could be a normal individual—that I'd never again have to sit at home and look out the window, as I was destined in my homeland, only because I couldn't walk. Or, if I wanted to talk to somebody, I would no more have to wait for my mom or my brother to come and "translate" for me. Now I could be a part of this world! And this is the greatest feeling of them all, ladies and gentlemen!

So, for the first time in many years I had INDEPENDENCE IN MOBILITY. From then on I could go to school and everywhere I wanted. But by then I began to feel more acutely than ever the need for a better way to make myself understood, because I was away from home more often, in school, and in the hospital. So I was introduced first to a language board, and then to the SpeechPac, a small Epson communicator with voice output. Then came a laptop computer which helped me a great deal with my school work.

But all those devices, although a million times better than nothing, lack one important quality that is vital for conversations—SPEED. What I found from my own experience and from talking with other people was that in order to hold a conversation you need to talk or otherwise communicate your ideas fast. My typing is a lot slower than other people's talking. When I tried to participate in conversations with them I trailed hopelessly behind.

Therefore, people either had to stop themselves and wait for my comment or go on, and often my response was out of place and uninteresting. I needed to communicate fast. And last year I was given the opportunity to participate in a 2-week program on learning TouchTalker with Word Strategy at Temple University in Philadelphia. There I met a wonderful man, Mr. Bruce Baker. From the very introduction (which was brilliantly conducted by Mr. Baker) I understood that the TouchTalker was the very thing I needed.

Word Strategy (or Minspeak, as it is now called) is the language of symbols smartly put together by very logical and sometimes funny rationales. It takes no more than three hits to produce a word or phrase; compare this to typing letter by letter. This speeds up the communication tremendously. So this is the key to a whole new world for thousands of people with speech disabilities.

In these short 6 years in the U.S., my life has changed tremendously. When I entered Widener, I was just a little scared kid who didn't understand much English. Now, as you see, I'm a determined young man, a senior in high school with a bright outlook to a college and career future and a known speaker in circles of augmentative communication and beyond. None of that would be possible without assistive technology. I used many different augmentative communication systems until I found the one that works for me: my own voice (namely, the Liberator)! The Liberator represents a new and more sophisticated generation of communication devices. It combines a new version of Word Strategy with a larger word selection and a mini PC with such features as a notebook, a calculator, and interchangeable voices. Having 10 interchangeable voices and a special software that allows it to produce words and phrases in two or three hits, it brings me as close to having normal speech as I ever dreamed possible.

What are my plans for the future? They are to get a degree from Temple University in computer science, land a good job, get an apartment in some skyscraper, and travel. I would also like to do my very best to play my part in bringing assistive technology to as many people worldwide as possible.

I think everybody deserves to be heard!

9

My Early Life and Education

Sharon P. Price

*In 1972, when Oregon was considering a
special education law, I sat on the committee
that helped write it because I didn't want
anyone else to go through what I had
gone through.*

Sharon P. Price, who has severe cerebral palsy, has lived on her own for 25 years. She has written two books, *Just Being Sharon* (1994) and *Sharing More Sharon* (2000). An advocate for rights for the disabled, she helped sponsor an Oregon law giving scooter and wheelchair users the same rights as pedestrians on public streets and sidewalks.

I was born on October 27, 1947, in Snohomish, Washington. My birth was difficult for both my mom and me. It was labeled a "forced birth" because the doctor put mom asleep after she had only one labor pain. Then he pulled me out of the womb with forceps.

Each of us stopped breathing several times during the delivery. The Snohomish Fire Department was called to save our lives. When the firemen came to the hospital, they walked right past my dad, who was standing in the waiting room. Many of them were his childhood friends, as dad had been raised in Snohomish. But not one of them told dad that they were there to save his wife's and his baby daughter's lives until it was all over.

Mom was in the hospital for a week, and I was there for 3 weeks. Because of the doctor's careless actions, I came out of the birth mishap with a black eye and a crooked right foot, which turns in to this day. I was also left with profound cerebral palsy.

When it came time for me to turn, roll over, sit up, stand, and walk, I didn't. When I was 11 months old, my parents took me to the Orthopedic Hospital in Seattle. The doctor told mom and dad that I had suffered brain damage during birth that resulted in my having severe cerebral palsy. After she heard the diagnosis mom was so angry that she threw the doctor's bill for $75 right back at him.

In the 1940s, most doctors gave cerebral palsy victims the same basic prognosis: They would all wind up to be "vegetables," so they should be placed in institutions and forgotten! My parents received the same advice.

Mom and dad were planning on having more children, so they told the doctors, "No way!" and took me home. In fact, 13 months after I was born, my sister Susan was born. Mom said it was like having twins a year apart! Within a few years, my parents also had two sons. My parents worked hard to raise me as normally as possible with my sister and brothers.

One of my biggest difficulties was in being understood. I had a severe speech disability, so I began speech lessons at the age of four. A family friend who planned on being a speech teacher wanted to work with me as part of her student teaching project. There were no elevators in the building where the speech lessons took place at Western Washington University in Bellingham, Washington, and mom had to carry me up several flights of stairs, leaving 3-year-old Susan and 1-year-old Mike in the car. Mom didn't like that at all. She later said the whole thing had been a waste of time in many ways.

Still, different types of speech lessons continued until I was 15. The lessons mostly consisted of the same thing. I was supposed to learn my sounds like "da" for /d/ and "ta" for /t/. I was always told to talk slowly and to think about what I was saying, but I can't think and talk at the same time.

When I was 5, we moved to a town where dad got his first school teaching job. There was a school for the handicapped 10 miles away in Burlington. I attended for 2 years and received an excellent start to my education. Along with the educational part of the school, I also received physical and speech therapy every day. Mom drove me and a couple of my classmates to school until the school hired a permanent bus driver.

There were only 10 other children in my class. Besides myself, there was a blind girl my age who was teachable. The rest of the students were mildly to severely retarded. When the teacher, Mrs. Johnson, realized Julie and I were "teachable," she gave us most of her attention.

I entered the first grade at the same school with the same teacher, but Julie's parents sent her to a school for the blind so she could learn how to read Braille. With Julie gone, Mrs. Johnson concentrated on me. It was like having a private tutor for my entire first grade. By the time I left first grade, I was reading at a third-grade level.

During the summer between my first- and second-grade years, we moved. The new three-story house had three acres of land with it, and in the evening we could look out the front room window and see the city skyline. But that was about the only thing the place had going for it. I was quite unhappy for the 3 years we lived there. Part of the reason for my unhappiness was that I entered the second grade, and public school, for the first time there. The school was old-fashioned with two grades to each classroom. That meant that while I was in the second grade, my "baby" sister Susan was in the first grade. We sat two rows apart all year long. Susan started school reading at a third-grade level because when we were supposed to be sleeping, I had been teaching Susan everything I learned about reading from Mrs. Johnson! The teacher, Mrs. Woodward, broke the second grade into high, middle, and low reading groups. Mrs. Woodward was a very nice lady but must have assumed that I was a slow reader because of my handicap. She assigned me to the low reading group. Because of my speech problem, she could not understand me when I tried to tell her that I had already read the book we were assigned.

Well into the spring, when my reading group finally got to where I had left off in the first grade, I announced to the teacher, "I have already read this book, last year in the first grade!" Finally, she understood me. She said that if I would do extra reading and do the tasks in the workbook, she would let me move up to the middle group.

I was in a hurry and did only the workbook part. She caught me, but she did eventually let me move up into the next group anyway.

Why didn't I tell my parents what was going on? I don't know. I'm stubborn and somehow felt like it was my own battle, so I didn't tell them.

My problem with Mrs. Woodward was mild compared to what my parents and I came up against with the third/fourth-grade teacher! In the spring, while I was still in the second grade, that teacher went before the school board and simply told them that she refused to have me in her classroom for the next 2 years.

I did start school in a handicapped boarding school in Seattle in the fall of 1956. I was only there for 3 weeks. It was a school mainly for the mentally retarded, and it nearly killed me to be there. I was so nervous the whole time I was there that two bumps on my right foot developed because of nerves. The bumps are my permanent souvenirs from that experience.

For the next 2 years, third and fourth grades, I was home-schooled with a tutor because mom was busy with my new brother, Matt. Dad made the laundry room into a classroom. After Susan and Mike came home from school, we would play school and have a great time. In the fourth grade, the school district did hire a home-school teacher for me, but she wasn't that good.

When we moved to Oregon in the Summer of 1958, I reentered the public school system which I dearly loved and had missed. Because I had officially missed the fourth grade, the school's principal decided that I should repeat it. At first, I didn't like this decision because I felt like I was butting into Susan's class and territory. But in the long run it was the best decision that my parents ever made on my behalf.

Because of my cerebral palsy, my handwriting is illegible, so in my "second" fourth grade, I was introduced to the electric typewriter. In the fourth and fifth grades, a typewriter was kept in the coat closet at the back of the room. When it came time to take a test, or if I needed to type something out, I would use the typewriter. An electric typewriter has been my second pair of hands ever since.

Once, while I was out in the hallway in the fifth grade, a little first grader took a look at me and started screaming. For that reason, in the sixth grade I went to school each morning for a 1-hour reading class, then returned home. Every afternoon for 2 hours, I went over to my home-school teacher's house for lessons while her three young boys were taking their naps.

This home-school teacher, Mrs. Ontko, was the best teacher I ever had. She worked my buns off. She would give me homework every night, which was a challenge that I loved. Only once did I not complete all of my homework, and when I walked into her house that day, I had tears in my eyes. Mrs. Ontko assured me it was no big deal and assigned the work to me again that night, and she added some more homework besides.

At the end of the school year, even though I had missed a week in December because of the flu, the school district gave me a Perfect Attendance Award because I had done "double duty" all year long.

Mrs. Ontko planned to take me clear through my senior year in high school, but during the summer between the sixth and seventh grades, dad got a teaching job in another city, so we moved west. My elementary school years were like a yo-yo on a swinging door, but thanks to a lot of caring teachers and family, I finally made it through. Susan and I graduated from Corvallis High School with the Class of 1967.

These incidents happened before they had special education laws to protect disabled students like myself. In 1972, when Oregon was considering such a law, I sat on the committee that helped write it because I didn't want anyone else to go through what I had gone through. In 1975, the Education for All Handicapped Children Act was passed. This law shaped both special and regular education for two decades after it was enacted. The law requires the state to provide a free, appropriate public education for all children between the ages of 3 and 18.

LIVING ON MY OWN

Even though I have severe cerebral palsy, I always dreamed of living on my own. For years before I was able to move out, mom and I would talk about the idea of my being out on my own on a daily basis, but deep down inside, I didn't know if my dream would ever come true.

> Even though I have severe cerebral palsy, I always dreamed of living on my own.

Then one day, with the help of my sister Susan and her husband, Gary, it happened! They were concerned about my welfare and future. It bothered Gary to no end that I was still living at home at the age of 27, and they set out to rectify the situation.

What was to be a weekend visit to Susan's house in Eugene turned out to be the biggest and the most important weekend of my life. Susan had made an appointment for me with a city official in Eugene. The man told us that he could do a lot for me, but before he could even start to help me, I had to set up residence in Eugene. By the end of the weekend—and before I hardly knew what had happened—I was living on my own in my very first apartment.

WHEELS

I knew from the start that I needed some special provisions to survive. First, I had to get some transportation for myself. I needed some "wheels." In the sixth grade, when we were living in Prineville, our school janitor came and got Susan's old blue bike. I was at home sick with the flu and as usual didn't have a clue about what was going on. I thought Mr. Owens had stopped by to see how I was, as he often did.

One evening a few weeks later, mom and I were summoned to the school. I was presented with a "brand-new" tri-wheeler that Mr. Owens had constructed from Susan's old bike. It had one wheel in the back and two wheels in front, with a basket between the front wheels. I was thrilled! Mom was so happy she let me ride it home—four blocks—in the dark! I rode that tri-wheeler until I entered high school.

I have had several tri-wheelers since moving out on my own. In the 1980s, the makers of tri-wheelers started to make vehicles that were not as sturdy, probably to make them more presentable. One was purchased for me, but for the life of me, I couldn't balance myself on it. Several times I had to ride it in heavy traffic. At the time, I was living in a suburb where traffic was a nightmare to begin with, and being on an undependable tri-wheeler made me very nervous. At any given moment, I didn't know if I was about to tip over. Once, as I entered the courtyard where I was living, my tri-wheeler did tip over on me. I was so mad, I left it right where it had tipped over and walked back to my apartment. The manager saw my tri-wheeler when he came home and knew exactly what had happened. He brought it to my apartment for me.

The best mode of transportation I have ever had is an electric scooter. These little vehicles came out in the mid-1980s. I have had three of them over the years, and they have been a real blessing. I can take them into a store or ride them down the street. For me, it's like having my own car. I can't describe the freedom it gives me, but oh, how I love it!

WORDS

The second thing I knew I needed was an electric typewriter. The typewriter has been my second pair of hands since my second tour of duty in fourth grade. Now that I was out on my own, I needed one for letter writing, check writing, and for writing notes to people with whom I needed to communicate.

When I was in high school, mom supposedly bought a typewriter for herself. That typewriter soon became mine. I had a lot of home-work in high school because I couldn't do any in class like the other students. I had to take it home each night and do it on the typewriter. In my junior year, I had to write a term paper for Human Biology. My subject was cerebral palsy. I spent my whole Christmas vacation working on the paper. Mom made me take Christmas day off, even though I wanted to work on it.

During the summer before my senior year, I had a clerical job at the school. My job was to type the tests for the business teacher who would use them for the next school year. One day the typing teacher, who came in regularly to work in her classroom during the summer, saw me typing the tests on stencils. (Remember those messy things?) As soon as she saw me typing, she insisted that I take her class the coming year. My yearly plan was already in, and it didn't include typ-ing, so I told her I didn't have time to take her class. Before I knew it, the teacher had gone to the office and changed my schedule! I had wanted to take a "fun" class my senior year, but ended up taking typ-ing instead. To my amazement, my typing improved during the year, and in the long run, I was better off taking the class!

When I was living in the suburbs, I got the bright idea one day to start writing a book. It seemed like the very minute I started to work on it, my typewriter went out on strike. I spent a lot of time at the local typewriter shop, and sometimes the kind people there even made house calls.

Eventually I went through three different typewriters. The first typewriter, the one I had used in high school, kept losing its key caps. They just fell off, making typing very difficult at times. The second typewriter would hit the page so hard with the keys that when I took the page out, it would be full of holes. It looked like a golf course from the back side of the paper. I got so mad and frustrated that I took a 2-year break from my writing.

I had not told anyone what I was doing. Then one day I showed my friend Mimi the first draft. After she had read it, she told me to immediately get back to writing because she felt that I was a good writer and that I had a story to tell. She told me to use toilet paper if I had to, but to write on!

With renewed energy, I decided to get back to work on my book. But before I could start, I had to get a workable typewriter. So down to the typewriter shop I went. They were willing to let me buy a typewriter and make payments, so I selected a memory typewriter that was really a computer. It had a four-page memory and a 5,000-word dictionary in it. It was the best typewriter I ever had. When my church found out that I was buying a typewriter on time, they presented a check to me for the full amount, which was unbelievable to me. This was my typewriter for years, and I wrote most of my book on it. I eventually moved back to Corvallis, and mom talked me into taking one term of a class called Write Your Life Story from the local community college. The class met at the Senior Center. I took the unfinished manuscript along and asked the teacher to take a look at it. She said she would tell me what she thought about it the following week.

Little did I know then that during the following week, I would be in the hospital having an operation. Because I had ulcers in my stomach, I had to have half of my stomach removed in an emergency operation. While I was on the operating table, mom went to my class to tell the teacher where I was and to get the teacher's reaction to my book.

The teacher told her I had a "hit" on my hands and that I should finish the manuscript as soon as possible. Mom was so excited she rushed back to the hospital to tell me! I was doped up to the eyeballs when mom came back and couldn't comprehend anything she said. She had to repeat what the teacher had told her several times before I caught on.

It was approximately 3 weeks after I got home from the hospital that I started back to work on my book. My work schedule is a little different than most peoples', and my dad gives me a hard time about it nearly every day. I start to work after the sun goes down and work into the wee hours of the morning. I love every minute of it! In fact, my e-mail address is "nightowl!"

Each night during the summer, I would put two to four pages of text into my memory typewriter. It was hard because I could see only one line at a time on the typewriter display. So I would print out the final draft on scrap paper and try to correct it.

After a year or so of this, a friend and her husband bought their family a new computer. They offered to lend me their old one so that I could get my book ready to be published. With a computer in the house to help me, things went a lot faster and smoother. Even before I got a computer, I knew I had to eventually get my manuscript put on a disk. To transfer the manuscript onto my borrowed computer, I had it scanned by a service center near campus. It took them a week to do it. When I told them that I had typed my whole book on a typewriter, they couldn't believe it.

It took me 12 years to finish the book, and I called it *Just Being Sharon*. I found a local publisher, and I was on my way to seeing my dream come true. The book was published on January 1, 1996. Almost immediately I started on a sequel. And I am still writing!

Nearly 600 copies of the book sold in the first 4 months of its release! Most went to family and friends. But it has continued to sell, and mail orders come in from all over the nation.

Because of my situation, the publisher made a special arrangement for me. His time and services were donated, and friends and family came up with the money to manufacture 2,000 copies of the book. Not just royalties but all the revenue from sales comes back to me. It's the first time in my life that I've been able to earn a substantial amount of money.

The first thing that I bought myself was—you guessed it—a new computer! I found out that with the difficulties I have with my hands, I could not use a mouse, so my new computer has a trackball instead. The trackball is more steady for me, and it is more sturdily built.

When I got my new computer, I also got hooked up to the Internet and to e-mail. My world changed overnight! At the time, I was very much involved with the local Disability Services Advisory Council. With my speech problem, they had a very hard time understanding me. When I got e-mail, I had no problems. When there were questions that the council wanted my input on, all they had to do was send an e-mail, and they would get an answer right back from me.

> E-mail has allowed me to communicate with people on equal terms! It's a blast!

I also took an e-mail and Internet class. The class was held at Corvallis High School, my old high school. It really felt strange going back there after 30 years. When I first got Internet service, I couldn't figure out how to use it. After taking the class, I'm proud to say that I have become a computer junkie!

Having e-mail and the Internet has opened up a new, exciting world to me. The Internet has so much to offer that sometimes it's overwhelming. I can spend hours looking up things. Some of my friends who are not on the Internet have heard horror stories about what is accessible. I always assure them that I am very careful.

I use e-mail daily. I e-mail friends, relatives, and even people I don't know. In recent months a woman in New Zealand who also has cerebral palsy found my web page on the Internet, and we've started to write frequently.

10

To Play Music

Gregory M. Haslett

Gregory M. Haslett is a physical therapy assistant and father of two teenage daughters. Greg was diagnosed with amyotrophic lateral sclerosis (ALS, or Lou Gehrig's disease) about 2 years ago. He now lives at home with his family in Portland, Oregon. Greg has been using a keyboard emulator and single switch on a personal computer for speaking, writing, and Internet access for about 6 months. Greg was a musician who enjoyed expressing himself without words. His contribution here is as lyrical as any musical composition that he has ever written or played.

To Play Music

Was a joy that hardly I can express

Akin to a pristine spring day

With visual, auditory and olfactory

Enhancement. Guitar, classical with its

Complexity, steel string with applied

Rhythm or complex skill, clarinet, sax,

Recorder or harmonica, keyboard and

Singing in our parish choir. Idle all now.

Miss all so very much.

11

Reflections on a Kayak Expedition in Scotland

Spencer Houston

I never forget my disability, and I sometimes have difficulty expressing something I assumed was automatic. It trips me up, and I think about the thoughts themselves. However, I believe that technology will eventually meet most of the needs I have been experiencing.

Spencer Houston lives in Fortrose, Scotland, with his Collie/Alsatian, Maida. He has three grown-up children: Angus, a Naval Architect; Neil, at University studying food management; and Shona, at University studying medicine. He is retired, having changed from a career in avionic electronics to teaching mathematics in residential special education. Following an active career, Spencer now has time and space to reflect on the increasingly spiritual part of his journey through life.

My speech therapist, Mrs. Alison Gray, gave me the entry form for this disabled essay competition and said in her understated way, "Think about it." With my amateur speech therapist, Mrs. Heather Hurt, writing down my ramblings, my subconscious became conscious, and I benefited. I was diagnosed with atypical motor neuron disease (MND) in 1989, when I was a senior instructor in sea kayaking. Then in 1996 I suffered a stroke that left me with dysphasic difficulties. My speech therapist's challenge led me to decide to weave my thoughts on MND and canoeing. I was greatly helped by Alison, who had painstakingly re-taught me to think, read, and write, and Heather, who spent hours re-teaching me, among other things, to read poetry with expression and emphasis. Once the essay was finished, I knew that I had put something to rest. This is the result.

I had just been told I had atypical anterior cell disease or MND. Every spare minute when I was not working, I was on the Hill or on the sea. This is the story of what I can remember at the time and my feelings looking back.

For the previous two summers I had gone up to Caithness, hoping to cross from the mainland of Scotland to Orkney, and these two summers the weather had been too bad to make the trip. It was 1992, and we were trying again. For some time we had been watching the sea and the sky. The kayaks where packed with tents, sleeping bags, food, and water, and, mine, with a bottle of whisky. Then the decision was made—we would cross. From Gills Bay, a tiny village just west of John O'Groats, we passed round the east of Stroma out to Swona. This small island was populated until the 1930s. The people who had lived there left their home as a summer sheiling. That is what we found. I didn't go in, but looking in at the window, I beheld a 1930s scene in the sitting room and kitchen. In the sitting room the far wall was dominated by a shoulder high mantelpiece, with period vases and candle holders, while in the kitchen the only piece out of place was a plastic bottle of Saxa salt. There was a valve radio, and outside were the remains of the generator.

In the south part of Swona the sea was tumultuous, the seals plunging and diving, while on land the puffins were not frightened, and I took photographs right up close. The cattle on the island were friendly, but as no one was resident, when they died they were not buried. I came across several animals in various states of decomposi-

---

This essay was written by an individual with aphasia who had a stroke and regained the ability to read and write. Hence, between the language formulation problems and the Scottish English, the reader may find some of the narrative confusing. However, the editors have chosen to leave much of the original writing intact to illustrate Mr. Houston's personal use of language.

tion. I am getting my thoughts together to make a living will. Maybe, like the cattle on Swona, it would be nice to die simply. We'll see.

In the Pentland Firth, the sea behaves like a fast river flowing between islands. On Swona we had to wait for the tide to push us up to Hoy. There we would have time to mentally prepare for what was ahead. In the Firth, there was a growing eddy, where the water goes in two opposing directions. We had to launch out of this eddy into the fast-moving water. If one of us capsized, the nearest island would be miles away. We had a buddy system. If I went over, my buddy had to rescue me, and vice versa—no fooling about, a time for complete dependability. It's like the team of relatives, friends, and professionals I have with me now—dependable.

We approached Hoy from the southeast. After quite a long day we quickly made camp beside a lighthouse and soon there was the aroma of food. We all cooked individually. After the inner men in us had been fed, some went off to make phone calls home or to visit the War Museum. I chatted with the ones who stayed, some of whom were old friends. We were joined by two local Orkney paddlers. I was among the "elder statesmen," so I bedded down early.

The next day saw us going south, west, and north to Rackwick, just short of the Old Man of Hoy. Within a quarter of an hour a friend's boat was letting in water just on the water line through a broken pump outlet. We dawdled on while Ken sprinted to the shore, fixed it, and re-joined us. Every hour or so we had a break on the water. In addition to our own "mixes," we sampled from boats next to us—mixed dried fruit, mixed nuts, mixed nuts with dried banana and chopped chocolate. There was, of course, also the usual, "Have a piece of my Mars bar!"

The shore became more and more inhospitable. Then a sandy bay made us decide it was lunch time. A leisure stop was called for. At sea again, the bay fell away, and the shore became cliff. We stopped "boulder hopping"—going close to the shore—and went out a bit. The spray rose higher and higher the further north we went. Then round a corner we were in Rackwick Bay. The dense sea spray reaching to the top of the high cliffs was something to be marveled at. But there was no time for marveling—we had to get ashore. However, there was a problem: There was big surf between us and the shore. Four of us went in close. With loaded sea boats, we were reluctant to land unaided on boulders, the smallest one a meter across. One of the Thurso surfers (surfed for Scotland) landed. The three of us remaining went out to the rest of the party, describing the arrangements. The "real" leader numbered us off in the order we would go in. The trick was to get on the back of a green unbroken wave and ride it on top to just past where it would break. It was EXCITING!—or as we say, "a brown trousers job!"

It was too much for one paddler who, after coming through the big stuff, capsized in the soup—the foam on the shore line. After we had tea, my bottle of whisky was demolished in 2 minutes flat!

I can remember going out to rejoin the party on the water, the big surf relentlessly coming in and me trusting my boat, my paddle, my strength, my experience. I am now building a different but similar kind of experience—in disability. When I kayaked, I found it easier to go into the waves rather than to go with them. At that time it was easy to have challenges, but now I feel I have had enough of them. I used to think when I was first diagnosed that I was on top of some big, unstoppable wave in a never-ending sea, and I had to stay behind the middle of the wave, or I would get washed out! That was then. Now, I'm getting to the stage that if I get washed out—so what. I reckon my God and I and those that surround me have got what it takes to stand up—or lie down (some things can't be changed)—to anything. We'll see.

The next morning, four guys to a heavy boat, we handed the fleet down to the waters edge. Fresh from a good night's sleep, I was edgy to go. I was among the first to launch. My spray deck was fitted, my paddle put into my hands, and I was off—with adrenaline pumping, no warm-up, straight out into breaking waves, then the green waves, then the swell bobbing us up and down 20 feet. We passed about a half of a mile seaward of the Old Man of Hoy. We went north then east into Scapa Flow, past the sunken hulks scuttled in the Second War. We had a break, then the final paddle to the campsite. Of the whole trip, I don't remember anything as uncomfortable, as downright painful as my left shoulder. I can quite clearly remember the "locked feeling." The boat wouldn't go, and I knew it would be downhill from here on in. In that hour the sea was calm but my mind was in tumult, leaping ahead to what could be but wasn't as of yet. For a start, I was to have a stroke!

The next and final day we would cross Scapa Flow to South Ronaldsay then to the Pentland Firth. There was no wind because the fog was down, with visibility to 200 meters. The distress flares were taken out from behind my seat and put on the foredeck. Collision with shipping was a real possibility, so plans were made against that eventuality. We were told the journey time would be 1 hour and 45 minutes to John O'Groats. We were also given the compass setting.

I'm learning to live for the here and the now rather than for the future, though accepting the future with its vagaries and uncertainties.

Looking back, there was something prophetic about the next hour or two. I was part of a group but still paddling my own canoe—quite literally! The fog—of the future—at one time overwhelmed me. I'm learning to live for the here and the now rather than for the future, though accepting the future with its vagaries and uncertainties. In a whole fleet of things I have changed. I'm less unbending and more easy at forgiving myself and others, to name but two. Some things about myself have not changed—my dogged persistence for one.

An hour and 50 minutes later John O'Groats Hotel loomed out of the fog. I have occasionally remarked that I am now, in living with my disabilities, on one of my biggest expeditions. The outdoor expeditions contributed to preparing me, I think, for the social, emotional, and spiritual journey of a lifetime. We'll see.

My life's journey has taken me through the natural seas to a sea of professionals at the Biennial Conference of the International Society for Augmentative and Alternative Communication held in Dublin, Ireland, in August, 1998. My professional and amateur speech therapists urged me to share my thoughts regarding this journey, and they helped me greatly.

I'll begin with my background and education and my social and medical history. I am 53 years old. I have three grown children, and I live independently with my dog, Maida. I started my career as an electronic engineer, later switching to the more exciting option of teaching mathematics in special education. I was also a senior instructor in sea kayaking and roamed mountain and sea, summer and winter. As mentioned earlier, in 1989 I was diagnosed with atypical MND, and in 1996 I suffered a stroke which left me with dysphasic difficulties.

For the past 30 years I have been computer orientated, having worked for a military avionics company. Technology held for me no fears. Over the last 25 years I have taught children with social, emotional, behavior, and educational difficulties, and the determination of some of these children to become integrated affected me long term. Immediately following my stroke, I imagined that, like them, I would become as normal as I wanted to be. Watching their determination to overcome their problems inspired me. This class in determination is the largest one I have taken.

Let me now share a few insights into my speech and language history. Prestroke my speech was okay. A speech therapist had warned of speech deterioration and had explained that artificial voices were available. At that stage I had not personally owned the phrases "MND resulting in loss of speech" and "technology can be used to speak," but I appreciated the frank and open approach of those around me. In the 2 years before retiring from education, I used a computer to assist me with administration, social work, and teaching.

I understood the availability of technology; but whilst I used it, had made no personal connection. I had been provided with a computer to assist me at work by the Department of Employment—the contracting technician dumped the machine on me and left. I had no say in the specification. The technology did not daunt me, but a program of familiarization would have benefited me practically and emotionally. As computers are normalized in society, the backup should be commensurate with the user's knowledge and skill.

I can now give you an idea of my communication after the stroke. Although speech therapists had warned me about the problems I would have communicating as a result of my MND, the stroke had forced me to face up to the reality of these difficulties sooner than had been expected. One of my first requests in the hospital was my computer. I could not speak. Requesting my computer was my way of attempting to get back to normal and to send a message to those around me, both literally and metaphorically.

Shortly after my stay in the hospital, I had a meeting with my lawyer and took my sister. To my amazement they were discussing my future. I signaled and interjected, stating my wishes, and whilst not fluent, left them in no doubt. Even with significantly impaired speech, I realized that I could still communicate in a real-life situation—that I could cope.

> *Requesting my computer was my way of attempting to get back to normal and to send a message to those around me, both literally and metaphorically.*

The four months after discharge were traumatic—sorting out somewhere to live, renting then buying, signing papers for my legal separation, and knowing there were aspects of MND which my speech therapist had alerted me to but had not fully discussed. As things settled, however, it became appropriate to tackle them. Generally, it was crucial that my therapist was prepared to be challenged, allowing me to question her methodology while we worked on the rapport between ourselves.

I'll tell you a little about my current communication. My speech is still clear and fully intelligible, although sometimes when I think of what I am going to say I have difficulty fishing out the right words. Other times I know the meaning of a word but can't find the word itself. I also have difficulty planning and constructing a sentence.

You have to listen carefully to me; the vocabulary is at times surprising and unusually complicated. My listening sometimes involves asking speakers to slow down or repeat what they have said. About 5% of the time I struggle to fully understand them, depending upon the speaker, situation, and message.

My reading is now quicker, and my comprehension better. Silent reading has become more expansive, as I understand not just the words and difficult grammar, but also the ideas behind them. My writing is also improving. Words flow more easily, especially on the computer. I use my predictor and spell check in a specialized software called EZ Keys supplied by the Scottish Motor Neuron Disease Association. I can write formal letters, but I always have them checked to prevent major problems.

I never forget my disability, and I sometimes have difficulty expressing something I assumed was automatic. It trips me up, and I think about the thoughts themselves. However, I believe that technology will eventually meet most of the needs I have been experiencing. If I had not had this practical input, I would not be so well adapted to my disabilities. Also, I used to be very talkative, but there I can see a change. I listen more and am getting more out of life by listening.

Whilst facing up to the advances in my deterioration, I have found difficulty in accepting the practicalities of switching access. I could still laboriously use a keyboard, and I have at times fallen back on this. My speech therapist suggested acquiring a keyguard as an interim to help my fingers separate the keys. My computer has many functions. It is my writing system; my communication system (e-mail, fax), especially for family further away; my information system; my database for addresses and other lists; my financial and legal organizer; my entertainment system; and, lastly, my speech system.

And now some comments about technology. I am imagining people with little or no technical information, and I think helping them is a "try-it-and-see" type of activity. That is, you only stop at the technology that he or she is interested in. Information needs to be simple and succinct, especially for stroke victims, with time allowed for assimilation. It is important not only to talk to the person in advance about technology, but to show him or her that technology in operation.

I have been provided with Internet software by the Wigram AAC Internet Surfers (WAACIS) project. This includes both e-mail and the World Wide Web. E-mail is something I access frequently. However the Web presents me with problems. It has been difficult for me to know whether the fault has lain with my computer or the servers, and the way my disability has restricted my competence in describing the problems has exasperated me to the point of giving up. One of the difficulties of WAACIS has been the lack of information provided on the web site by individual users. It is difficult to engage in dialogue when you know so very little about someone.

Then there are my current technological issues. Purchasing a computer presents many problems for people with disabilities. It is difficult for the supplier to understand the complexities of matching not only the computer to the person, but also the trolley to the seat. The experience of having my first computer delivered without a program of familiarization has led me to realize how important this is. The commercial aspects of buying a computer and trolley have badly frustrated me. It was difficult to know if I am getting the right value for my money.

With my new computer I have firsthand knowledge of what I would like, and I am so much further down the road of MND that the increased specification of the computer will see me through. I am of the opinion that at present the disabled who need a computer will find that professionals with the necessary skills to help them are in very short supply, and therefore a heavy reliance will be placed on "computing" friends.

Apart from the WAACIS project, there has been no professional with the relevant training to do this. There needs to be an identifiable role within the National Health Services (NHS). Their computing departments are not presently available. The nearest AAC center is 200 miles (a 3-hour drive) away where there is good support, but it needs to be closer. I can hear the professionals say, "On top of all I have to do—computers and the Internet!"

Often I am aware of my thinking strategies, and they seem to be improving. When I was diagnosed with MND, my prognosis was very important to me. Now I take each day at a time, and right from the beginning of the stroke I have never expected things to return to normal.

The point needs making that success is up to the patient as much as the speech therapist. It is by rising to the challenges set by the speech therapist and the challenges that I introduce to the sessions myself that I have enjoyed any success. Amateur speech therapists have augmented my professional speech therapists regime, and I have benefited from this voluntary help immensely.

Sharing jokes is very much part of the normalizing process. On the other hand, peace and tranquility are very much a feature of my future. By "peace and tranquility" I don't necessarily mean silence, which is not something that I am afraid of. In the past, I was

Until recently I thought that I would only be able to communicate with high-tech devices. Now I realize through experimentation with family and friends that smiles, frowns, and other expressions can convey a lot, and my family is so in tune with me that I have no qualms about future communication.

very verbose and always contributed at meetings. It is remarkable that I am so composed about this.

What about my future communication? My experience with the living will issue has changed. Initially I thought that it had to be a definitive statement about the way I wanted the final stages of my life to be lived. Although part of this remains, it is insignificant. I will not call it a living will but my wishes at the terminal stages of my earthly life. These wishes are not morally or legally binding on those who treat me. My psychologist is also my advocate. Until recently I thought that I would only be able to communicate with high-tech devices. Now I realize through experimentation with family and friends that smiles, frowns, and other expressions can convey a lot, and my family is so in tune with me that I have no qualms about future communication.

I submit that this is just one more contribution from the hearts, minds and souls of those, like me, who you are trying to help to communicate.

12

The AAC Manufacturer's Tale

Toby Churchill

Wherever possible, AAC users should use the alphabet for communication (as opposed to learning an icon-based language). The alphabet is a powerful 26-symbol system which has evolved over thousands of years and has the ability to express anything under the sun. Literacy can grow with the user, from school to university and beyond. Literacy unlocks the world of books, ideas, and independent living.

Toby is the Managing Director of Toby Churchill Limited, which he founded 25 years ago (manufacturers of the LightWRITER AAC device); he now runs the company with his wife Sheila and brother Simon.

I have been disabled and without speech for 30 years. I am going into some detail about my (perfectly ordinary) story because it may encourage the younger disabled. A disability does not mean the end of life.

I run the company that makes and sells LightWRITERs. I "invented" the first LightWRITER 25 years ago, but that is too grand a word: I prefer to say "put the bits together." I've always been a do-er. At the age of 5 my parents gave me a construction kit. The first thing to be done was to throw away the instructions. The next task was to invent a potato peeler ("put the bits together"). Like many boys with some practical skills, I went on to build a bicycle, a go-kart and a motorbike; it was fun.

My college coursework included 6 months per year in industry, which I loved. Instead of the ongoing educational slog, I was doing Real Things, learning Real Lessons: If you displease people on "the shop-floor," they take industrial-action, and the managers give you a hard time. This seemed like a very practical lesson to me. One of the options was to do a 6-month industrial stage in France, which I lept at. What adventurous 20-year-old would turn down the opportunity to live alone in Paris? To use the vernacular, "bloody yeah!"

I turned 21 in 1968, and a few months later was flown home with a virus (thought to be from swimming in a polluted river, not that the cause matters). The virus spread quickly through my brain. Within a week, I had lost speech and all movement, and a plastic feeding tube was pushed unceremoniously up my nose. No big deal, I had been in hospital before; that's the sort of thing they do. For the next couple of days I didn't sleep at all. I lay awake listening to the nurses changing shifts, catching snippets of conversation, and wondering what to do. I wasn't afraid or angry. I just wanted to solve this problem.

I built up a mental map of the ward—the doors, the nurses' station, the kitchen. The kitchen was very tempting since I was tasting no food or drink at all (it was administered via the tube). There was a heat wave, my throat was dry, the windows were shut tight, and the heating was full on (why do hospitals DO that?). I yearned to get out and be active, but it appeared to be necessary to adapt to a different plan. It really was that simple; there was simply no choice in the matter. Other people use the words "brave" and "courageous" to describe the disabled, but I've no idea what they mean (have you?). There was no choice. I didn't object to my situation—I could think of worse.

I spent 5 months in the first hospital (Addenbookes, one of the best in England and conveniently only 2 miles from my parents' home). I spent those months mostly in bed (slowly regaining movement and, with it, communication by head movement). I wanted to be outside, of course—even the ability to go down to the hospital foyer would have been very highly prized. Activity, new scenery, fresh air! Despite this, I wasn't bored. I was in a neurological ward (mostly for patients recuperating from brain operations), and the other patients were endlessly fascinating. One of them climbed out of bed completely naked during visiting hours and proceeded to wash his blankets in the hand-basin. ("Is he supposed to be doing that?" said a visitor.) I let my mind drift, counting the holes in the ceiling. "Aha, here comes a nurse with something for me, but why is she wearing rubber gloves?"

These months weren't all bliss. Hospitals find it necessary to use very hard mattresses (and are surprised when patients get bed sores). I never lost full sensation, and so bed sores were never an issue. But lying immobile for great lengths of time meant a buildup to a blinding pain as the pressure site needed attention. I simply needed to be turned over, a 2-minute job. I would be comfortable for an hour or two after having been turned. Then the aching would begin and I'd start to moan. Over the next hour, the aching would grow to agony and the moaning would grow to an all-out furious scream. Why couldn't the nurses see the pattern? Turn Toby = Instant Quiet. The other patients on the ward must have thought I was enduring all sorts of horrible internal torment. Little did they know they were bystanders to a communications war.

A casualty of this war was a school friend who passed through the ward briefly for a minor operation. He walked over to my bed and looked down at me but was powerless to help. I've never seen him since. He probably suffered more than I ever did. I was trying so hard to demonstrate the pattern to the nurses, but the message just wasn't sinking in. I had limited communication at the time, and I did explain it all in words. I was told to be more patient, the nurses were "busy." One problem was the nurses came and went in shifts with the minimum of communication, as I supposed, but I learnt of a more profound reason: I overheard a nurse say, "Oh he just screams. He can't help it." Right! This is war! It was important to me that I win it.

Every day a posse of doctors came round who were, of course, completely unaware of all this. A devilish plan was born: I timed things the next day so that my bladder would be full in the morning. When I heard the doctors approaching, I opened up. I had a rubber mattress, so the beautiful yellow liquid didn't soak in but trickled up my back, into my hair, and lapped round my ears. Excellent!! It couldn't have worked better. The doctors peeled back the covers ready to smack my knees with their rubber hammers. Instead, they were met with a pool of stinking urine. The ward sister was politely admonished, the nurses scurried, and I was told I was a very naughty boy. But victory was total. We never had a communication problem after that.

I spent the rest of the time there watching life come and go. New nurses made friends with me and brought me beer. I formed loose plans to design an AAC device. My first ideas involved thousands of tape recorders. I knew that wasn't the right way to do it, but I knew I couldn't further my knowledge from where I was. It would have to wait. I spent the next 7 months rehabilitating in Stoke Mandeville, gaining independence, getting out, and taking interest in the work of some local universities.

Thirty years later, I have one arm, four wheels, and a very bad head for heights (I have always had vertigo, and the virus has exaggerated this to the extent that I now can't even look up at high buildings). I can enjoy food and wine, I still have my wits about me, and I am very healthy in the sense that I am never ill. I don't want or need to travel much, and when I do travel, I use whisky to control my vertigo. I have been seen at airports getting drunk at 9 o'clock in the morning, as much to cope with the huge building as the flight. But mostly I don't travel. I don't want to. It's a lot of work for everyone, and tempers get frayed. When I do, it's with a lot of people to share the workload—I'm heavy.

> *Thirty years later, I have one arm, four wheels, and a very bad head for heights.*

I have a television set hanging over my bed and another one so I can watch it when up (but I rarely do; I prefer to work). I can do both at once, of course, as any housewife knows. I have all the computing power a person could need at my place of work (which is 5 feet from my bed). My mother Ruth loves gardening, and I have a large south facing window onto the garden. I can't go to concerts, but I can organize parties and have local bands play for me. I have a nurse—who is also willing to clean my room for some extra money. I have a great family life and a very full career: What more could I want? I have enough money. I have all the brain cells I need. Life is good. And I'm biodegradable. Death will be good, too, I hope. I live in the house that my father designed (he was an architect) with my mother, wife (from Oregon), daughter (Lucy), and three wild animals (cats) who love having their bellies rubbed. I am 52 and need to decide what I'm going to do when I'm grown-up.

After my year in hospital, I went home (my parents adapted the house), resumed the last year of my college coursework (interrupted by illness), obtained my degree, and went to work on my main mobility task—converting a car. "Your disabilities are too severe—can't

> *I have a great family life and a very full career: What more could I want?*

be done," I was told. Huh! I remember demonstrating my one-hand joystick control to the designer of a competing system. I drove very fast at a concrete block and nipped round it at the last moment. "Jeez, slow down. You're scaring the living daylights out of me," he said. "I think that's what he's trying to do," muttered someone else in the car. I could now get about but was limited to a portable typewriter when I got there. A lot of searching revealed nothing remotely suitable, though I did come across a computer terminal which the Chicago police were putting in their cars to computerize that city's felons, and the device had the flavour of "car-ness," which I was into at the time.

However, I could see that the Chicago police wouldn't be committed to supporting me on a continuing basis. Other avenues fetched up in the same place—the only way to solve the problem was to design and build it myself. Out with the soldering iron and the textbooks. Friends were put upon and contacts were made. A car, a portable computer, numerous other gadgets to help me—my disability hadn't stopped me building things, but the reaction to me was very different. Everyone now thought I was joking, that it was a hobby that wouldn't get far. I carried on. I understood what they were feeling. A bank manager refused me a loan for that very reason. Never mind. I decided to do it myself.

Shortly after I built the first LightWRITER for my own need, people started asking, "Where? How much? Who do I make the cheque out to?" It dawned on me that someone would need to start making them commercially. It also dawned on me that the somebody would be me. I'd be wasting my time if I tried to get another company to do it. Sales grew slowly to about 50 a year by 1980. I designed and built them all myself, learning my craft along the way. In 1982 I realized it was time for a change. We needed a more powerful systems approach. I met Nick Bane, who is still with us today (Technical Director). He is still creating magnificent software for us, still the backbone of the technical side of the company, and still e-mailing Microsoft to tell them that their software is broken "here, here, and here." "Oops," they say, "So it is. How very silly of us" (or words to that effect).

In 1986 it was time for another change. We needed a smaller, more appealing case. Enter Clyde Millard (Industrial Designer), and the SL1 was born. The electronics were designed by a 16-year-old named Martin Stevens—I bought him a computer and off he went, eyes sparkling. The National Health Service (in England) imaginatively bought 24 SL1 devices and placed them in demonstration centers.

They called it "pump priming," and that's exactly what happened. The effect was that many more than 24 LightWRITERs found their way into users' hands. Twenty-five years later, the LightWRITER has developed into the optimum portable communication tool for me, and seemingly for tens of thousands of others. The company is now run by me (Design); my wife, Sheila (Manager); my brother Simon (Marketing); and his wife, Tricia (Sales). Perhaps Lucy will want to join us one day, who knows?

My original dream remains to make LightWRITERs available to all who need them, worldwide. If I achieve even a hundredth of that in my lifetime, I will die happy. Meanwhile we hear some wonderful stories over the phone. "User A has thrown his LightWRITER out of the window and a car ran over it. What shall I do now?" "User B has vomited chicken soup into her LightWRITER."

My first few weeks in hospital gave me a sharp lesson in the need to communicate, anything from "Move my left foot while you are passing" to "Please open the window" to "No, I meant 'I'm sorry to hear about your husband,'" and not "I'm hungry." Over the years, I have learned how to communicate using an AAC device. Short, unambiguous statements are best for most people—a bus driver or shop assistant doesn't need the user's life story. One idea is ideal ("Let's do this"). Two ideas are all that most people can manage ("If this then this, if not then that"). Three ideas usually confuse ("Well, after all that discussion, what do you want me to actually do?"). The same rules apply as in normal conversation: Learn to read the signs; the other person will eventually want to move on, and from that point on, one's status changes from "an interesting person" to "a bore." This transition can happen early on (reading an AAC device is tiring), and can be quite abrupt in some people—they suddenly absolutely need to go shopping. Let them. It is the responsibility of the AAC user to steer the conversation in a way that leaves the partner feeling that they have had a pleasant or useful conversation and would be willing to do it again.

> *My original dream remains to make LightWRITERs available to all who need them, worldwide. If I achieve even a hundredth of that in my lifetime, I will die happy.*

I believe that wherever possible, AAC users should use the alphabet for communication (as opposed to learning an icon-based language). The alphabet is a powerful 26-symbol system which has evolved over thousands of years and has the ability to express anything under the sun. Literacy can grow with the user, from school to university and beyond. Literacy unlocks the world of books, ideas, and independent living.

There are other methods of communication that are more powerful than portable AAC devices: letter, fax, e-mail, and, of course, telephone. The LightWRITER can do most of these things. For example, it can make phone calls. But I prefer to use the phone with an assistant reading out the words on my computer screen. This means that I can be silently typing my next thought while the person at the other end is talking, and my assistant can reply almost immediately. The conversation is thus more fluid (and quicker, cheaper, less tiring, and more productive). The human voice can give my words intonation, spontaneity, humour, and wit. Machines can't do that (yet).

My assistants have to have considerable forbearance to work out what my shorthand means, to speak words they have never encountered, to pass on ideas they might disagree with, and to try not to guess what the drift of the conversation might be, because if they plant a completely wrong idea in the mind of the person we are speaking to, the conversation becomes very confused. And most importantly, they report my actions to the person: "Toby nods, 'yes;'" "Wait a moment, please. He's typing a reply;" "Hang on, he is just looking it up for you." Above all, they need to relay everything that I say. The natural assumption is that the person at the other end can see and hear the same things that they can—not true, of course!

Communication is a powerful tool (I use it to explain how I want to build things). As with three-way phoning, much skill is required on all sides to build what I want built, not what other people think I might want built. This sounds dictatorial, and it is, but I also try to make it pleasant, like a conductor and an orchestra. I tell myself that I listen to the opinions of others (but all dictators think that, don't they?).

We are surrounded by the pure magic of electronics, but are largely unaware of how they work and how they are transforming our lives: telephones, televisions, computers—electric and electronic gadgets of every kind. They enable man to see deep into outer space or deep into the human body and to communicate with others anywhere in the world, to share knowledge or ideas, instantly. The applications for the disabled are particularly startling: Electrons have "no real objective form at all," yet can be made to speak if the user is unable to speak, print if the user is unable to write, and communicate any idea or emotion under the sun provided the user has language skills (if necessary, with a single switch). The engines that perform these tasks are fantastically complicated—so many things are going on inside a communication tool, most of them at the same time. Making it all work is exciting, challenging, rewarding, and extremely difficult. I enjoy it.

13

Partners with a View

Laurence C. Thompson
and M. Terry Thompson

If I had one word of advice for AAC specialists, I think it would probably be to help the patient learn to use everything he or she has. You don't need to completely forget speech. If you can just say "yes" or "no" or maybe just one word, it helps.

Dr. Laurence C. Thompson is retired as Professor Emeritus of Linguistics from the University of Hawaii. His stroke, at age 57, occurred in 1983. M. Terry Thompson, his wife and professional collaborator, lives with him in Hawaii during half of the year; they live the other half in Oregon.

Editors' Note: The Thompsons are partners in more ways than one—
married for 33 years, linguists and authors together, and now communication partners since Larry's stroke in 1983. As the self-described
"vocal" member of the team, we interviewed Terry who, with Larry,
gave us the following advice and opinions. This essay is transcribed
from our conversations together. While the style is different from the
rest of the essays, we trust you will find the insights valuable.

OUR COMMUNICATION HISTORY

We have been communication partners for decades, as professional
colleagues, as student and teacher, and as husband and wife.

Larry had a stroke at work in 1983 at the University of Hawaii,
so he's on worker's compensation for the rest of his life. They agreed
to continue with his therapy as long as it seemed to be profitable to
him.

We've been using AAC for about 7 years. We communicated for
10 years even before he got a DynaVox. So we don't only use the DynaVox by itself. He has a way to say, "Ohhhh." He uses that when he
knows that an hour or two or three or maybe a day later I'll say,
"Ohhhh, that's what you were talking about." So he'll say, "Ohhhh,"
and I know that he knows that I know what he's talking about. Also,
he can answer "yes" or "no" or "maybe." He also writes things down.
He'll copy off a bottle or a box or something when he wants to add
things to the shopping list.

We always worked together before he had the stroke; we're also
very good friends. We did work together professionally. He had his
bailiwick and I had mine, but we often worked at the same table or
the same desk and we know each other pretty well, so it's not as difficult as it is for some people. For some couples, the wife has worked
at one profession and the husband at another, and they really don't
know too much about the day in, day out things. For that reason, I often can guess what he wants to write about. Sometimes I do a fairly
good job, and sometimes he does get very frustrated with me.

Larry has always been good with maps. He loves maps. In order
to get me to discover what he is telling me, he will draw a map, either a city map locating something within the city or a map of the
U.S. locating it within the U.S., or perhaps a map of France or England wanting to talk about someone or something there. We play a
lot of guessing games. He's been very patient with me about letting
me find the clues. And sometimes I absolutely drive him into hyster-

ics because my clues are so far from the point. Fortunately, he's got a great sense of humor, so he is able to laugh about it.

Things changed over the years; now he's a lot quieter since he had the stroke. I talk a lot more. I've always been talkative, but now even more. He communicates well with other people, and he's gotten very vocal in the last few years, although he doesn't say many words. He gestures and smiles and points and makes noises and people realize that they are communicating with him. He's not a dummy. One of the things that always amuses us is when he sees a doctor for the first time. If it's not a doctor who is familiar with strokes, the doctor immediately starts talking louder, and we both begin to chuckle. When people don't understand him, Larry will come and get me and take me to where somebody is because they've asked him a question that he simply isn't equipped to answer at the moment, but he knows I can. When he does that, I tell them that "Larry wants you to ask me that question," because I know that's what he wants.

> *One of the things that always amuses us is when he sees a doctor for the first time. If it's not a doctor that is familiar with strokes, the doctor immediately starts talking louder, and we both begin to chuckle.*

Larry is so independent. If he wants something, he goes and gets it. In fact, he's often more able physically to do that than I am. For example, when we go to a restaurant he really doesn't have trouble ordering; he looks at the menu and points to what he wants. Very few waiters will insist that you say what it is you want. At Willamette View, the retirement place where we're living now, he has learned to order from the posted menu. He either nods that he wants the same thing that the person before him wanted, or he looks at me and I order for him. He's learned to say that he wants "a mini," which is a small portion. He can say "decaf" and "water," and most of the other things he might order are things that we pick up at the salad bar.

Larry uses many modes of communication. He's still very determined to speak, and he does occasionally, too. We keep encouraging him to use the words that he can say. The problem is that under pressure they don't come easily. He practices and practices and practices and then when the time comes to use the word everything flees. The syntax just disappears—it still does. That's very frustrating. He still practices writing (copying) words and sentences in excellent penmanship.

TELLING STORIES

Larry has become a great storyteller. I never realized what a powerful communication technique storytelling is. This past weekend I went with a group of four other people my age on a trip. It was a 2-hour trip and during the whole ride (we all didn't know each other that well), I was kind of analyzing our conversation. I would say a good 85% was storytelling. You know, "Oh when I was in college," and just constant storytelling. There was very little of the touchy, feely type stuff or new, recent activities; it was all this retelling old stuff. We do a lot of that at Willamette View where we live in Portland. You know, you have lunch or dinner or breakfast with different people all the time and somebody says something that reminds somebody else of a story about something that happened a long time ago or last week, or of a joke.

We don't have as much chance to use the storytelling in Hawaii because so many of our friends have moved away; they've retired and moved away or died. People in our financial group often move away because of the high cost of living. When we're in Portland, Larry's very busy. He has a very full schedule. He goes to physical therapy twice a week and has massage therapy every week. He comes to speech therapy once a week, and he swims every day. His swimming takes about 2 hours. Then there are meals three times a day, which entails going to the dining room. So it's about an hour or a little more for each meal. You begin to add all of that up. He does a lot of homework with his DynaMyte, and he practices writing every day because, you see, he's had to learn to write with his left hand. He's taken up oil painting so he spends time painting when we're in Portland. He went around and took pictures of his oil paintings. He has them all in a little portfolio and tells people "these are the things I have painted." He not only learned to paint, but he learned to do it with his left hand. It's something he'd always wanted to do. Actually, if he had been painting before, it probably would have been just too frustrating to relearn with his left hand because he was always very right handed.

The last time he went to see his physiatrist, Dr. Ward, he had everything he wanted to say programmed in his device. He had broken a bone in his arm up close to his shoulder, and he wanted to tell Dr. Ward about that. It was just a hairline crack, not a bad break. He had that programmed in. Then he brought along his little portfolio of pictures to show Dr. Ward what he had been painting, and Dr. Ward was so impressed with this that he asked if Larry would paint one for his house. Larry has also started doing latch hook rugs. This he started while he was still in the hospital after he had the stroke. The physical therapists, occupational therapists, and recreational therapists all thought that this was just something that he shouldn't try because with one hand it would be too frustrating. He simply took it as a challenge and sat down and did it. He has made three large rugs, 6 feet long and 3 feet wide; they're used as wall hangings. The nurse practitioner at our nursing home saw one of his rugs and asked if he would take a commission to do one for a treatment room in the nursing home because it echoes. (She was trying to find something to keep that echo down because of all of the hearing aids.) So he did that for her. Now he's working on another one; it's about a third done. The design was printed on the canvas, but it was printed on crookedly. It's a very geometric design, a rather complex geometric design, so he's having to figure it out as he goes. It's worse than a jigsaw puzzle. He's doing real well on it so far, but of course it gets more difficult as it goes along.

UNIVERSITY CONTACTS

After years teaching at the university, his academic work and colleagues continue to be important to him. His former students are very good; some of them are getting up toward retirement age now. They come and talk to him when they see him and tell him what they're working on and ask his advice on some of their puzzles. So that sort of keeps him in touch. Some of his students are very good about sitting down with him and telling him what they're doing and writing things out for him and asking his advice on things. And, he's still very good at proofreading things. He can't really read, either, but somehow the typographical errors seem to jump out at him, and he's very good at catching them.

His colleagues at the university are fascinated by his communication device, but they're more interested in answering all the questions he asks. He has programmed many questions into his device so he can control a conversation somewhat. Then they stop talking across him to me, and they talk to him and ask him questions. He mostly does social interaction with questions. When we're seeing people that he hasn't seen for a while, he'll put in questions for friends who are still teaching, such as, "What courses have you been teaching? Do you have any good students? What are you writing? What are you working on?"—that sort of thing. And each one of these questions is good for 10 or 15 minutes. And he listens; he doesn't interrupt with his own stories. He's become a very good listener since he can't talk!

DynaVox/DynaMyte

The AAC device is only part of his communication. It's a smaller piece of the pie than sometimes we wish it would be, but the reality is that it's a very useful piece. It has its place, but it is only a part of his system. I remember when I came to the hospital, I kept talking about "the boxes" and "the system." Dr. Melanie Fried-Oken kept saying, "That's not the system; that's his device." She said, "A system is saying 'yes' and 'no' and looking over to Terry and all the other ways to express yourself. There's a whole system that you use and that you go back and forth among. If somebody doesn't get it, you go to a backup. This is only one of the tools in the toolbox. We like to think it's the most important because it's kind of what we do. It's not all we do." Our speech-language pathologists, Melanie Fried-Oken and Jane Murphy, obviously are involved in other things. I kind of get technology-focused. But it really is just one of the tools.

It's a very useful tool, but only one of his tools. I think it's been very good for his brain. It's been a nice challenge, a nice mental stimulation to learn all the programming tricks—he's still learning! He gets the manual out and looks up how to do things. He does most of the programming and he copies words. He's using a lot more of his brain because of the programming. The DynaMyte is much more of a challenge than the old DynaVox. It is organized quite differently. It's much more flexible, too. For one thing, he can copy things from one page to another. He used to really growl about the old DynaVox, the fact that he would want to put things from one page to another and there was just no way to do it except to do it over.

It's interesting at Willamette View, the retirement place where we live, that more and more people have computers. It's not unusual at all to overhear a couple of people talking about their problems with e-mail or their problems with getting their new computer set up. Many of them have had computers given to them by children or grandchildren who want to keep in touch, and e-mail seems so much simpler. They get very frustrated before they learn how to do it, and then they're so proud of themselves when they finally learn. It just seems so alien to them at first. We didn't have this problem with the DynaVox. As academics, we got into using computers in the mid-1970s, when punch cards were still being used. So we've been at it for a long time. We've always had at least a computer at home and a computer at the office since the mid-1970s.

So many people who use augmentative communication devices were born disabled, and they used them as children in school. Of course most of the machines are designed for children. And so many of them are designed to be used with a wheelchair where you have a simple way of getting it from place to place. Larry walks, so it's only with this new machine that we've had this last year that Larry is able to carry it around. The DynaMyte is not necessarily easier, it's just better. Also, it's lighter and easier to carry. He dropped the old DynaVox on his foot once. I was afraid he'd broken his foot.

For most of our social interaction at Willamette View, the device is actually not very useful. Larry swims, and he can't take it in the water, or in the dining room with the food, or in the art class where he'd probably get paint on it. We tried taking the DynaVox to the dining room, which is where most of the socialization at Willamette View goes on, and it just didn't work out. A lot of people wear hearing aids, and it's hard to hear something like that (machine language) in a large room with a lot of people talking, unless you're right up close to it. And you can't do any lip reading; there's no redundancy there. It wasn't particularly successful. And there's no room on the tables for it. The thought originally had been that Larry could order his meals himself. Well, he can do that without the DynaMyte. If we go to a restaurant, he simply points to what he wants on the menu.

The DynaMyte is so much more flexible than the old DynaVox. It can do so many things that it gets a little confusing. He has to memorize the various paths you take and then remember those paths. And, sometimes he doesn't remember, and then he has to experiment to find them again, and he gets things all messed up, and then he gets really frustrated. One problem that he has is that he gets a page almost finished, and then he realizes that he wants something that's in the first column down near the bottom to be in the third column up near the top. With the old DynaVox you simply erased one and typed it in in the other place. On the DynaMyte you can swap those, but it takes remembering how to do it. The new machine simply doesn't work the same way, so there isn't an old way to do it anymore except for erase and retype. I discovered that under one of the things that was in the wrong place, when I erased it there was another one under that. You can stack them up. Yesterday morning we were both having computer problems, and he had this page that had gotten in a real snit, and I was trying to work my bookkeeping program on the computer. I was having all kinds of problems and we both were fit to be tied by the time we went to lunch.

SPEECH THERAPISTS AND AAC

The traditional speech therapist doesn't really know about these machines, and many of them really don't trust machines. I went, with the encouragement of the first speech therapist that Larry had in Hawaii, to a conference in Hawaii that was about the various types of techniques for using a machine of one sort or another or learning boards. It was a new world for me. I'm sure it was a new world to most of the therapists that were there. It was just 2 days, and that was all they got. They do have one fellow in the education department at the university who works with augmentative communication and they have a few children in the school system who use these things. But it's practically unheard of in Hawaii and this was very frustrating. (We still spend the winter in Hawaii.) When Larry got the old DynaVox, he took it with him faithfully to sessions with his speech therapist. It would just sit on the desk. I knew she really didn't understand how to use it. At that point she was getting into a new career of teaching debate and that sort of thing at a community college. She really wasn't interested in learning anything new. She was in her mid-fifties and one of our favorite people, but the technology just was a conundrum to her. She really was enjoying her teaching but wasn't doing much work in the way of speech therapy. So, we just sort of stopped going to her. He did see one of the university professors in speech therapy for a little while, and then one of his students for about 2 or 3 months. But that was not terribly useful for Larry. It was very useful for the student, but Larry had spent an awful lot of time teaching classes to speech therapists when he was still teaching at the university, so he sort of figured he'd done his due with that, and he was ready to move on and find somebody who would do something for him.

> I remember one day Larry and Melanie came out of a session almost in tears. They were so pleased because they had had a real conversation using the DynaVox with Larry using real sentences. That was a real breakthrough for him.

We met our present AAC therapist through a speech therapist in Oregon who was looking for someone who might be interested in trying one of these new devices. They did a project together with a couple of speech therapy students. They felt that Larry was a good prospect for this type of thing, and so Melanie helped write a proposal to get one. I remember one day Larry and Melanie came out of a session almost in tears. They were so pleased because they had had a real conversation using the DynaVox with Larry using real sentences. That was a real breakthrough for him.

THE POWER OF PERCEPTION

I noticed how small changes in Larry make big changes in people's perception of him. We had some friends visiting over the weekend from Seattle. They're both computer experts. She works for Microsoft as a consultant and has a master's in library science using computers. He has his doctorate in linguistics and has written all of the programs for the American Indian dictionaries that we've been working on for all these many years. He was a colleague of Larry's at the University of Hawaii. They're good friends, and they also know technology. So, Larry brought out his DynaMyte and some photographs that he knew they would be interested in and shared these with them. They were just really pleased about it. We had a visit with this friend of ours that was Larry's best man—you know, a longtime friend. We spent a few days with him and his wife in San Francisco several years ago when Larry first had the DynaVox. Larry worked out a little scheme to use, and he and Steve went off in the living room by themselves and Larry had some questions set up, "What have you been working on? Have you been teaching? What courses have you been teaching?" and each one of these questions would set Steve off for 15 or 20 minutes. They just had a fine time. And it only took half a dozen questions.

If I had one word of advice for AAC specialists, I think it would probably be to help the patient learn to use everything he or she has. You don't need to completely forget speech. If you can just say "yes" or "no" or maybe just one word, it helps. It was so funny—at this retirement place where we live we walk to and from meals. We go to breakfast, back from breakfast, go to lunch, and all three of these trips are in the morning. So several years ago Larry practiced and learned to say, "Morning." People immediately commented, "Oh, Larry's talking so much more now," and it's the sort of thing that encourages other people to communicate with him instead of talking past him at me and asking me, "Can he so and so?" Well, he can nod and say "yes" and "no" if he's not really pressed. And now more and more people will talk to Larry. Everybody started talking about how much more Larry's talking. People's perceptions are so important.

I think you should never "give up on speech"—I think persistent speech practice is very important. One of our friends worked with him over a period of a year and a half or so, and she had him working on a dialogue with her. Whenever she saw him, she'd say, "Hi," and he'd say, "Hi," and she'd say, "I'm going home," and he'd say, "I'm going home; I'm tired." And a lot of people didn't realize that this was a routine just between the two of them.

Larry started walking without a cane, and people immediately noticed and their perception was that he had improved tremendously. His walking was the same, but he was not using a cane to stabilize himself. He takes a cane with him when he's going to a strange place in case the ground is uneven—you know sort of up and down; then he needs a cane. But around where we live he goes walking around without a cane. He does say "yes" and "no" very clearly, and he asks for coffee or decaf or water. I think the perception before was that others weren't sure whether he understood, and when he says things, then they think, "He's with us again."

14

Liberating Myself

William L. Rush

Only once in our relationship have I given my wife, Chris Robinson, reason to be jealous—when I laid eyes on the Liberator. I actually drooled over it, and my drooling was unrelated to my cerebral palsy.

William L. ("Bill") Rush lives in Lincoln, Nebraska, with his wife, Christine Robinson. He is a freelance journalist and disability rights advocate. When he is not writing or tilting at windmills, Bill enjoys listening to music and mystery novels on tape, playing chess, and traveling with his bride.

Only once in our relationship have I given my wife, Chris Robinson, reason to be jealous—when I laid eyes on the Liberator. I actually drooled over it, and my drooling was unrelated to my cerebral palsy. A consultant from the Prentke-Romich Company (PRC) showed me the Liberator on a summer night. I was impressed with its many functions. It even could sing the University of Nebraska's fight song. However, I already had a voice output communication device, my TouchTalker. It had served me well for 4 years, so I didn't want to change horses or devices in midstream. The consultant respected my choice.

That following Easter, Chris pointed out the call in our church bulletin for 13 men to recreate da Vinci's *Last Supper* for Maundy Thursday service and suggested that I might give it a try.

"It says here that the men have to memorize something," Chris said. "You could maybe program whatever it is into your Touch-Talker."

That Sunday the coordinator/director gave me the speech that I was to "memorize." Storing it in the TouchTalker might seem like an advantage, but it was as hard as committing it to memory. I tried to program it in myself. The biggest problem was that the TouchTalker wasn't designed to store whole paragraphs. Plus, my TouchTalker's editing software had not been upgraded, so I couldn't do any sophisticated editing.

I even called PRC's service department in hopes of getting a hint on how I could download the speech into my TouchTalker. The tech said that it could not be done. "However, if you had the Liberator," the tech said, "you could do what you are talking about. The Liberator can download any text file from your computer and store it as a notebook."

In about 3,500 B.C., the Sumerians invented the wheel. The wheel consisted of two or three wooden segments held together by transverse struts that rotate on a wooden pole. It transformed transportation, warfare, and industry. However, about 400 B.C. to about 300 B.C., a Chinese work described wheels with 30 spokes, dished wheels for greater strength, and the shaft chariot. I thought I knew how the Sumerians might have felt if they had heard about the Chinese wheel.

Using my out-of-date TouchTalker wheel, I started on the speech, which was 3,726 characters, at one o'clock in the afternoon, and when Chris came over at six o'clock, I was still working on it. The results didn't please me.

"Here, why don't I help you since I have 10 fingers that work?" Chris said after she saw how frustrated I was. Besides having 10 coordinated fingers, Chris had a good ear. She could hear what programming sounded the best. If we put in the speech with only the usual punctuation, the TouchTalker would say it too fast. If we put a comma after each word, it sounded so monotonous that Chris started to rock when she heard it. Fortunately, Chris was an experienced pianist and had a feel for the rhythm of my speech.

At first we were going to split the speech into three parts, but that didn't work. The TouchTalker took too much time between selections. The result was two undesired pauses in the speech. I solved this problem by combining the three parts into one big selection. However, I was happy that we had used three selections as we were entering it. That way, if the device failed while we were typing the last word, we would have lost only the last part of the speech rather than losing the whole thing. Had I had the Liberator, I would have used the Liberator's notebook to enter, edit, and store the speech.

"Maybe it's time to get a Liberator," I said to Chris. "Well, you are getting into doing more and more stuff with your voice," Chris said thoughtfully. "It wouldn't hurt to look into getting a Liberator."

I started with the rehabilitation technology specialist at the Nebraska Assistive Technology Project. I thought he would be supportive. He wasn't. "Do you know how many people want a communication device who don't have one, yet you're asking for a better one?" he said. I felt like a Sumerain being chastised for wanting to try a Chinese wheel. Shame on me. I looked at the rehabilitation technology specialist. I wanted to introduce him to Thomas Henry Huxley, a British biologist who was best known for his active support of the theory of evolution. Huxley said, "The rung of a ladder was never meant to rest upon, but only to hold a man's foot long enough to enable him to put the other somewhat higher."

It became clear that I would have to make the case of why I needed the Liberator myself.

It became clear that I would have to make the case of why I needed the Liberator myself. As a journalist, I knew that a good solid story had to answer six questions: Who? What? When? Where? Why? and, How?

The who, what, when, and where of this story were obvious. I decided to concentrate on two questions: 1) Why did I need to change communication devices? and 2) How would the Liberator improve my ability to communicate and my life?

With the TouchTalker I had started to give speeches for my local independent living center. To give a speech, I would have to dump a majority of my device's vocabulary to fit the speech into the machine. Then after the speech, I would have to load the vocabulary back. In between, I would have to pray that I wouldn't need the part that I had dumped. With the Liberator I could have about 75% of the Bible or 100,000 words at a time.

Besides the better communication options, the Liberator, I had learned through several conversations with the people at PRC, could be used to take notes. This interested me because for a decade and a half I had been looking for a way to take notes when I was away from my base computer. I had tried using a tape recorder. The problem with that was that I couldn't transcribe fast enough, and the tapes sometimes failed. This left me without notes—a nightmare to most journalists. However, the Liberator has the means to store large blocks of text.

This meant I could go to where a story was and type my notes into my Liberator. Since the Liberator could upload to my base computer, I could upload my notes into my base computer's word processor via a radio link. Then, I could write the story. Not only would the Liberator help me with my face-to-face communication, but it would also help me with my journalistic efforts. It would be my communication device and my laptop computer.

The Liberator also had the advantage of using an icon-based access language called Minspeak—the same icon language my TouchTalker used, so I wouldn't have to learn a different system. I was beginning to feel like Pavlov's dogs. The more I learned, the more I drooled.

I started to make my case to the state. I asked the people with whom I worked to write letters to the Division of Vocational Rehabilitation saying that getting a Liberator would enhance my communication. They did. I needed a speech pathologist to sign off on my work. I found a speech pathologist. She insisted on doing her own investigation because it would be her name and her reputation on the line, both figuratively and literally. Her research proved me right— the Liberator was the best communication device for me. I resisted telling her, "I told you so," and was amazed by my maturity. The State of Nebraska was, too. It bought the Liberator for me in August, 1992—13 months after I had been introduced to it.

Even before my Liberator came I started to call it, "My Libby." Chris pointed out that I had never named another piece of my equipment. I laughed, but then realized that she was right. I have called my old dilapidated manual wheelchair "a hunk of junk," but I have never called a piece of my equipment a name of endearment because I had always believed that inanimate objects shouldn't have endearing names.

The Liberator could do so many things for me. It was almost as if PRC had taken the deepest communication needs and wants of my soul and made a device to satisfy 80% of them. I remembered an old television series called *Knight Rider,* which was about a car that had been infused with a person's soul. The car had a name of Knight Industries 2000, and its owners called it "Kitt." It seemed only fitting that I named the Liberator because it seemed like it had been infused with my spirit, and because anything that I could dream of doing was possible with the Liberator.

One of the first things I did was to load Shakespeare's balcony scene from Romeo and Juliet from a CD-ROM into my Liberator. I edited out all of Juliet's lines. Then I went to Chris's apartment, sat outside her second story window, and recited Romeo's lines from the balcony scene. When it became obvious that the mosquitoes would have eaten me all up before Chris heard me, I went inside the apartment building and sat outside her apartment door and recited Romeo's lines.

> *The Liberator could do so many things for me. It was almost as if PRC had taken the deepest communication needs and wants of my soul and made a device to satisfy 80% of them.*

It has been more than 6 years since I got the Liberator. In an age where things have been designed to become obsolete in 2 or 3 years, this is remarkably long. I credit this with my close involvement with the selection process. I knew what would work for me. I also credit the Liberator's flexibility and expandability. The Liberator has grown with my needs and desires.

I have grown considerably with the Liberator's help. I occasionally serve as worship leader at my church. I look up the week's scripture in my Bible on my computer. Then I select the scripture that will be used, copy it to a text file, and download that file into the Liberator. I also have just recently started helping with the church's puppet ministry by doing the voices of the puppets. I get a copy of the script on a computer disk, edit out all the lines of the other characters, and save only my lines to a text file. When it comes time to say them, I use a macro that says a sentence, moves to the next sentence, and waits for me to activate it again.

I haven't put any limits on how far the Liberator and I can go. In fact, a friend who is active in the Disability Rights Movement has said that she and her group have gotten the National Republican Party to promise that it would have a person with a disability address its national convention in the year 2000. I think my Liberator and I would be up to that, even if it would mean we had to change our party affiliation!

15

Empowerment

David Chapple

AAC doesn't make successful people; people make AAC successful.

David Chapple is 30 years old and lives in Garfield Heights, a suburb of Cleveland, Ohio. He is employed by a small software company named CyberAccess where he works as a software engineer. During his spare time, he enjoys traveling, listening to music, and watching sports.

With the help of augmentative and alternative communication (AAC), I have achieved my goal of starting my career as a software engineer. Although I have the strong computer skills to get a job and to work competitively, AAC has helped me with all the other facets of my job: my interview, my programming work, and my relationships with peers. At my interview, I was able to respond to the questions quickly and intelligently. With my voice output communication aid (VOCA), I can store programming commands under icon sequences so I can type a programming line within seconds. Finally, AAC has helped me to express my sense of humor and technical ideas to my co-workers.

When I was growing up I had a lot of dreams and goals, not un-like any other kid. Some of those goals were going to college, living independently, and getting a job. I knew I had to work very hard in order to achieve each of those goals, but AAC has helped me to reach every one of the goals. As you all probably know, Minspeak is one lan-guage system for VOCAs that enables people to speak quickly and clearly. It was important while I was going to college because I had to communicate with my professors if I had questions or comments during class. Also, I had to communicate my answers to test questions to a proctor. Of course this level of communication is also important to live independently because I have to be able to communicate my everyday personal needs. These are big achievements. I believe one of the biggest dreams of anybody is to have a successful career, but people who have speech problems need help to reach their dreams.

Last October the dream finally came true for me after a long up-hill battle. Although I had a bachelor's degree in computer science and was a registered student in graduate school, people still won-dered how I would fit into the business world. After I graduated from college and got my bachelor's degree, I started to work with many vo-cational rehabilitation counselors and specialists to help me to find a job. Many times my hopes got high with their ideas that ranged from starting my own business to working for some huge company to getting more education. But my hopes were quickly smashed for one reason or another. The biggest letdown was when somebody, who shall remain nameless, said to give up on me because nobody would hire me. But with the help of Minspeak and my strong will, I have proven that I can get a job, maintain the job, and be an integral part of a company.

From about July to September I went on countless interviews and by the time September came around, I was getting discouraged. I was beginning to think maybe the computer field wasn't the place for a person with a severe disability, and I started to think about other options. You know that old saying, people who can't do something usually teach it. So one of my thoughts was to become a computer professor, but I had a lot of silly thoughts during that time. One day in September I received an e-mail from Wayne Largent from a company named CyberAccess (my present employer) asking me if I wanted an interview. Thinking I wouldn't get the job anyway, I wrote him back a description detailing my disability and the Liberator, and I even sent him my web site address that has my picture on it. After all this I really didn't expect an interview, but in a couple of days I received a call to set up an interview.

In the past when I did get a call for an interview, I would ask somebody like my vocational counselor to make the first call to the company because I thought they would be afraid of my Liberator. Many times when I use the telephone the person on the other end has no idea what to make of my Liberator. A lot of times I get hung up on or they say get my attendant to talk for me although I do have a prestored message in my Liberator trying to explain how I communicate. I think when people hear a computer voice on the telephone they automatically think I am trying to sell them something. When you think about it, it is kind of funny, but it is very frustrating when it actually happens. Instead of risking a potential job opportunity, I had to swallow my pride and ask for help. Not so with my present employer: they were impressed that I could describe my disability myself without somebody speaking for me.

> I think when people hear a computer voice on the telephone they automatically think I am trying to sell them something. When you think about it, it is kind of funny, but it is very frustrating when it actually happens.

After 3 years of looking for a job, I finally got that call with the job offer that I had been waiting for. I am going to tell you a funny little story that my boss didn't know about until he read this essay. I pretty much knew I would be very much considered for the job after being interviewed for 4 hours. For that week after the interview I was sitting on pins and needles, and every time the telephone rang I almost jumped out of my skin. I guess it was fortunate I planned to go out of town for a few days because I wouldn't think about getting the job. I did call my sister to check my answering machine once during the trip, but the call didn't come. Anyway, the morning after I came home the telephone rang, and it was finally the call! After waiting a week—no, years—for this moment when my boss offered me the job, I was so excited I lost control of my wheelchair, hit the telephone, and hung up on him. A minute later he called back thinking his cellular telephone was going bad. After that little snag he did offer the job to me, and I started a week after that. Since that day I have been thinking about what I would say to that person who said just to give up on me. I think I would say never underestimate a person with a strong will and a Liberator because they can do anything they want.

Though I did get the job with CyberAccess, I had been on many interviews before this one, and I would have been lost without my Liberator. When I was doing my undergraduate studies, I had an opportunity to have a mock interview at the career services center at Cleveland State University. At that time I had a manual board with Blissymbols and I needed somebody to go with me on the mock interview to read what I was saying. This was awkward at best and was very hard on the person who was reading the board. I feel if I had a Bliss board for a regular interview I think it would be even more awkward because it might seem like I couldn't talk for myself and it would be a lot slower. On the other hand, with my VOCA and Minspeak, I can express my thoughts and skills myself during an interview, which makes a better impression.

Even though the Liberator and Minspeak were godsends during interviews, I don't think anything could have helped during those interviews from hell. I guess anybody that has gone on a lot of interviews or that will be going on interviews at some time in the future can relate to my experiences. Of course there are interviews that last for 15 minutes, and you know there is no way in hell you will get the job. Or there is the famous line, "We will be in touch," and they never call. But when the interviewer is more interested in your Liberator rather than your job skills, I think I can say this doesn't happen to everybody. During that interview, not unlike other interviews in the past, they began with asking me a lot of questions about my Liberator. However, usually the Liberator questions stop, and the questions then turn to be job related. But in this case, the interview turned out to be a half hour Liberator training. Needless to say, I didn't get the job, and I don't think I would have accepted a job from the employer because the person who interviewed me didn't recognize my computer skills. Then, when I did have a good interview, and I thought I had a chance of getting the job, it was either one other person had a little more experience than me or the job required some physical work that I didn't know about. I don't know if my interview at CyberAccess was actually my best, but I guess it was my most effective because I got the job.

When I got the job there was little question that I was qualified, but there was an issue about my speed. On my computer, both at home and work, I have the device that hooks to the computer to act as an interface between my VOCA and the computer. I am sure most of the people here know what I am talking about, but there could be a reader new to computer access, so I am going to take a minute or two to explain it. I use a program that is in my VOCA for mouse interface and keyboard emulation. With this program, the Liberator keyboard is transformed into a computer keyboard with the function keys and fancy characters. I can also operate a mouse with the program. Although I'm sure that thinking about how people with physical disabilities can possibly use a mouse was an afterthought to Bill Gates, I find the Windows 95 accessibility options also helpful. I like to use mouse keys when I have to move the mouse in precise movements or when I need more control of the mouse buttons.

I did have some experience with programming for a very small computer company on a very part-time basis, but I just got two assignments in a year. During that time I stored a lot of the most common programming commands under icon sequences, which makes me a relatively fast programmer, so I did get something out of that job experience. However, some of the programming commands are a part of everyday language and therefore are already in my VOCA program. Some examples are the "if-then-else" statement, the "do-while" statement, and the "for-next" statement. Wayne, my boss, has been very impressed with how much I can do in a week. When I first started he thought my speed could have been a problem, but he took a chance on me anyway. His worries quickly diminished. He discovered my work output equals that of a programmer without disabilities!

I also have to write weekly reports on what work I have done. With the device I can type those reports quickly, and I am able to use the appropriate words without spelling too much. In addition to the weekly reports, I communicate with the people in the office primarily by e-mail. This is true because I mostly work from my house and go to the office for meetings and special events. Anyway, I can type long and detailed e-mails to my boss or another programmer who I may be working with on a project.

One of the most important things at CyberAccess is whether or not a potential employee will fit in with the workplace personality. With my VOCA, I can contribute in meetings as well as make an occasional joke with my co-workers. An example of this was at the Christmas party when the company usually provides a movie. This year the VCR was broken, and nobody knew what to do. I suggested that I could sing Christmas carols. Everybody thought that was very funny, and they still talk about it to this day. Another example is when groups of employees had to do skits during a training exercise about a certain situation that happened in the daily operations of the company. This turned into a big satire of those situations, and that was the purpose I believe. I was able to take part in my group's skit because I was able to save my lines and recite them on cue. This was very fun for me, and I think my co-workers enjoyed my participation.

Besides being the comedian that I am, I can communicate my thoughts and ideas to my boss or co-workers, and I have become a part of the CyberAccess family. Even though my VOCA enables quick communication, it is a fact that I communicate slower than people without a communication device. When I am talking to somebody one-to-one, they know they have to be patient and wait until I complete typing what I am saying. Usually, they still give me complete attention while I am typing, and I really respect that. But other times they can't always stop whatever they are doing and just stand there. I realize the company can't stop whenever I have something to say, but they don't want to make me feel what I have to say isn't important. At those times we both learned it is okay for them to do something else while I am typing my message. Usually this doesn't happen that much.

On the other hand, I think it would be ludicrous to think that while I am in meetings with a lot of people, like project meetings, department meetings, or company meetings, everybody should wait in silence while I type in what I have to say. The employees at CyberAccess realize that when they hear my clicking, I am going to say something, but the meeting doesn't come to a halt. The discussion continues until they don't hear the clicking. At that time, they acknowledge me, and I speak what is on my mind. I'm not trying to find fault with any other augmentative communication device. Without my VOCA it would be very hard for me to contribute in meetings at all. I guess my point is that Minspeak gives me the tool to give my knowledge and input to my co-workers, and they have learned to adapt to make me feel my input is valuable.

> *The employees at CyberAccess realize that when they hear my clicking, I am going to say something, but the meeting doesn't come to a halt.*

Despite doubts by many people, I have reached my lifelong dream of finding full-time employment. Although I had the knowledge to become a software engineer, the Liberator gave me the opportunity to demonstrate that knowledge and to express my personality so I could reach my dream. A VOCA is just an incredible tool that enables people to achieve their dreams. Without those people, a VOCA would be nothing. Maybe if I didn't have a VOCA I would be where I am today anyway, and I am sure I would be. But the Liberator and Minspeak have helped me to reach my goals more easily, and I can really show people my personality. We should always remember: AAC doesn't make successful people; people make AAC successful.

16

Reaching for the Stars and Almost Touching Them

Arthur Honeyman

Arthur Honeyman lives in Portland, Oregon. He received his bachelor's of science in history in 1965 from Portland State University and his master's of arts in literature in 1974. He began his career in creative writing in 1966 by composing poetry. Art has been a door-to-door salesman, an educator, a state civil servant, a candidate for state political office, and is now a noted author, word processor operator, writer and literary consultant, and owner of Wheel Press, Inc., a small publishing business in Portland. The author says that writing is his "most beloved activity," and he is always working on a book. He has published 15 books in addition to engaging in ghost writing, advertising, sign writing, and customizing resumes.

Reaching for the Stars and Almost Touching Them

if you are anything like me

by the time that you perish from this earth

you will have spent an entire lifetime

setting goals far beyond your eager grasp

straws slipping through your clutching fingers

yet you realize with all your primitive instincts

that it is probable you are quite fortunate

that the big one ingeniously got away

for if you were to actually touch the stars

that you covet and for which you reach

you would be burned if not cremated

and you also know that the act of reaching

is infinitely more valuable than touching

for reaching stretches you more and more

while grasping or touching stops you short

17

Others Say So, Too

Peg L. Johnson

*We all have visions and dreams whether we
are able-bodied or disabled. I have learned
that to accept challenges and to embrace the
future, you must never cease to "express
yourself."*

Peg L. Johnson lives in Minneapolis, Minnesota. She has been employed by the Minneapolis Public Library since 1979. A college graduate, she is the author of a book entitled *Express Yourself* and the founder and coordinator of a support group for AAC users. She enjoys theater, travel, and college and professional basketball and football. Go Gophers and Vikings!

Until my high school graduation, I never really admitted, deep down, that I had significant problems expressing myself. In fact, I wasn't even aware of it. This may seem strange to those who know me or to those who have read my other essay (see Chapter 4). However, growing up, my circle was very small and consisted of family, friends, and teachers who knew and understood me well. After graduation, that small comfortable circle did not prepare me for the realities of the world. The world did not have a place for me. I did not belong. I did not fit in. I had no job. I had no career. Unlike today, the vocational rehabilitation instructor told me that all I could do was go home and weave rugs! In the late 1960s and early 1970s, it was unheard of for a person with a severe physical and communication disabilities to obtain employment. After I cried (nonstop) for 15 months, my family and friends helped launch me on a path of self-employment, self-determination, and self-direction that has motivated me to this day.

My first taste of the business world was to establish an arts and craft business with a lifelong friend. Learning the skills to operate a successful business for 12 years was no small feat. The business grew so large that we needed to employ eight able-bodied people to work out of their homes. After learning much from this entrepreneurial experience, I felt the need for a new challenge, so I enrolled in college.

In the late 1970s some of my friends with disabilities were finding employment, so, while I was still in college, I began a 13-month search for a job. Not only did I want to be a contributing member of society, but I needed to prove that a person with a severe disability could be a part of the workforce. Every single Monday for 13 months, I called my employment counselor to inquire about available job opportunities. Finally, the Minneapolis Public Library hired me in September 1979, and I have been working there part time ever since. I feel like one of the library's icons.

While in college, I took an introductory computer class. The final assignment was to write an eight-page term paper dealing with any aspect of computers. Needless to say, I selected the topic "computers that talk." When it was time to research the topic, I found only three pages of printed data on the subject. I panicked, but I was up for the challenge! A professor at the University of Minnesota was kind to meet with me and steer me in the right direction. By the time I had exhausted all of the resources and interviewed the local experts in the field, my term paper ended up to be 35 pages with pictures. That course had a profound and lasting influence on my life.

After graduating from college, my house was still piled high with unused alternative and augmentative communication (AAC) data. Being disturbed and extremely frustrated about the lack of available information, I decide to expand my research and compile enough data to publish a 182-page resource guide on AAC. Writing a technical primer was no small feat either. Each and every detail needed to be precise and accurate. The assistance of many dedicated AAC "gurus" and professionals nationwide played an instrumental part in the book's content. After compiling all of the technical data, decoding the AAC jargon was another significant challenge. I understand much better now why textbooks are not written in plain, everyday English. It's "darn" difficult! For months, anybody who even walked by my keyboard was recruited to type or re-type a few pages into the computer. The typed text was then transferred onto some floppy disks, which then went to a printer. My dad had previously worked with a printer, so finding and hiring a printer was one of the easier aspects of this overwhelming undertaking. The printer was able to run text for the book directly from the floppy disks. We paid him to insert the photographs, design the cover, and bind the book, which was entitled *Express Yourself.* (When people ask me about writing a book, I always strongly recommend writing on a topic that is familiar to them.)

As I was interviewing people for my book, I discovered that a great many costly electronic communication devices were just sitting on shelves collecting dust. Once again, this disturbed and frustrated me. Inevitably, caregivers would state, "Those devices are too much bother and too hard to work—I know what they want, anyway." Something needed to be done! In 1988, a friend and I founded Express Yourself of Minnesota, Inc. (EYM), a nonprofit organization established to provide support services for individuals with severe speech impairments.

Individuals using AAC systems, and their families and therapists, expressed a need to create a supportive environment where users can practice and learn to be better communicators. It was determined that users were not effectively communicating outside therapy sessions and desired communication experience in real-life situations. It is recognized that communication device users need an opportunity for ongoing assistance to further develop their skills beyond the initial assessment and training. As a result, one of EYM's initial programs was to establish a support group for individuals using voice output communication devices. The name of the group is Your Expressive Society (YES). The first session

> *Individuals using AAC systems, and their families and therapists, expressed a need to create a supportive environment where users can practice and learn to be better communicators.*

was held in October, 1990, and consisted of eight augmentative communicators.

I remember the first few years, group members seldom brought their devices to the YES group meetings, and when they did, devices needed repair or batteries needed to be charged. Now most everybody is prepared to add their input to the discussion. At times, we all talk at once. Being attentive to 10 or more different people is quite a challenge. One appreciative YES participant stated, "It's sure nice to know that you're not alone."

The group wasted no time in becoming involved in the community. Right off the bat, our first public awareness event was singing Christmas carols at a shopping mall. It was so successful that it is now an annual event. Some of our augmented communicators took to the streets on Veterans Day and sold poppies as volunteers for their local American Legion posts' fund drive. Another time a few selected users spoke before the state occupational therapy (OT) conference on how OT had influenced their lives. Members of the group also used their devices to sell candy as a means of initiating contacts with friends and strangers. Two members and a facilitator made a presentation about the YES group and its activities at the annual Rehabilitation Engineering Society of North America (RESNA) conference in Las Vegas, Nevada. RESNA is a group of research engineers that is very influential in developing AAC technology. The YES group also sang and spoke at the annual celebration of the Americans with Disabilities Act.

As the group gained greater confidence and independence in their abilities to communicate, group members became braver and more outgoing. So outgoing, in fact, that one of our members took it upon himself to arrange for the taping of our meeting for a talk show for cable television! Needless to say, this surprised and dismayed the leaders and facilitators of the group and created a minor nightmare. After this "educational" incident, we knew we needed to draft guidelines for the group, which was an interesting experience to say the least!

The group's latest endeavor was to create a professionally produced video documenting the everyday communication interactions of our YES members. It is our hope that this video will inspire and assist others who are struggling with similar communication issues. It shows firsthand how successful communication affects the lives of individuals, enhancing their self-esteem, assertiveness, and sense of belonging. Viewers experience the pride and joy of the group members when, for the first time in their lives, they accomplish something they had only dared dream about in the past. This video was produced for the International Society on Augmentative and Alternative Communication (ISAAC) Conference held in Dublin.

As you can well imagine, all of these activities take money and physical assistance; the YES group has very little of either! EYM has received a few much-appreciated contributions along the way. The Minnesota Society for Augmentative and Alternative Communication has always been there to support the group.

Two trained AAC speech-language therapists are currently facilitating the YES group on a volunteer basis. They are in the process of training three support group members to take a leadership role in planning activities for the group. This is the start of an AAC mentoring program, which is the next goal of the organization.

When the group was formed, it was my dream to have graduate students from the speech disorder department at the University of Minnesota come to work with our group. This became a reality. The students not only bring their expertise, but they bring fresh blood and creative ideas. I believe they also gain some real-life experiences that can't be taught from a textbook.

> *It is difficult to think about the early days of feeling closed out and not fitting in. Now, I communicate with a myriad of people from all walks of life and feel I have a place and a purpose.*

I have been fortunate throughout my life to have learned and gained from so many interesting and challenging experiences. It is difficult to think about the early days of feeling closed out and not fitting in. Now, I communicate with a myriad of people from all walks of life and feel I have a place and a purpose. I hope my life experience has helped to open doors and to aid in greater understanding and opportunity for others with similar communication disabilities. We all have visions and dreams whether we are able-bodied or disabled. I have learned that to accept challenges and to embrace the future, you must never cease to "express yourself."

18

butt look

a different perspective

Arthur Honeyman

butt look: a different perspective

when you are in a wheelchair as i am
you have a direct eye view of butts
and if your thinking is anything like mine
you are darned grateful that most of them
are covered because you do not want to
look at bare butts not because they are
so bad to look at but because you like
to guess at their appearances by how
their clothing fits in conjunction with their
different bodies and the ways that they
move and the wrinkles or creases in their
pants or skirts or tights or other forms of
apparel or wardrobe worn by us
members of the human race to make us
look different from the animals that we
really are and that we pretend to not be
for we seem to have the idea that our
ways of adornment are superior and even
more seductive and appealing than the
rest of kinetic existence with no
ifs ands or butts

19

How I Communicate

Gail M. Grandy

FRIENDS SOME UNDERSTAND
TRY GOOD
BETTER COMMUNICATE
DIFFERENT WAYS GAIL

Gail M. Grandy lives in Portland, Oregon, with her husband, Tim; her beagle, Ruby; her cat, Kiwi; and her bird, Owl. She is a strong advocate for independent supported living and accessibility. Gail enjoys meeting new people, dancing, babies, animals, and parties.

Editors' Note: This interview was conducted between Gail Grandy and her augmentative communication specialist, Susan Livick. Because Gail is congenitally deaf and has severe cerebral palsy, Susan would ask Gail questions using ASL; lip reading; and pointing to symbols, letters, or words. Gail would respond by pointing to symbols, words, or letters on her communication board or by using her DynaVox. Her interview is transcribed here using the notational system for multiple modes of communication that has become policy in the ISAAC journal, *Augmentative and Alternative Communication*. The specific notational rules follow at the end of this chapter.

Susan: How do you communicate now and what role does AAC play?

Gail: *BIG ROLE*
COMPUTER USE PICTURES UNDERSTAND I
SAY WORDS UNDERSTAND PEOPLE

COMPUTER TIM WORK PAGES PICTURES WORDS MAKE
TAKE TIME
SLOW

BOOK COMPUTER PICTURES WORDS NOT END
PICTURES LAPTRAY SHOW PEOPLE
PICTURE WORDS SEE UNDERSTAND
BODY ARMS NOT WORK

SIGN NO
I UNDERSTAND SIGN I

LEGS FEET POINT
MAKE FACE

I USE MY VOICE
I YELL LAUGH CRY
PEOPLE ONLY UNDERSTAND SIGN "yes" (okay) *PEOPLE*

Susan: How does communication with symbols on the DynaVox differ from sign language and written letters?

Gail: *I LIKE PICTURE SYMBOLS AND COMPUTER SPELLING*
KEYBOARD SAME I

PICTURE SYMBOLS SAY THE WORDS MAKE ME THINK
MAKE ME MORE THOUGHTFUL "woman new"
I LIKE PICTURE SYMBOLS AND SPELLING ON MY TRAY THE SAME I
MY THOUGHTS FEELINGS IDEAS MAKE PERSONAL
SPELLING WORDS ADD TO PICTURE SYMBOLS MY
"new" b-i-g i w-a-n-t v-a-n *"happy excited"*
I UNDERSTAND ASL SIGN LANGUAGE I
ASL MY NATIVE LANGUAGE ASL
I CAN'T SIGN ASL SAME I
DISABILITIES STOP ME
MY DynaVox USE EASY UNDERSTAND PEOPLE MY
SYMBOLS PEOPLE UNDERSTAND BETTER EASY
I LIKE SPELLING WORDS AND WITH SYMBOLS USE I
I LIKE SPELL WORDS BETTER I
g-o o-n b-u-s h-e-l-p
i w-a-n-t s-o-n r-u-b-y

Susan: How has your communication equipment changed your daily support?

Gail: *GET DRESSED*
I CHOOSE CLOTHES COLOR PANTS SHIRTS SOCKS SHOES
FOOD BREAKFAST LUNCH DINNER DRINK
WATCH TV
GO SHOPPING
WALK DRIVE CAR

SAY NEEDS
TELL STORY
I WANT EAT WHAT WHEN I WANT
WANT DRINK WHAT WHEN I WANT
I WANT DRESSED WHAT WHEN I WANT

DYNAVOX TV POWER CABLE ON
TELL TIM TURN ON TV RADIO PLAYER
SLEEP
GO TO BATHROOM
TOILET
TIRED
SLEEP I WANT

CALL MOM SISTERS BROTHERS
MAKE TTY CALL FRIENDS MAKE

TELL DOCTOR HURT BIG
MAD SAD HAPPY BODY LANGUAGE USING MY VOICE
SAY DON'T UNDERSTAND DISRESPECT "ignore"
THINK DIFFERENT "misinterpret"

Susan: What role has your communication system played in your ability to use supported living and supported employment?

Gail: *BIG*
I SAY WANT
PEOPLE UNDERSTAND BETTER
GET WANT
PEOPLE UNDERSTAND HELP GAIL PEOPLE
FIRST TRAY POINT TO WORDS ONLY
PORTLAND COMMUNITY COLLEGE LEARN ASL SIGN LANGUAGE
ROOMMATE HELP TEACH ASL SIGN LANGUAGE

COMPUTER FIRST OLD WORDS+
COLOR NO
VOICE BAD
LEARN HARD NO

TRAY PICTURES
WORDS SPELL BETTER
PEOPLE UNDERSTAND NO
GAIL TRAY BETTER PICTURES HELP
UNDERSTAND PEOPLE GAIL

DYNAVOX WOW!

Susan: How is your communication equipment used when planning for your future with your husband?

Gail: *USE DYNAVOX LAPTRAY BODY LANGUAGE VOCAL-IZATIONS*
ALL TIM UNDERSTAND
FAMILY GO PLACES
FRIENDS VISIT
CALL FRIENDS FAMILY

> *PAIN*
> *DOCTOR HELP MEDICATION*
> *SHOPPING MAKE PLANS*
> *TRIPS*
> *DYNAVOX LAPTRAY HELP SO DOES BODY LANGUAGE*
> *AND MY VOICE*
> *TIM UNDERSTANDS ALL*
> *"Tim is my everything, my one and only"*

Susan: What are differences in your communication over the years?

Gail: *FAMILY*
BODY LANGUAGE
POINTING
GRABBING
VOCALIZING
STAFF AT FAIRVIEW (Editors' note: Oregon's state institution for people with mental retardation where Gail lived most of her childhood and young adulthood until she sued the state and advocated for herself to move out)
BODY LANGUAGE
POINTING
GRABBING
VOCALIZING

DYNAVOX SURPRISE
PEOPLE LIKE
DON'T LIKE

LAPTRAY OK
PEOPLE LIKE
UNDERSTAND PEOPLE

HUSBAND BETTER
WORK HARD
COMMUNICATE DIFFERENT WAYS GAIL

FRIENDS SOME UNDERSTAND
TRY GOOD
BETTER COMMUNICATE DIFFERENT WAYS GAIL
WILLOW TREE (Editor's note: Gail's previous residence)
COMMUNICATION BOARD SMALL WORDS SPELL
BODY LANGUAGE
POINTING

GRABBING
USING MY VOICE

UNITED CEREBRAL PALSY GROUP HOME
COMMUNICATION BOARD SMALL WORDS SPELL
BODY LANGUAGE
POINTING
GRABBING
USING MY VOICE

FIRST HOUSE
TWO ROOMMATES
LEARN SIGN ASL
SOON COMPUTER WORDS+
NEW BOARD PICTURES
REBUS BOOK

Notational System for AAC Journal

1. *Naturally spoken elements* are italicized.
2. *"Words and sentences produced with digitized or synthesized speech"* are italicized and placed in quotation marks.
3. MANUAL SIGNS are in capital letters.
4. *GRAPHIC SIGNS* and *PICTURES* are in capital letters and italicized.
5. Some manual signs or graphic symbols need more than one word in translation. When the gloss of a sign or symbol contains two or more words, these are hyphenated, for example, YOU-AND-ME or SIT-DOWN.
6. S-p-e-l-l-i-n-g is underlined and has hyphens between letters.
7. "Interpretations or translations of meaning" are indicated by quotation marks and are used for interpretation of manual sign or graphic symbol utterances. They are also used when giving the meaning of facial expressions, gestures, pointing, etc., for example, "yes" (nodding) or "no" (shaking the head).
8. { } indicates simultaneous expressive forms (e.g., speech and manual signs) or manual and graphic signs. For example, {GLAD *I am glad*} means that the manual sign GLAD is produced simultaneously with the spoken sentence I am glad.

20

Our Lives, Our Community, Our Caregivers

Sharon Jodock-King and Alan R. King

Behind every successful person with a disability, there have to be hard-working caregivers. This statement is most certainly true for my husband and me.

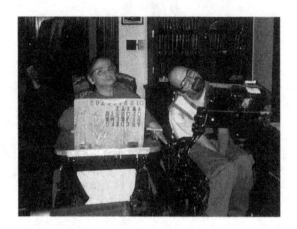

Sharon Jodock-King is a lifetime advocate for herself and other people with disabilities. Sharon has helped with many projects that have bettered the lives of people with disabilities, including serving on the committee that got Seattle's metro buses to install wheelchair lifts. She also got curb cuts put in along her street for 10 blocks. Sharon is also an artist and has held many art exhibitions and sold many of her creations. She loves to travel and hopes to make it to Europe someday.

Behind every successful person with a disability, there have to be hardworking caregivers. This statement is most certainly true for my husband and me. Alan and I were married on June 4, 1983. We were residing in a 110-person residential center in Seattle, Washington. Both of us had spent most of our lives in state institutions and hoped one day to be able to live in the community. Cerebral palsy is our disability. Alan runs his electric wheelchair, his communication device (the Liberator), and does art with his feet. I've got pretty good control of my left hand, and that is how I do my thing. We both need a caregiver for all of our personal needs.

In 1981, the residential center started training programs for placing residents out into the community. Alan and I took all the classes that were offered. In fact, we ran out of classes to take. They had built accessible apartments which I would have been eligible to move into, but then they changed the caregiver rules. I would need 24-hour on-call care, but the rules changed to self-help care. I was very disappointed with this change, and I even shed a tear or two.

I went on with my life at the residential center. Alan and I met and fell in love. We dated for a year before we became man and wife. We were allowed our own room, which we fixed up like an apartment. There were several other married couples in the building also. It seemed like we all got bit by the marrying bug around the same time. There is a 15-year difference between Alan and me, and I'm still being teased about "robbing the cradle." Anyhow, Alan and I continued our daily activities of attending a nearby community college, plus physical therapy and recreation, and we joined a group that also was planning to move out to the community.

There seems to always be something that drives a person to want to make a change in his or her life, and I was no exception. One day I came home from school and found that two of our favorite drinking cups had grown feet and walked off into the sunset, so I thought. I was not delighted about the situation, and I let my feelings be known to our social worker. Things had been disappearing out of our room, so when the cups came up missing, that really set a fire off within me. I informed Susan, the social worker, that she could immediately begin the paperwork for Alan and me to move out. Later, I found out that the cleaning lady had taken the cups into the utility room to clean them.

Moving was not an overnight event. It took us 2 years to get everything in order. We had to obtain funding from the state that would pay for our housing in the community. Alan and I organized a support group in case everything fell apart. As the time drew near for us to take the big plunge, we lived out of boxes for 6 weeks waiting for our new apartment to be emptied. The person who lived in the apartment we were moving into also was on a waiting list for an accessible apartment in the community. It was like a vicious circle. We were moving into a six-unit apartment complex which housed people with disabilities.

Finally the big day arrived, and I sat in the middle of our room with tears streaming down my face. I was having second thoughts—"what ifs." I dried my tears and headed my electric wheelchair down the hall to the waiting van. I didn't look back over my shoulder because I knew I would make it just fine. Alan and our friend Mark were already in the van. Mark had taken the day off just so he could move Alan and me to our very first home.

Our first live-in caregiver was Pete. We had hired him from the residential center, which was an okay thing to do back in those days. Today the policy is that a person can't hire anybody from the residential center until the employee has been gone for 6 months. This is so the residence doesn't lose all of its best employees. Anyway, Pete got Alan and I unpacked and settled in our apartment, and he also moved some of his belongings into his own bedroom. We communicated our needs and desires to him on our electronic communication devices. Pete was used to how we communicated, so that was a plus on our side.

Living out in the community wasn't a bed of roses. The first hurdle we had to cross was getting our first Social Security Disability Insurance (SSDI) check. Alan and I thought the check would be in the mailbox the beginning of the month following our move. NOPE! No such luck. We were 6 days into a new month and yet no SSDI check. We voiced our concerns to Pete with our communicators, and his advice to us was to wait another day to see if anything showed up. Next day came and Alan and I looked long and heavily into the poor mailbox. When we realized it was looking pretty hopeless, we instructed Pete to call the residential center and inquire if the main office knew ·anything about our check. Sure enough! Our check had gone to the residential center and was being kept for the last month we had lived there. They did give us our monthly allowance together of $70. Thank goodness we lived across from a school that had a food bank. Alan and I lived out of it for the next 2 months. Pete would go with us a couple days a week, and Alan and I would pick out what we could eat without choking. Most people with cerebral palsy don't do well with hard-to-chew vegetables and fruits. We got through the SSDI check crisis okay. Our future would hold more of these types of situations.

Pete was with us for 6 months until the romantic bug hit him square between the eyes. It was hard for all of us to have to break up the relationship, but the apartment wasn't big enough for two married couples. Pete had a van, which he took Alan and I in daily, because he also worked at the community college which Alan and I attended. Pete found us a person named Andy, and we interviewed him. He seemed to be an okay guy for the first 5 months. He would take Alan and me in his car to different places. We managed to overlook Andy's moody spells because it appeared he was communicating with us well and always did what we asked of him. I guess we should have been more perceptive during the last week he was with us, because all hell broke loose one Sunday morning. Andy got me up as usual, and I went out to the living room to wait until he got Alan up. I did notice that all of our pill bottles were sitting on the kitchen counter. I thought it was a bit weird, but thought Andy was checking if we needed to go get more pills. Alan and Andy joined me and I told Andy what I wanted for breakfast using my communication device. Old Andy's face turned white, and he said, "Can we talk? I've got something to tell you guys that you will not like to hear, but I need to get it off my chest." Andy proceeded to tell us that the night before after he had put us in bed, he had taken his car and went down to the lake to commit suicide. Something inside him told him not to do that, so he had come back to the apartment and had gotten out all of our pills to take them. He said he had sat for hours looking at our pills. Most of our pills wouldn't have done any harm, but maybe Alan's Valium would have put Andy to sleep for a few hours. I immediately started thinking what to do with this information. Thank goodness for our support group, because now it could come in handy. All Andy said was, "Am I fired?" I nodded my head, "Yes," and went over to our speaker phone and called one of our group members. She was over within an hour, and Andy was gone that afternoon. We gathered the whole group together to figure out a plan how Alan and I would get care. Each member took turns for the next 2 weeks. Our case worker was called, and we all decided it would be best if a nursing agency could come in until we could hire a new 5-day attendant. Alan and I didn't think too highly about different people coming in and out of our home from the agency, but we tolerated it until we found a full-time person.

Bill was an attendant from a nursing home. He was between jobs and was working for a nursing agency. Alan and I met him on an organized group outing to a People First self-advocacy convention in Idaho. We got to know each other and one thing led to another and before we knew it, we were interviewing Bill and hiring him. He didn't know what he was getting into when he came to work for us. Shortly after he started, I found out that I had breast cancer and had to have chemotherapy for 7 months after my surgery. I became sick as a dog after each treatment, and Bill would get up many nights to clean me up or listen to me moan. He had patience and hardly left my side. During this time, I usually used an alphabet letter board to communicate to Bill. He learned my voice sounds well enough that we didn't have to use any letter boards or communication devices. There were still rotten days that I had to turn to the old board, but it was very few times. Bill was with us a year and a half before things began to deteriorate between the three of us.

Lloyd helped Alan and I find the duplex we are living in at the present time. The apartment was a 2-year transitional place. We had to sign up for subsidized housing funds, which took 2 years. Alan and I, plus a housemate with a disability, would pay a third of our monthly income towards the rent. Subsidized housing money would pay the rest of it. Bill had helped us start the ball rolling by filling out the miles of paperwork. It took us quite a while just to find an accessible house, and it was Lloyd who took his faithful measuring tape out into several houses to measure the width of doors, hallways, and bedrooms. He always came back with the news that the measurements were too small or there were too many stairs which would have to be ramped. One day a light suddenly went on when we found an ad in the newspaper which said, "A duplex near Greenlake for rent." My heart skipped ten thousand beats. I had always wanted to live near the water, but I didn't dare to get my hopes too high. Lloyd came back to the apartment with a wide grin on his face after he did his measuring duties. The doors measured just right. The hallway was wide enough for our chairs. The bathroom was a bit on the small side, but it would be workable. Lloyd said a ramp could easily be built on the side of the porch which had a driveway going up to it. The next thing was to contact the landlord, Kathy, who we found out later was a registered nurse. Kathy's dad, Paul, built a temporary ramp so Alan and I could get into the house to see it for ourselves. It was an instant love affair with the house and me. I didn't want to go back to the apartment that night, but I finally gave in on one condition, and that was that the house would be ours in a couple of weeks. The agreement came to pass. We have lived here now for 6 years. We've had several housemates who have developed their own wings and made their own nests. Their disabilities have been real severe, but we've all made it. Jim, our present housemate, is hearing impaired and uses a wheelchair but is capable of caring for himself.

Kevin is our present full-time caregiver. He works 4 days a week and has 3-day weekends. Both Alan and I have grown by having Kevin around for the last 3 years. (He began as a weekend person.)

He is 23 years old and has his own opinions. He and I have gotten into some real heated discussions. He rattles off a mile a minute, while I yell for him to shut up so I can get my opinions in with my new communication device. There have been times when I'm sure the neighbors have heard us yelling at each other. The funny part of it is, we both have grown stronger in mind and spirit. I feel we have grown more like a family. Most of our caregivers have been younger than 25. I'm probably thinking of them more as children which I sure did want, but just wasn't able to produce.

21

Life with Cerebral Palsy

Chris Featherly

*Please don't think small when it comes to
communication for a person, whether it is a
tiny tot, an older child, or an adult. Look
into their eyes and see what is there;
you will be surprised.*

Chris Featherly is an 18-year-old student at Bremen High School in Midlothian, Illinois. He has changed schools recently hoping that the new school will meet his physical needs and take him into an independent adult life. He has lived with his grandparents for the last 12 years in Illinois. His spare time is always spent on the computer trying to get the skills he will need to enter to working world.

My name is Christopher Glen Featherly, and I'm going to try to give you a little overview of life with cerebral palsy as I know it.

I'm 18 years old and was born in Fort Worth, Texas. I'm currently attending Bremen High School in Midlothion, Illinois. I came to the Chicago area when I was a little boy of 5. My, how I've grown! I was born prematurely at 32 weeks of gestation. I developed hydrocephalus and was shunted at 3 weeks of age. The prognosis on discharge was as follows:

> Prognosis for this premature infant with severe hydrocephalus is, in the long run, poor. However, at the time of discharge the infant does seem to display some purposeful cortical activity and may do well for some time. At present, it is expected that the infant will be able to undergo chronic care at home with training and instruction.

And again, another doctor fooled.

When I came from Texas to live with my grandparents at the age of 5, I only had five generic signs for communication. My grandmom wouldn't put up with that, and so she went to the library for a sign language book. Now she learned that there really was something upstairs! The school system wanted me to use a 48-page, three-ring binder of pictures for my communication. Can you see me, using my right hand, to flip between 48 pages to talk to someone? I don't think so! My grandmom took me to Siegel Institute in downtown Chicago for a speech evaluation. They said, "This kid needs a TouchTalker, from the Prentke-Romich Company (PRC)." Well, guess what! The school speech clinician said, "No. He doesn't have language, and if he has it he won't use his own voice to talk." So guess what grandmom did? She took me to Homewood to see another speech therapist. What do you think she said? You got it! She said, "TouchTalker." So back to school, and again the answer was, "No." Grandmom then told them she was going to take me to Shriners. If they said TouchTalker, that would be the mode of communication I would have. Well, what do you think they said? Yup! It was TouchTalker. Now, we knew how school felt about it, which meant it was in our ball park. It was time to save money and purchase it so that I could get stuff out of my head and stuff into it. By now, do you sorta have an idea what kind of grandmom I have?

Grandmom saved, and when she had half of the money it was time to find the other half quickly. Through talking to people, she found out about a fund through the trucking company my grandpop was working for. She called them and left a message with the president of the association. In the meantime, the president of Frozen Food Express heard about my situation and called to say that they would pay half of it. So, between the two companies, it was paid for.

Darn! Now grandmom had her half of the money saved. What did she do but buy another piece of equipment to put me in to stretch my hamstrings. Oh well, it helped. I started using a Minspeak Application Program (MAP) with my TouchTalker. A MAP is a software program for the communication device that teaches you how to put pictures or icons together for messaging. There are different MAPs for people with different language levels. It wasn't long before I needed a new Minspeak Application Program. I upgraded the software, but again, I outgrew that MAP. I went to the Word Strategy MAP, and I am presently using it. So, I went through the MAPs, but I also went through the TouchTalker, and now I need more funding.

At this time PRC was offering $1,500 for a TouchTalker to be used toward the purchase of a Liberator. This was a good deal, as I needed the more powerful communication device called the Liberator with its many new functions and extended battery life. This came about by just making a telephone call to the insurance company and asking if they would help. We offered to give them the TouchTalker toward the purchase of the Liberator or else give it back to PRC directly and they would take the $1,500 off the price of the Liberator. As I mentioned, grandmom used her savings for the TouchTalker to buy a piece of equipment to stretch my hamstrings. Each time that she purchased equipment for me, she would ask the insurance company for the money. Before they answered her, she would call them back and say that she had found funding for it, but she wanted it to be noted in the file that she had done that. Now, do you see what happened when she asked for the Liberator? She mentioned the notes in the file. Their answer on the Liberator was, "It is ordered." If you remember, I mentioned that school said I didn't have language, and I wouldn't use my voice. Also, when I came to live in Chicago I had only two words—I could barely speak. They were "yes" and "no."

Now it is hard to keep me quiet, whether it is with my voice or my Liberator. I used the Liberator to learn the parts of speech. Oh, how I remember grandmom drilling into me what a noun is—a person, place, or thing. Then it was the verbs, and so on. I found that if I used the icon sequences over and over I became automatic with them. The speech therapist at Shriners taught me a story that was called, "This is a Story." It used a lot of core vocabulary, plus "anybody," "everybody," "nobody," and "somebody." I can't tell you how that helped me. She would time how long it took me to tell the story using the Minspeak icons; then she would let me time her while she did it. I really enjoyed it when she did it because I always beat her. It was nice to have her care enough to learn the MAP along with me. I use the icon tutor in my Liberator to teach myself the icon sequence for new words. I also use the word prediction program to give me the fringe vocabulary that I don't use everyday. If I find I'm using a fringe vocabulary word a lot, I store it as an icon sequence. I also have a lot of slang stuff that I like to use with my friends; I store that, as well. I have been on America On-Line for several years. From there, I am able to get some age-appropriate jokes. I got tired of the old elephant and chicken jokes. My friends now ask me for jokes, knowing I'm up to date with stuff. I also store food icon sequences in my Liberator. That way I can order my own food when we go out to eat. I use my Liberator with my answering machine to talk with my friends. It's too hard for me to hold the receiver on my shoulder and use that hand for icon sequencing.

All I hear from grandmom is that, between my on-line time and phone calls, the bill keeps going up. Remember back when I didn't talk at all and how hard she tried to get me to talk? I remember back then. I look at where I am now and where I'm going, and I think it's amazing what technology can do for a person.

Please don't think small when it comes to communication for a person, whether it is a tiny tot, an older child, or an adult. Look into their eyes and see what is there; you will be surprised. I'm sure glad my grandmom looked into mine and pushed me as hard as she did. We don't have enough time here for me to tell you how hard she pushed me. Did I say pushed me? I mean how she is still pushing me.

22

Down Memory Lane

Thomas J. Boumans

I think it is important for people to become acquainted with AAC early in their careers.

Thomas J. Boumans is a graduate of the University of Louisiana at Lafayette with a degree in psychology. He lives at home with his parents, Daniel and Phyllis Boumans. He enjoys swimming, camping, shopping, and traveling with his family.

Would you like to take a trip with me down memory lane? Great! But before we begin, I must warn you that, as a 32-year-old man in a wheelchair because of severe cerebral palsy who uses an augmentative communication device to communicate with strangers, my life experiences have been different and my recollections may strike you as somewhat unusual. If you are still interested, hold on to your hat and buckle up your seat belt as I take you on a whirlwind trip into some of my past experiences.

My childhood was fairly unusual, to say the least. Although my mother and father tried to make it as normal as possible, and I thank them for that, the fact is, it was not. Everything had to be adapted or modified for me in some way in order to compensate for my disabilities. I can still remember riding up and down our driveway in a little green car that they had rigged up with some straps on the pedals to hold my feet on as I rode. In those days, it was not easy to find the things that a child with a handicap needed.

School was a major problem that had to be addressed. Because of my severe disabilities, I could not go to school like all the other children, so school had to come to me. Remember that this was before all the educational reform regarding children with disabilities. I was, however, able to get a very good education. In the first grade I had only a homebound teacher who would come in two or three times a week as she thought I needed. Luckily this only lasted for 1 year. When I started second grade my parents found out about a service offered by our local phone company. They would hook up a special open phone line from my school to my house. This way I was able to hear everything going on in the classroom and talk back with my mother's help, if necessary. This is how I went to school from second grade through high school. Of course, the homebound teacher still came as usual to monitor my work and to administer the tests. Fortunately, I had the same teacher for 11 years, so she became experienced in communicating with me. She would set up my work so that I could respond to true/false tests or select the appropriate letter for multiple choice questions.

During this period of time, I was having speech therapy to improve my vocalizations, which were easily understood by my family, but were not effective with strangers. I also tried working with several communication devices in the 1970s which were not very good (at least not for me). Remember that this was before technology hit AAC, so most of the devices were mechanical. They all required motor skills, which I did not have. One device that I used briefly included a scanning display for basic needs and another was a scanning strip printer. Both were very slow with no memory capabilities and took a lot of effort on my part. So much so that by the time I responded to a question, the person had either lost interest or forgotten what he or she had asked in the first place.

After I graduated from high school, I decided that I wanted to go to college. My homebound teacher made special arrangements with the school board so that she could serve as my assistant and test marker for the ACT. We also made contact with the Director of Special Services at the University of Southwestern Louisiana (USL). With the help of all the nice people at the university, I was able to set up my classes in accessible classrooms and have my tests administered to me either by the professors themselves or in the Department of Special Services. I was thus able to complete the requirements for a bachelor of science degree in psychology.

Once I had graduated from college, someone told my mother and me about a new professor in the Department of Communicative Disorders at USL who probably had some new ideas about communication devices. Everyone knew that I was looking for a better way to communicate. It was through this contact that I met some people who have become great friends. First was Dr. Peter Payne, the head of the department, who got the ball rolling to find me a device that I could use. Then there was Millie Zimmer, a graduate student, who did the initial evaluation and made the arrangements for me to be seen at the Louisiana State University Medical Center in New Orleans, Louisiana. It was there that I met Diane Bristow, speech pathologist and company representative for the Prentke-Romich Company, the company which manufactured a switch activated voice output communication device called the LightTALKER. With the help of all these people, I was able to set myself up with a communication device and a talking computer, which I needed because of poor eyesight.

Dr. Payne suggested that once I had my LightTALKER, I should spend some time at the university getting and sharing experiences with some of the graduate assistants and clients in the Speech and Hearing Clinic. This would benefit both me and the graduate assistants who would learn from working with me. Initially, I worked one-to-one with Darlene, one of the graduate assistants. We would do some creative exchanges where we would pretend that we were in certain situations and react accordingly. For example, we would practice ordering things at a restaurant or going down to the post office to get a stamp to mail a letter. I do remember that this was in the summer and we had a room that had no air conditioning (this is in south Louisiana where summers are very hot and humid!), so my memories of this time are not the most pleasant, although I mean no insult to Darlene. Later, I remember that I did have fun with Darlene and Anne, another graduate student, and Bradley, a client who was learning to use another VOCA called the SpeechPac. We would all gather around a table and play cards. Since neither he nor I could talk or hold the cards, Anne and Darlene would hold the cards and follow the directions that we gave using our communication devices. Sometimes we played "fish" or "poker" and we all had a great time. I think experiences like these were the most helpful because we practiced with our devices and had fun at the same time.

As I mentioned earlier, the communication device that served me the best for many years was a LightTALKER which I customized to fit my needs. After trying with limited success to use the light pointer for direct selection, I decided that row column scanning was easier and more accurate for me. I could use a wobble switch mounted to a flexible bracket on the back of my wheelchair and by merely hitting it with my head could scan very quickly and accurately. My LightTALKER had software in it so I could program my own words, phrases, and sentences. All this was done in 1986 before a lot of the newer programs were in use, but in a way it all turned out for the best because it was done by me and contained exactly what I used and needed. If I had gotten my system later, I probably would have had to adapt someone else's ideas to fit my own. The software allowed me to use a form of storage which gave me access to numerous pre-programmed sentences with only three keystrokes. In addition to this, I programmed commonly used words and computer commands so that I could be more efficient when using the LightTALKER as my input device for my computer. Armed with this system and technology, I felt that I was able to address most communication needs that I might encounter.

As far as communication goes, the thing that I enjoy the most is making guest appearances at the university. Every semester I go over and meet with some of the classes in the Speech and Hearing Department in order to demonstrate to the students what augmentative communication is like and how it influences people's lives. These classes usually consist of future teachers and speech pathologists, and, I might add, they are mostly female, which was an added incentive for me. But all jokes aside, I think it is important for people to become acquainted with AAC early in their careers.

> *As far as communication goes, the thing that I enjoy the most is making guest appearances at the university.*

That way they will not be intimidated when they encounter a similar situation in the future. It gives me a great deal of pleasure to know that these students will go out into the world with a better understanding of what technology can do for the disabled person.

Let me now address another issue that seems to be very important to many people who use AAC. How does the personal care attendant fit into one's life? Because I am an only child and live at home with my parents, they are my primary caregivers. However, I do have a wonderful attendant and friend, John, a graduate student at USL, who comes in daily to help with my care. He is employed by Respite Services and is paid by them. When John is with me he is usually bathing, shaving, or feeding me, so I do not use my device to communicate with him for obvious reasons (electronic devices and water do not mix). We get along very well with simple questions which I can answer with either yes or no responses. I do, however, think that, in general, attendants should allow a person to do as much of his or her own communication as possible and come to their aid only when asked to do so. This point should be established at the beginning of the relationship.

These classes usually consist of future teachers and speech pathologists, and, I might add, they are mostly female, which was an added incentive for me.

Now that we have covered our whirlwind trip down memory lane, let's move on to the present and the future. Because technology is ever changing, and I hope to keep up with what is available, I am now making some major changes in my use of AAC. I will describe my current AAC technology, using all the jargon and terms to impress you! Recently I got a new Apple Powerbook 520 computer with a fax modem. The software that I am using includes: Ke:nx, Co-Writer, and Write Outloud. I am planning on later adding Talk:About. The whole unit is mounted on my wheelchair with a Daessy mounting bracket. I will still use my head to activate my wobble switch. I am really excited about getting everything together and being able to customize it myself. This new system gives me greater opportunities than I had before.

23

How I Got Here

Mike Ward

All in all, my life is okay despite being a total quadriplegic. My advice to anyone newly diagnosed with amyotrophic lateral sclerosis (ALS) is to plan ahead. Find out what is available before you need it, and get it early. Life as a ventilator dependent quadriplegic can be rewarding and pleasant if you are prepared!

Mike Ward is 54 and recently widowed after 30 years of marriage. He has two children. His daughter, Alethia, is 29 and works in research. His son, David, is 26 and is a professional photographer. Mike has had amyotrophic lateral sclerosis for 12 years. He still works part time for Intel, his employer of 18 years. He enjoys reading, traveling, and watching the seasons change. He has been in Rotary 17 years and greatly enjoys the meetings. His goal is to have and see grandchildren.

In early 1986, when I was 40 years of age, my voice started going bad. Through a long series of doctors, I was diagnosed with amyotrophic lateral sclerosis (ALS) on October 27th, my wife's birthday! I had no idea what ALS was, but my wife did, having had a neighbor die of it in high school. It was clearly not a good birthday for her!

I was a manager at Intel, running laboratories. At this point, I was managing 20 people and just about to start developing a new instrument. As time went on, I learned more about my condition and got a second diagnosis from the Muscular Dystrophy Association (MDA) clinic in Portland, Oregon. They told me to go out and live life, that I did not know what was going to happen. This along with my bosses' support gave me the desire to continue on.

I went to various therapists, including a speech-language expert. I learned swallowing techniques and was introduced to various AAC devices. The message was, "Prepare for things before you need them." As a physicist who develops instruments, I immediately started looking into the devices that were available.

Meanwhile, my two kids took the diagnosis very hard. My daughter, Alethia, was a junior in high school. She got help from the teachers in school. My son, David, was in eighth grade and had a harder time with it. We were very active in scouts and went camping a lot as well as sailing. Luckily I did not decline very fast, and we got in another year of camping, sailing, and canoeing. They could easily see my strength decline but could still talk with me.

At Intel, my bosses were very supportive of me. I could keep working as long as I wanted and continue with my projects. I cut down the number of people I supervised and started the development of my Ion Mill project. In addition, I started investigating augmentative communication. Luckily, during this period, by using techniques my speech-language pathologist taught me, I could continue to be understood.

I got an early model of a personal computer and borrowed a DECtalk speech synthesizer from Digital. With this I learned how to send a serial stream of data to the DECtalk and have it speak. I decided I liked the Huge Harry voice best. We also tried some software voice generators, but they did not work very well with unusual words and sounded too Swedish!

About this time I started thinking of how to make the large rack-mounted DECtalk box more portable. The Digital Equipment Corporation (DEC) representative told us that Boston Children's Hospital was developing a portable DECtalk. We immediately tracked it down, the Portable DECtalk II, and purchased one as soon as it was available. Now that I had a voice, it was time to buy a portable personal computer.

My speech-language pathologist had shown me a lot of input devices and speech systems. The one that seemed to meet my needs best was a Toshiba 1200 running Words+ software. We got the personal computer system with back lighting and a hard disc. I then received a selection of Words+ software and proceeded to experiment with it. I tried Equalizer software and various forms of keyboard emulation software in the EZ Keys family. I spent a lot of time on Morse code keyboard emulation (WSKE) but could never develop a rhythm. Around this time, my occupational therapist made me a hand splint to extend one finger for typing. This greatly improved my typing. I could now type on my office computer using a simple version of WSKE.

The next challenge was to mount the computer on my chair. After looking at the options, I chose the swing away arm by AbleNet. At first I used my finger to run the computer; later I used a pillow switch and finally a lever switch mounted on an adjustable arm.

My colleagues at work seemed to accept these changes. When they could still understand me, I gave presentations in meetings. Once I needed the voice synthesizer it got slower but they would wait for me. The transition to AAC was accompanied by my responsibilities getting smaller. When I could not be understood speaking was the point at which work seemed to give in to my disability. Wheelchairs and needing help was tolerated as long as I could speak. Once AAC came into the picture, my job responsibilities effectively ended. I became a consultant and a mentor, but my group was just me. I expected and tolerated this because, by that time, my speech rate was so slow that conversations had to wait on me.

About this point, my personal friends changed also. My Rotary club continued to support me and does so to this day. However, my friends all but stopped coming to my home. This was due to my needs being so high that it took 2 hours to get up or to go to bed. Also, I was not good company to be around. I used a feeding tube in my neck and was embarrassing to be around during meals. All in all, this did not bother me because I understood what was happening.

Meanwhile at work I continued to refine my work system. I needed access to both a personal computer and a mainframe computer at the same time. I settled on a TurboSelect made by a Canadian company in Vancouver, British Columbia. They had a unique concept of a programmable scanning box. It worked quite well and was just on the verge of success when the company went out of business.

This forced us to keep trying. The problem was memory limitations on the PC. I could not run the programs I needed with the Words+ software running. I tried memory expanders and so forth with no success. Then I found the TTAM by the Prentke-Romich

Company. This was a hardware keyboard emulator. So now I ran one PC with Words+ software and drove a second PC using the TTAM. This solved everything! I used the equipment to set up big meetings and receive inputs for a newsletter I published.

By now, all of my input to the computer was through a single switch in my lap, which I activated with my right leg. At one time I was very fast on single switch input. But the nature of ALS is progression over time. So I knew this would go! I kept looking and found the Eyegaze by LC Technologies. Intel ordered me one without much persuading. We ordered it with the second computer option and discovered the software had been written but they had not found an interface. We suggested they try the TTAM.

The system was installed 4 months later. At first it was hard to use. Some adjustments were made, and I started learning the system. It took about a month to get familiar with eye gaze selections, and then it was easy to use. Over the years, the software has been updated and customized extensively. One of the things I really like about the Eyegaze system is they will customize it for you! I have my Dectalk voice on it and people come in my office and chat with me.

Unfortunately, the world has moved from DOS to Windows requiring a mouse. LC Technologies found that the mouse option in the TTAM did not work. Their software solution using the handicapped features of Windows 95 was not too reliable because of problems with Windows. I never chose to use it. Recently, a new keyboard interface was developed at Stanford and implemented on the Eyegaze giving me a mouse. I still use keyboard functions whenever possible but now I have a mouse when needed.

This is how I have remained productive and employed. I have relied on 24-hour care for 8 years and have been using a ventilator for breathing for 6 years. My life is drastically different than what I had expected it would be when I was 40! But it is still okay; I have a lot of help from my family and all my friends and nurses.

Away from work I communicate with a letter board. I still have my laptop computer on the wheelchair and can use it for preprogrammed messages, but my leg is so weak now I cannot reliably use it. I have an eye blink system I could use but find the letter board suffices. There are now portable eyegaze systems available and I am starting to look at them.

All in all, my life is okay despite being a total quadriplegic. My advice to anyone newly diagnosed with ALS is to plan ahead. Find out what is available before you need it and get it early. Life as a ventilator dependent quadriplegic can be rewarding and pleasant if you are prepared!

24

With Communication, Anything Is Possible

Jim Prentice

*I firmly believe that language and the ability
to use it well are two of the great equalizers
for a severely disabled person.*

Jim Prentice earned his bachelor's degree in information management and graduated with high honors from Carlow College. He was employed for 10 years in the Reprographics Department at Westinghouse Energy Center in Monroe, Pennsylvania, during which time he communicated using the Liberator. He has also provided consultation for Barry Romich, President of Prentke-Romich Company, on the development of an electronic communicating device for nonverbal individuals and has lobbied on Pennsylvania House Bill 1305, "Proposal for Funding for Personal Care Attendent." He was named the "1989 Disabled Pennsylvanian of the Year" and in 1990 was recipient of the "State Victory Award" for the State of Pennsylvania. He maintains sole proprietorship of a printing businesss called Jim's Business Services and is presently pursuing his master's degree.

To first get over the nitty-gritty part of this essay, I believe you should have a mental picture of me. (Now, it's not that bad.) I am handsome and debonair, and I lie a lot.

Really, I am 44 years old and have cerebral palsy. For the past 8 years, I have been employed as a professional by the Westinghouse Electric Corporation as a statistical record keeper. On my jobsite, I use an augmentative and alternative communication (AAC) device called the Liberator to interface with my computer and make me a productive employee. My Liberator was the most instrumental asset in changing my lifestyle and assisting me when I went on interviews seeking employment.

In my earlier days, my sister was my communicator. When we went out to play, she always translated what I was saying to our friends. This made it easy on me, but I was stubborn and wanted to be able to talk to them myself. Seeing my aggravation on not being understood and the determination I had to keep trying, my parents enrolled me in the elementary school for the disabled. Here began the making of Jim Prentice. I was taught the alphabet, spelling, and reading. This was done by using a letterboard. I was then able to spell and answer the questions that were asked of me. I was even able to make conversation. At ages 6 and 7, I really had no interest in girls. But as I grew older, girls started to look better to me. That's when I decided I had to do something about my sister, so I replaced her with my communication device.

I have used some form of communication device since I was old enough to learn the alphabet. As I progressed, I graduated from an alphabet board to a lap spelling board to an AAC device called the TouchTalker. The TouchTalker had a voice similar to mine and a large storage memory, which enabled me to communicate with the public quickly because I could store many sentences and phrases used in everyday conversation.

With the Liberator, especially at my interview at Westinghouse, I did not need anyone to explain what I was saying. I was able to answer all questions posed to me by my interviewer. This made me feel quite independent because my interviewer felt comfortable in asking me questions and could see that I was self-sufficient and didn't need an interpreter. I guess I made a good impression, or he was curious to see how I would handle a job, because I was hired. I guess I'm showing that a severely, physically disabled person can still be very productive.

When I started to work, I'm sure that all the employees surrounding my work station probably thought I was someone from Mars. I rode in on my motorized wheelchair and had some sort of device attached to my chair. I rode past them, and they really didn't know whether I was able to talk. If they did talk to me, they weren't sure that I would be able to answer them. They never saw someone coming to work with a communicator. I stopped them in their tracks, before they were frozen on the spot, and said, "Good morning, my name is Jim. How are all of you doing today?" Big smiles came on their faces and they seemed to answer in unison, "We are fine, and it's nice to have you working with us." That sure broke the ice. I felt like one of the team then. I made sure I programmed a few jokes into my communicator so that it would make my conversation more friendly and comfortable for them. It worked!

I started to use a personal assistant at age 22. That was the same time that the Attendant Care Program originated in our area, and I was selected to be one of the first to have an assistant assigned to me. I felt like my life was flowing, and I wasn't just another statistic, but I was a part of the real working world. This is when I realized how important it was for me to have my assistant. I would need him or her to get me ready for work and to drive me there in my van. I would also need to have my assistant at noontime to help me with my lunch and personal needs. At the end of the day, I would need for him or her to pick me up from work and drive me home.

The duties of my assistant are not only for my work purposes, but also for any social activities, meetings, and conferences I attend, and for driving me to my classes that I attend at college one night a week, as I am working towards my master's degree in information management. Many of the functions that I attend are dinner-oriented. I need help; therefore, I cannot be without my right hand (my assistant, that is). They even travel with me anywhere in the United States or abroad.

I remember the time I went on a vacation with friends and I took my assistant. That night all my friends gathered in our room and afterwards some of them decided to stay overnight. One of my friends was acting as my personal assistant. Since we had about 14–17 people in our room, they drew straws as to who would be sleeping in the van. He was the unfortunate one, or fortunate one, depending on how you look at the situation. My friends left early the next morning, knowing that my assistant would come up in a little while to dress me. In the meantime, the maid came to clean up and found me still in bed. She called the manager and told them that my friends left me behind. The manager called the police. I was trying to tell them that it wasn't yet checkout time and that my assistant would be here in a few minutes. But they didn't try to understand me and just kept screaming. Then they called my parents and said everyone left and left me behind. Meanwhile, my assistant came up and started to yell that if they had taken the time to let me get my words out, I would have been able to tell them that everyone told us a different check-out time. He even told the police off for not having more sense than to think that he would have left me behind. My assistant then gave me my communicator, and I used a few choice words and told them to get out of my room. Sometimes people are too hasty to take time to listen and instead just judge the book by its cover and not by its pages or its contents. What I mean by that is that people see a severely, physically disabled person, and immediately they classify him as being mentally retarded.

MY ASSISTANTS

Let me explain a little more about these "angels from heaven," my assistants. We have a government project that operates through an organization called the Independent Living Program. You can qualify for this program if you are living independently and need assistance or are treated as living independently in your parents' home. I advertise, interview, hire, and train my own assistant. I am allotted so many hours per week for my assistant—this depends on what one's needs are, but the paycheck is handled by the Independent Living Program. I record the hours worked onto a timesheet, and they issue the check minus any federal deductions.

It was quite an interesting experience for me the first time I relied on an assistant, and probably a difficult experience for my assistant. It was the first time I had had someone beside my parents dress me and do all that was necessary to get me mobile. Incidentally, speaking of mobility, I use a motorized wheelchair, and, I must say, I think I can keep up with the speed the teenagers use in driving their parents' cars!

Back to my assistant. At first, the real problem came in getting me dressed. I was in bed and in no way could I have my communicator. I had to rely on my natural voice, which she was not familiar with. Naturally, after a few tries, I had to resort to spelling with my finger. Of course, she didn't realize that I was spelling, so she didn't pay attention to my hand movements. My mom had to come to the rescue and explain. I wanted to be independent and train my assistant by myself and had warned my mom and dad to stay out of it. But, bullheaded as I was, I had to resort to some help, and after that, it was like a piece of cake. I have no trouble using a personal attendant in my parents' home. My parents understand that the purpose of this program is to allow me some more independence. Knowing I like to be independent, my parents leave my assistant and myself to handle the whole thing our own way. They are giving me my freedom, and I am giving them freedom to do their own thing and not worry about me any more when they are on the go. Also, I have a few things to iron out before I can go on my own.

Once, I had an assistant who felt she was already thoroughly trained and knew everything. But, as she started to do things for me her way, she soon discovered that her way didn't coincide with my disabilities. I had to take time to train her how to do the things for me my way and to put her way out of her mind. For example, when she was putting me in the wheelchair from my bed, I had to tell her all that was necessary was to put me in a sitting position on the edge of the bed, pull me up, and just pivot me into the chair.

All of my assistants who have worked for me were not familiar with my mode of communication. This also presented another training challenge. Here, too, I prefer to train them myself. The words and phrases that I have stored behind the icons are ones that only I can manipulate. I only use my assistants as interpreters if I do not have my communicator, which is rarely. Unlike some AAC users, when I am talking to my assistant I don't mind if they finish my sentence because I feel it's faster. I do get angry, however, when they get too busy guessing and not listening to what I am trying to say. I do not use my assistant while I am having a conversation, either on the phone or in person. I don't feel that there is any time that is appropriate for an assistant to speak on my behalf. My communication device is all I need to use. I need no help, and I can control it all my way. My privacy is very important to me, and I feel that the right to privacy is something that is entitled to all, including severely, physically disabled people. Among the factors that I explain to my assistants when I am instructing them on the "do's" and "don'ts" and explaining rules and regulations that I want them to know is the concern that my privacy is my first priority.

I am a very independent person; therefore, I do not feel that I need my assistant to make telephone calls for me. In order to avoid having the other party on the line hanging up on me, especially when they answer and it takes me a minute to get started, I have preprogrammed an explanation. As soon as they say, "Hello," I press the icon where I have stored the message that says, "I am using a communicating device so please be patient and listen carefully." It's amazing how that message can bring about such good results. They inevitably answer, "Thank you. I will, and you just take your time."

I would just like to mention an incident that happened to me before I started to use any form of communicators. I went out in this huge world that I had been dreaming about and felt that I could be as independent here as any other child my age in our town. But embarrassing moments always have a way of creeping into one's life. I had only been out in this wonderful world for about 2 hours, when a young boy my age came up to me and looked and wondered what I was doing out there riding around in a wheelchair. Of course, as curiosity got the best of him, he asked, "What are you doing in that wheelchair?" Not being able to speak coherently, I tried to explain, but to no avail because all I could utter were strange sounds to him, and these he couldn't understand. This is where I wished the earth would open up and swallow me and my wheelchair. From that early age, mentally, I set a goal for myself and hoped to convince my parents that there must be some way that I could be understood and not just be another statistic watching the world revolve around me.

Not to get on a soap box, but I firmly believe that language and the ability to use it well are two of the great equalizers for a severely disabled person. Another area I'd like to address is expectations. When an individual first gets his or her communication system, he or she is filled with high hopes and great expectations about what can be done with it. The family is excited, too. Together they dream of the new worlds that the device will open up for them. Soon, however, disappointment starts to creep in as both realize that the new system isn't the magic box they had hoped it would be. Situations such as this should be anticipated and handled at an early stage of the AAC intervention process. Both the person who uses AAC and the family should be presented with a clear picture of what the selected device can and cannot do.

They should be reminded also that communication is the basis of all human relationships. Augmentative and alternative communication can provide a person with the ability to have and develop strong and rewarding relationships with others. Deny a person the ability to articulate intelligibly, and that person is sentenced to live in social, intellectual, and emotional isolation. You must use the communicator constantly and not just once in a while. Don't get me wrong, I am

> *This power of communication that we acquire through the use of the augmented communicator is giving us the freedom of speech that we thought we would never have. It's a long, grueling struggle to get it working for you, but everyone has to work together.*

not saying a communicator makes a person, but that the person makes the communicator, and the communicator helps them to be what they want to be.

Hopefully, I have pointed out to you how communication is the basis of all human relationships, and that freedom of speech is the first right guaranteed to all Americans. Using the right communicator and having the aid of a good assistant makes for a good team in helping a disabled person to compete with others in such things as education, independence, and, the most important step of all, employment. This power of communication that we acquire through the use of the augmented communicator is giving us the freedom of speech that we thought we would never have. It's a long, grueling struggle to get it working for you, but everyone has to work together, the disabled person and his or her family, assistant, speech-language pathologist, Office of Vocational Rehabilitation, and others. Soon the bright star will shine that spells, INDEPENDENCE, SUCCESS, COMMUNICATION, FRIENDS, and hopefully, EMPLOYMENT.

25

Making People Laugh and Cry

Rick Hohn

Unfortunately, as you know, most people think that a person with a disability can't do much except sit around all day. For the first time, they are able to look past my wheelchair to see the person that I really am.

Rick Hohn, of San Diego, California, is a pastor of two retirement homes and a house church. Besides speaking to other churches, schools, and organizations, he consults with DynaVox Systems, Inc., on various projects including product development. He also participates in public presentations and writes a regular column in the *DynaVox Voices* international newsletter. He has recently published his autobiography entitled *More Than a Watchmaker*. His talents include painting, and he has taught art classes.

What a difference there is now in public speaking from I was growing up! My classmates made fun of me because the teacher printed
on huge poster paper the speech that I was going to deliver so that
the audience could read what I was saying for my eighth-grade graduation ceremony in 1960. A friend teased me that these signs were
my idiot cards that I needed for cues. "Idiot cards for the class idiot,"
is what I felt they were all saying about me.

At home, I memorized my speech about the duties of the post-
master general that my teacher had to physically write for me. The
speech was impossible to prepare by myself. There was no way I could
write even my name with my hands being affected by cerebral palsy,
and hardly anybody could understand what I was saying with my severe communication disorder. It was easy to concede that I couldn't
prepare it myself, but I tried my best to memorize the speech at least.
This was so I wouldn't need idiot cards, and I practiced saying each
word clearly. But when I sat in front of a microphone at a practice
session, refusing to look at the idiot cards, I heard what my voice
sounded like for the first time. I jumped as I scared myself. My voice
that was garbled and obscure echoed around the auditorium that had
been converted from a lunchroom. It was obvious, as I didn't understand what I was saying myself, that the signs were necessary. I could
still speak without looking at the so-called idiot cards, but the audience definitely needed them. I would have given anything if people
could have understood me verbally. My parents felt the same way because they knew that plenty was inside of me
if only there was some way to dig it out. I envied my friends who were paralyzed from po-
lio or muscular dystrophy but could express
themselves freely. If they were uncomfortable in their wheelchairs, they could easily
tell the teacher or anyone exactly how to
move their bodies to make them comfortable.
I would rather have been paralyzed than be
without speech for the sake of explaining
where I hurt and how to rectify the problem,
not to mention being able to deliver a speech
myself.

> *As a child, I
> would rather
> have been para-
> lyzed than be
> without speech
> for the sake of ex-
> plaining where I
> hurt and how to
> rectify the prob-
> lem, not to men-
> tion being able to
> deliver a speech
> myself.*

The only speech device of that day was
an apparatus that was held on the voice box
for magnification purposes. Although my
speech therapist had me try the aid, I knew
that it wouldn't work. My problem wasn't enough volume but was
coordinating the muscles for my lips and tongue to work together

properly. So, in the disappointment with my graduation, I never dreamed that I would make audiences laugh and cry as a motivational speaker 40 years later.

In 1993, long after my college education, the executive director of Community Interface Services in Carlsbad, California, offered me a job teaching art to adults with developmental disabilities. The director saw some of my paintings and thought I would be good at teaching art. My speech disorder was a big hurdle and was going to be an excuse for me to turn it down. How would I give instructions about the various techniques of painting without the ability to speak? That would be silly, like expecting an audience to understand my speech at my eighth-grade graduation ceremony. Just before I was going to let the position go, however, I heard of a communication device that I received on loan through the local phone company. Although it took me about a week to preprogram everything that I wanted to say to my class on the first day, I was surprised that I could successfully instruct students through the voice output of an augmentative communication device. I switched to a different voice output communication aid (VOCA) called the DynaVox by Sentient Systems Technology, Inc. This VOCA made my teaching even easier. Because teaching art made a reality of what I thought was once impossible, I wondered if I could use my augmentative device for public speaking. I knew that my heart was full of messages that I could give in church to give people hope and encouragement. The attempt at speaking for my eighth-grade graduation long since faded, but sometimes at church I would get frustrated with myself for thinking that I could make a point or two better than my pastor!

In recent years, I have spoken to small gatherings by typing my messages and having someone read them. Because people seemed to be lifted up by what I had to say to them, I thought more about using my DynaVox to speak. Friends from my church encouraged me along these lines and invited me to teach an occasional bible study. So, in January of 1995, word got out that I was speaking with an augmentative device. Teen Challenge, a substance abuse rehabilitation center in Riverside, California, asked me to come and speak to about 75 men, and I was delighted to do so. After singing for 20 minutes at the chapel service, I was lifted in my power wheelchair onto a small stage by three men. One of them carefully adjusted a mike in front of my DynaVox speaker. When these men returned to their seats, I felt tense and had stage fright. For a half of a second, I hoped that I wouldn't sound obscure like I did that one day at my practice session when I spoke in the microphone. Before I had a chance to think about this for too long, though, I forced myself to press a button on my device that said, "Good morning!" My greeting sounded clear, unlike years ago. Everybody responded cordially—enough for me to relax and deliver my message paragraph by paragraph on my device. I paused at appropriate times and tried to look everyone in the eyes at least three times.

After sharing about my life, and about everybody having a disability of some kind, I could see that men, of all ages, were being touched by what I was saying. They had tears in their eyes and were constantly wiping them. Most of these men had been in prison before, but apparently I must have gotten through somehow. I finished the message, about 5 minutes early, so their professor asked them to take the time to meet me. All 75 men swarmed around me and congratulated me, one by one, with a hand shake, a hug, or a kiss. Hand shakes were rare, as their eyes were still filled with tears which they were still busy wiping. One burly man approached me. I recognized him because when I was speaking, I had admired the big cross that he was wearing. It was beautiful! Now, with streams of tears running down his cheeks, he took off the cross around his neck and carefully draped it around mine. All he could say, in a shimmering voice, was, "The Lord told me to give this cross to you." As I hugged him in appreciation for what he had given me, I sensed that this ability to move a group of people, in addition to my painting and writing, symbolized a new stage of my life.

So far, this is turning out to be true, as I slowly get more and more invitations to speak. My pastor asked me to share at my church, and I loved that especially. Most of the people there cared about me, but never thought of me other than as a man in a wheel chair. So when I speak now, their minds are boggled and jarred. I love it! Tripping them out is fun. Unfortunately, as you know, most people think that a person with a disability can't do much except sit around all day. For the first time, they are able to look past my wheel chair to see the person that I really am. They are excited to hear more of what I have to say. My speaking ability has branched out to include schools, organizations, and anybody that wants me to share with them. I enjoy talking to people because I have been longing to do so for more than 30 years.

I enjoy talking to people because I have been longing to do so for more than 30 years.

Sometimes, when I go to my speaking engagement, I take some paintings and, perhaps, sell one or two of them. I have also showed my paintings in art shows. One of the best ways to promote my art work was to find a business that planned to have an open house. If a store or an agency was about to open, I would ask if I could exhibit my paintings and do a demonstration of how I paint with my head. This became a win-win situation for everybody as local newspaper reporters came to do write-ups about my art and the open house, and, as a result, more customers attended.

The art classes that I enjoyed teaching were being cut back because of the agency's downsizing. I was looking for something else to do. I believed that I would fit in naturally working in the AAC field because whenever I got a spare moment, I went to my nonverbal students to try to improve their communication systems. I applied at Sentient Systems Technology, and they offered me a consultant position that I absolutely love! Even in working for them, I get to show people my art, sometimes.

Before my employment opportunities started, I wrote my autobiography that I have self-published. The title of the book is *More Than a Watchmaker* because the doctor who diagnosed me with cerebral palsy told my parents that I would do everything besides making a watch. Now that it is published, my plan is to take my book to the speaking engagements that I have and sell them with my paintings. Everything is starting to snowball, and I am beginning to see the realization of my goal, the goal of getting off of government assistance that has limited me.

26

I Almost Died, but Somehow I Lived

Alan R. King

My spelling skills had gone down quite a bit since I was so heavily sedated, but I still made my wants known.. . . . I would make an attempt to move some part of my body or make a facial movement.

Alan R. King loves to get to know people using his electronic communication device, the Liberator. He has been searching for years for a real job that pays real money. Alan is an artist and does his artwork with his feet. He just completed an art class at the Pratt Art Institute—a top art school in the United States. Alan serves on several boards as well as on his church council. He is very proud of the stereo that he just purchased.

The title to this story has fit me well once or twice during my 41 years. My mom said I was born dead, and it took the doctors 20 minutes to revive me. It was from this near-death experience that I became disabled with cerebral palsy due to the lack of oxygen to my brain. I am the middle child in a family of seven with three brothers and three sisters. I lived with my family until I was 9, and then it became too hard physically for my family to handle me. My parents placed me in a state school for disabled children younger than 21. It was at this school that I learned to communicate with my left foot. A very creative teacher put small picture symbols together on six ordinary rolling pins. She then mounted the rolling pins on a frame of small steel tubing and made it so the bottom two tubes fit into the ends of my wheelchair footrests. I would use my left foot to turn the rolling pins, and as years passed I became very quick at speaking to people. I was so used to the picture symbols that my spelling skills were not developed, which was not a good thing years later.

I spent my years at the school doing many projects, such as playing the guitar and sewing with my feet. Mom has a picture of an embroidery piece that I entered in a fair, which won a red ribbon. My feet have gotten me far in my life. I had a job going from the different departments of the school delivering mail, and my rolling pins came in very handy talking to people. When I turned 21 it was my turn to depart from the school in which I had made so many friends among the staff and residents.

Seattle would be my next destination with many opportunities to seek and the place where I received my first electronic communication device. Many more devices followed as I tried to keep up with technology. I am currently using a Liberator, which is one of the best talkers on the market today.

MY HOSPITAL NIGHTMARES

Living with a tracheotomy and a feeding tube is no picnic! It has been 2 years this last April 19th since my life completely changed. It all started when I was not feeling well one day, and I was throwing up dried blood. My attendant, Carrie, became concerned and called 911. She thought it was my old ulcer acting up. Soon we could hear the police siren roaring down the street coming to the house. They checked me out and suggested that I go to the hospital. An ambulance was called to come and get me, and off we went to the closest hospital, which isn't far from my home. I couldn't take my Liberator with me because it's attached to my electric wheelchair. The ambulance couldn't take my wheelchair, so there I lay on the stretcher with only Carrie to interpret my head shakes and eye movements to yes and no questions.

In the emergency room they tried to pump my stomach out, but they gave that up because of the involuntary body movements of my muscles. Putting an IV tube into my arms was a trip as well. I tried holding still, but the more I tried, the more I moved. The doctors and nurses who were working on me were trying to be patient and understand how my body worked. The doctors were going to send me home, but I was breathing hard so they took a chest x-ray and there was a spot on my lungs. I had aspiration pneumonia with a fever. The doctor wanted to admit me into the hospital to see what was causing the fever. Sharon, my wife, who also has cerebral palsy, had taken the city bus to the hospital. She gave hints on her Liberator to the doctors and nurses about how to make things easier for them to work on me.

> I couldn't take my Liberator with me because it's attached to my electric wheelchair. The ambulance couldn't take my wheelchair, so there I lay on the stretcher with only Carrie to interpret my head shakes and eye movements to yes and no questions.

I was admitted to the sixth floor, which deals with respiratory problems. I was just going to be on the sixth floor for a few days, but those few days stretched into six horrible weeks. Sharon was visiting me daily, but Monday night she asked if she could go Tuesday to one of her many meetings which she attends quite often. I agreed to it, because we thought that I surely would be home at the end of the week.

The doctors had taken me off all my medication in the emergency room and to this day we still don't know the reason for that move. I went to bed that Monday night, and the next morning I woke up in a hot sweat. Now remember, I hadn't had any of my medications in 4 days. The medicine was to help me relax my muscles and to help my respiratory system. I seriously can say that I was going through bad withdrawals. I was up all Tuesday in my wheelchair sweating and stressing out to the max. It was that night when all hell broke loose. They had put me to bed around 10:00 P.M., and the nurse came in my room to check on me a little bit later. I was breathing funny, so a couple of nurses put me in my wheelchair to see if that would help. I was still breathing hard, and I was feverish. One of the nurses called a doctor to come and check what was going on with me. By the time the night was over, I was wearing a neck brace, and I slept in my wheelchair for the next 3 nights. I really should say that I catnapped—because of my breathing problems, my muscles were always moving. Tuesday morning when Sharon came in to see me, I was talking to Kathy, the speech pathologist. Kathy told Sharon that I had had one hell of a night, which was the reason I looked so drugged up. I still wasn't breathing normally, and talking with my Liberator was becoming more difficult. Kathy brought in a small letter board, which I also had a hard time using with my foot. She showed the nurses how to position the small board so I could point to the letters and numbers with my left foot.

Up until then, I hadn't had anybody who knew me stay with me at night, which quickly changed when everyone saw what kind of shape I was in. It was like the night shift didn't take the time to get to know me as a thinking person. They just did what they had to do medically, and then they would leave. I felt I was just another body to them. When our main attendant, Kevin, and Sharon heard of my nightmare, they put together a list of friends and people who knew how to communicate with me. Kevin started calling people that very afternoon and soon I had a different person, who knew me, each night. Sharon helped me with communication on her Liberator during the day when she was with me. Most of the time she would ask yes and no questions that I could shake my head to answer. It was really helpful to have my attendants come to the hospital to assist with understanding what I wanted to tell the doctors and nurses. It was like we all had ESP with one another. The guessing game came in handy when I had spelled a word wrong or didn't know how to spell a word.

Doctors came to check me twice a day. On Friday I still was breathing weird, and my lady doctor came in about 1:00 P.M. Sharon and I were in my room alone talking about what might happen to me. I was able to use my Liberator a little that day. The doctor didn't bring good news. They had been taking X-rays of the spot on my lung which hadn't changed for the better, even with me on antibiotics. The doctor took a listen to my lungs and then said, "We need to talk, Alan." She proceeded to explain that the antibiotics weren't working like she had hoped they would, and she highly recommended I be transferred to the intensive care unit (ICU) down on the fifth floor. The first words which came out of my Liberator were, "Oh shit. Why me?" I was scared plus nervous. Sharon had a good cry from just hearing the words *intensive care unit*. She asked for Kathy, the speech pathologist, to be called to come for support. Kevin was paged to come as quickly as he could. Sharon went and had the doctor call my parents to tell them the latest. Mom had been calling all week to see how I was doing. It's hard having your family 300 miles away from you when you are so ill. My family called the hospital several times to make the arrangements to come and see me during the weekend. Mom, however, wasn't in good health, so she stayed home with one of my sisters and a niece.

My belongings and I were taken down to the ICU. They pushed me in my electric wheelchair because I couldn't lie down without my breathing becoming worse. Once in the ICU, they started evaluating me. Sharon followed me into the room, but was asked if she would leave for a few minutes until they got my blood pressure taken and took care of other things. In a little while they asked Sharon to come back into my room to discuss with the doctor which route to proceed with regarding my treatment. They asked if Sharon would give her written consent to put me on a ventilator. Sharon said it was my decision and that she would agree to whatever I wanted. I agreed to go on the ventilator, and then they told Sharon she had to leave until they got me ready. I was heavily sedated so that it would be easier to work on me.

> *The first words which came out of my Liberator were, "Oh shit. Why me?" I was scared plus nervous. Sharon had a good cry from just hearing the words intensive care unit.*

The next thing I knew I was in bed with a tube down my throat and a block in my mouth so that I would not bite down on the air tube. My throat was in pain from the tube, plus they had put a catheter in my bladder, which was really painful. I'm sure if I had had good hands, I would have had that thing ripped out of me in no time flat. I was pretty out of it for quite a few days. I remember a few of my family members when they came in and out during the weekend. They kept saying goodbye to me, and it sounded like they thought I was dying. I guess I was in pretty bad shape, because the doctors and nurses kept working on the spot in my lung. A respiratory therapist came in every 2 hours to use an instrument on my chest. The instrument wasn't painful, but it wasn't the most joyous sensation that I had ever felt. I used my eyes to answer yes and no questions when I was aware what was going on, and the letter board was used when I was fully awake, or if the person knew me well and had the patience to guess what I was spelling out. My spelling skills had gone down quite a bit because I was so heavily sedated, but I still made my wants known. During the first few days my eyes were completely shut, and I responded by rolling my eyeballs up and down and from side to side. Quite often I would not respond to the doctors and nurses, but when Sharon started yelling, "Alan," I would make an attempt to move some part of my body or make a facial movement, so she knew I heard her. There's something about a wife's voice that makes a husband listen, sometimes! Julie, a friend of many years, got a note pad of lined paper so visitors could write in it daily what was going on with me. It's interesting to read the note pad now. The nurses and doctors did explain everything they were doing to me. Sharon and the rest of my attendants made sure that was communicated to every shift that was working with me. There was nothing worse than not knowing what they were going to do with me. I also had many IVs stuck into me in the ICU only to have them come out in a short time. Finally the doctors got smart and put one in the side of my neck, and that one stayed in until they took it out on the rehab floor when I went home.

> *There's something about a wife's voice that makes a husband listen, sometimes!*

Sharon helped with communicating to the professionals. The second day in the ICU a social worker came and saw me, and being as I wasn't able to use my Liberator, Sharon took over talking to her. The social worker was respectful, and I felt she heard what Sharon was relating to her. The question of where I would go—to a nursing home or my home—when I was discharged came up right away, and there were lots of pros and cons to the question. My family was concerned that with my care increasing, it would make double work for our attendants. My first priority was to stay out of the nursing home and go home where I had my familiar surroundings and the people who knew my basic care needs. All the staff in the ICU were willing to train Sharon and my attendants in all of my additional care. This was the top discussion throughout the week.

It was around the third day in the ICU that they decided to try getting me up in my wheelchair with all my hookups of tubes and wires. The staff had not put me in my wheelchair, so Kevin was asked if he would come to assist. The first time getting me in my wheelchair was a big deal, being as I was all hooked up. I didn't have my Liberator on my wheelchair because it was easier to transfer me in and out of bed without it in the way. I couldn't use it anyway. I remained in my chair a good 5 minutes before I went back to bed. Sharon was there when all of this took place, which I wanted. It was also on the third day that they started weaning me off the ventilator. I was started out by getting less and less oxygen from the machine, and gradually I was breathing on my own. The morning came when they were going to take me off the ventilator altogether. The night before I had told Sharon and Kevin what time I wanted them to be there in the morning to support me on my big day. I had an idea that I would try and be off the ventilator by the time they came, so I had the nurse call Kathy to come and give me support while they took out the tube from my throat. When Sharon and Kevin came I wasn't in such a great spirit as I thought I would be. My throat didn't relax and let air come through when the tube was removed, so they had to put it back in.

Kathy observed that I had become nervous when they had tried it the first time and perhaps with Kevin and Sharon there they could help me to relax. Kevin suggested trying it again with soft music and him talking me through it. This was tried and again I could not control my throat. It was attempted a couple more times before a meeting of all of us was scheduled to talk about doing a tracheotomy on me, so I could get off the ventilator. The doctor said there was a chance that I would need it permanently, which made me start thinking that I would no longer have my voice to make sounds. I thought surely I could work to get off the trach.

On the morning they took me to surgery to do the tracheotomy, Sharon came to be with me until they came and got me and all my equipment. It didn't take that long and when I returned to my room, all of the equipment was gone and I had a trach in my throat which hurt badly. I was kept sedated for a couple days, but I could respond with my facial gestures for "yes" and "no." I was in the ICU a couple more days before I was transferred back up to the sixth floor until the rehabilitation unit had a bed for me. While I was on the sixth floor for the second time, I received a letter plus several word boards that stood and covered the foot of my bed. I could point with my feet to words and letters to communicate to people while I was in bed. Marvin, an engineer at the hospital, made the board for me. We've known Marvin for years, so it didn't take him long to figure out what I needed. It was also on the sixth that I received my biggest blow. I had always loved eating and ate big amounts of food whenever I felt like it, especially ice cream, root beer, and chocolate.

A huge discussion was held when my trach was put in whether to fix my throat so I could continue eating with the trach in, or take a chance that perhaps someday I could be able to take the trach out all together. I chose the latter and went with a stomach feeding tube. This decision set me into deep depression, and I lay in bed and cried while I thought about what I would be losing. Eating had been a big part of my life, and now that too was being taken from me. The doctor repeatedly informed me that I would experience very little pain with the feeding tube. The doctor was wrong with that information because I had a horrible stabbing pain that continued for months. I kept returning to see if he could figure out why I still had pain. We finally came to the conclusion that it was being caused by my cerebral palsy.

I received a new electric wheelchair while I was on the sixth floor, too. I was in that new wheelchair for the biggest part of the day, but there wasn't very much practicing space. I could work the foot switches pretty well, because they had been modeled after my old electric wheelchair. My Liberator was mounted on my new chair, and I could carry on a conversation, but I would require more training when I got on the rehab floor to come up to my previous communication capabilities.

My dad, my youngest sister, and my niece came to visit me while I was still on the sixth floor. In fact, they were visiting on the day that I was transferred to the rehab floor. I felt like I was going home when I moved up there because I had stayed on the rehab floor once or twice before when I was evaluated for my new Liberator. It was like going home after being on the floors of the hospital where people had to be trained on everything about my care. It was a big relief off Sharon's and my attendant's shoulders to know that I would be listened to, that the staff would take the time to let me communicate on my Liberator and really figure out what I wanted to tell them. The main goal on that floor was to discharge me either to my home, my top priority, or to a nursing home for people my age. My primary doctor had many team meetings over the next month with Sharon, Kevin, Kathy, two to three of my primary nurses, a social worker, plus other doctors to see what would be the first route to take. In order to remain on the rehab floor, one has to have a daily program. I chose speech and physical and occupational therapy. I was no longer in my room when visitors came like I had been on the other floors. Every time one of my pastors came for a visit, I was out doing something, so one day Pastor Nancy left me a note saying, "Alan, if you need anything, call." Sharon usually hunted me down and sat and waited until my therapy session was over, and then we would wait in my room for Kevin or Carrie to come so we could either go outside or down to the cafeteria. The subject of going to the cafeteria was a subject in itself. When I first got my feeding tube Sharon asked if I would rather not have her eat in front of me. I thought over her question and then shook my head. No, I wanted the company more than having people not eat in front of me, even though it was torture at first. It was hard on my family and friends not to offer me my favorite foods, which I have already mentioned.

I had worn my doctor down enough about me going home that at the end of the second week he said the respiratory therapists could begin training Kevin and Carrie how to suction my trach and take care of it. The first few tries weren't that easy, but as time grew nearer for me to leave, the task became easier. My feeding tube also required new training, which the nurses did.

The big discharge day arrived and I was happy but a bit afraid, too, about how everything would go once I got home. The rehab floor had become my place of security for the last month, but I knew I had to take the big step from my safe nest. I honestly felt that the staff had done a marvelous job training both Kevin and Carrie, and that it was up to all of us to carry the training on. My bags were packed and placed on a cart for transport. The social worker had made arrangements for a visiting nurse to be at my house when I got there. A nurse called for a wheelchair van to come and get me. The same nurse went down with me to the van, and as I got on the van we both started crying. I had wondered many times as I laid upstairs in my bed if I would see my home again.

I began crying like a baby when I drove up to my house in my electric wheelchair. They had made big old "Welcome Home Alan" signs, and the signs were up all over the house. In my head popped the song, "It Feels Good to Be Back Home Again."

The hospital experience has not stopped me from getting out and continuing to use my Liberator to talk to people. I've got plenty to communicate to those who take the time and have the patience to listen to me.

27

Just an Independent Guy Who Leads a Busy Life

Michael B. Williams

Hiring good personal care assistants is just as important to my living independently as are getting the right communication systems and keeping my wheelchair in good working order.

Michael B. Williams is a disability consultant and activist. He lives in Northern California with his wife of more than 20 years and his two children.

An interviewer recently asked me whether I thought I would ever be truly independent. Although I understood the words of my inquisitor perfectly well, I found his question most curious. I had just spent 45 minutes detailing my busy daily schedule. "Define your terms, sir," I said. "I do what I want and need to do in life."

I am an independent guy who leads a very busy life. I am married and have two children. I edit a quarterly newsletter on augmentative and alternative communication (AAC) that is aimed at consumers and their families. I also consult in the field of AAC and speak at conferences.

I am assisted in my activities of daily living by my personal care assistants (PCAs). Without the help of these folks, life would be slow, dull, and extremely frustrating. I have been hiring PCAs for more than 20 years. In that time, many PCAs have gone through my life: Some have been excellent; the majority have performed satisfactorily; and a few have turned out to be real creeps who had to be terminated within a few days. I consider this to be par for the course.

One of the most important things I've had to learn about hiring PCAs is that they're not friends, so I don't expect them to hang out all day with me having fun. That's not what they are here for. PCAs are here to help me with my basic daily routine so I can go out and do the other things I need or want to do by myself or with friends.

Whenever I'm hiring a personal care assistant, I immediately look for two things: 1) a willingness to learn new things right off the bat and 2) basic literacy skills. Everything else (except sobriety and honesty) is up for grabs.

As part of the hiring process, I do two screenings of my PCAs. One occurs when a prospective PCA makes his or her initial contact by telephone. At this time my candidate gets a basic overview of the job, including the fact that the prospective employer uses several modes of alternative communication. I also casually mention that I drool a bit. If a prospective employee hasn't fainted away by this point, he or she has qualified for a formal interview.

These interviews usually take place at a neutral site away from my home, such as a coffee shop or other social gathering place. This accomplishes two things: It allows me to size up my candidate without worrying if he or she is scoping out my abode for a future burglary, and it gives the candidate a chance to see me as a regular guy who can function in a social setting. This is also an opportunity to see my prospective employee's reaction to me in relationship to food. People with cerebral palsy sometimes have a proclivity to slop food on themselves. This upsets some people. The desire to satisfy my hunger is stronger than my desire to please the aesthetic tastes of others by keeping clean, and I don't want my employees walking around in a perpetual state of angst every time I partake of a morsel of food; therefore, I don't hire people who show displeasure with me and food.

When the appointed meeting time arrives, I am in place, sipping my coffee. I come armed with most of my modes of communication. I have my voice output communication device, my letterboard, and a piece of paper with a detailed job description of the tasks I want done. My would-be PCA usually has no problem spotting me. I stand out in a crowd. I am often the only older, significantly disabled person who's in a wheelchair and who's wearing a towel around his neck while drinking coffee.

I sit and drink my coffee until I sense the presence of a nervous person lurking about the fringes of my personal perimeter. I look around to see who it is and then hit them with the eye contact and a broad smile. It's too late to back out now; my candidate realizes I have spotted her, and she approaches with caution. "Are you . . . ?" she asks. "Yes, I am," I reply using my voice output communication device and flashing another big smile.

We're off and running. I bid my interviewee to take a seat and hand her the description of the jobs I want done. As my candidate is reading this sheet, I watch her face for any signs of discomfort. As the reading progresses, I slowly pull out my letterboard and lay it on the table, ready for the next critical step of the interview.

Some people believe it is a good idea to explain how their communication systems work. I don't share this view. On the contrary, I believe in total immersion. I don't mean to be cruel or unfeeling toward my potential personal care assistants. I just really think the best way to explain my communication techniques to people is to communicate with them. When my prospective employee is finished reading the description of duties, I switch communication modes and go to my letterboard.

This is the most critical part of the interview. If she makes it through this, chances are she has a good shot at getting the job if she really wants it. By pointing at the letterboard, I get her to focus on it. My first question is always, "Do you have any questions?" I ask this because I really want to know if she has any questions about the duties, and because the sentence is fairly simple to decode. It has four short words and one medium size word. They are words everybody knows. If my budding personal care assistant has difficulty with this, then we are both in trouble.

I point to each letter fairly slowly, pausing slightly at the end of each word. I look at my interviewee at the end of each word to see if she is understanding me. If I see a blank stare coming back at me, I know that understanding isn't taking place, and I will respell the word. It usually takes my prospective employee two or three tries to catch on to what I am doing; once she does, however, we start interacting quite well, and we both can concentrate on the business of the interview. If I see that the person just isn't getting the hang of my letterboard, I switch back to my voice output communication device and finish up the interview that way.

I have never hired a person who has flunked the letterboard portion of the interview. This is because I communicate with my personal care assistants by letterboard a good portion of the time. It's just easier that way, especially when I am in the bathroom. If I'm engaged in idle chatter with one of my personal care assistants while he is doing something else (which seldom happens) I use my voice output communication device so he can keep working as we talk.

Over the years, I have discovered that the best time to find out if a prospective personal care assistant will be able to communicate effectively with me is during the job interview. If I conduct a rigorous interview and insist my candidate interact with me, he should pick up on the basics of how I communicate. Then, when my new PCA comes to work on the first day, he can start concentrating on the duties of the job, rather than struggling with learning how I communicate.

Of course, there are little bits of etiquette that one just can't teach during the interview, such as what I do if my personal care assistant hovers over me while I am making a telephone call, or what I do if people in the community keep addressing questions to the PCA instead of to me. I think these are matters of individual communication style that can be taught quickly to the PCA during the first few weeks of employment.

My personal care assistant may hover over me once while I'm on the telephone, but that's the only time he'll do it if he wants to keep working for me. As far as letting my PCAs speak for me, they are not allowed to do that unless they are authorized to do so by me. They also quickly learn to redirect any question asked of them about me back to me. This is how I quickly establish with strangers who's really in charge of the communication process, a most important skill for an augmented communicator to have if he or she wants to live and work in the real world.

Hiring new personal care assistants is always a pain in the neck, and I hate to do it. But I also know that hiring good PCAs is just as important to my living independently as are getting the right communication systems and keeping my wheelchair in good working order. They are why I can say, "I am just an independent guy who leads a very busy life."

28

Spaghetti Talk

Gordon W. Cardona

*The AAC evaluation should be done . . . with
the AAC user involved in the process from
step one. . . . It is the augmented speaker who
will be using the device every day, both
personally and professionally, not the
AAC specialist.*

Gordon W. Cardona resides in Alhambra, California, with his family. He would like to thank his parents, Samuel and Waltraud, and siblings, Allison, Cameron, Stephanie, and Matthew, for all of their support, encouragement, and love. He currently works part time while looking for full-time employment, serving on three boards for nonprofit organizations, and publishing newsletters. He enjoys snow and water skiing, river rafting, parasailing, sailing, playing power soccer, traveling, and cruising.

EARLY BEGINNINGS

I had various communication boards when I was in school since I was unable to talk. I learned how to type on an old electric typewriter using a pencil to press the keys. It had a keyguard so I didn't accidentally press two keys at once. I practiced by writing stories I made up from picture books I borrowed from the library. I had come to realize that it was easier to use one finger to type than having to pick up the pencil and place it comfortably in my left hand. Soon, I completed all my school work on my typewriter, including math! This became my mode for communication by writing short notes, letters, and cards.

I received many speech therapy sessions when I was in elementary school and from California State University, Los Angeles (CSULA). My speech therapists tried to help me speak better and made lots of communication boards to suit my communication needs. I really liked most of the speech therapists I had. Most of them really tried to help me communicate my needs.

As I got older, they evaluated me for equipment, and I played with many communication devices. I thought it was fun and an honor! I was just about the only student in the whole school to whom they offered the communication device to try out and demonstrate. I wonder why. Actually there was only one other student with a speech impairment in the higher grade classes. I'm sure they probably thought I could use and play with the device to its potential.

EVALUATION EVALUATED

I think the AAC evaluation should be done by the AAC specialists or speech pathologists with the AAC user involved in the process from step one. All decisions should be made by the user with the specialist only providing the various devices, suggestions, and mounting options (if necessary). It is the augmented speaker who will be using the device every day, both personally and professionally, not the AAC specialist.

As they evaluated me for a device, I evaluated the various communication devices they threw at me. I didn't mind. I usually thought it was fun to play with and try out new devices. However, when they asked me to decide which device worked best, I had difficulty. Most of the devices were big and bulky and had strange sounding voices. I wanted something small with total control over it. I'm pretty sure most people who are not familiar with communication devices would not be able to understand the early voice output devices.

When I was 12 or 13 years old, my speech therapist and teacher thought I needed an effective way to communicate, so I tried out the Canon Communicator, a small machine that prints out letters on ticker tape. It was very small and portable. I really liked it even though I didn't use it much. I guess I am more of a listener than a communicator.

It wasn't until my freshman year at Bassett High School that I really began to use my Canon Communicator. I completed almost all my classwork using my device since someone else was using the sole typewriter with the keyguard to do her work. Do you want to know about the Canon Communicator? It's a small machine, about the size of a Sony Walkman. I would type my message and it would come out on a tiny strip of paper. These usually long strips of paper were all over the place! After my teacher graded my work, she stapled the paper strips from the assignment into my workbook. Soon my workbook was full of little strips of paper sticking out. You sure couldn't miss my book! I had to do this during my first 2 years of high school for most of my classes since I couldn't use the typewriter most of the time at school.

These long strips of paper came back 2 years later at my senior dinner. One evening just before my high school graduation, all the seniors and their families and the special education staff gathered at a nice restaurant to celebrate the occasion. In the front of the banquet room, there was a long row of tables for the staff with chairs behind them facing the audience. The graduates and their families were seated at tables in the middle and back of the room facing the staff.

The special education department at school usually has its annual senior dinner about a month before graduation for the seniors and their families. I did not know what to expect, since the staff do not tell the seniors what will happen. That year, there were about six or seven students graduating from the department. We were excited and curious about what would happen that night.

After dinner, each staff member gave a short speech about our career at Bassett High and recalled a few memorable moments, and some were very funny. Then each instructor gave one of his or her students a personalized gift which was meant to be taken as a joke. Usually, the instructor who taught the student the longest or knew the student best was the person who presented the gift.

I received a gift from one of my instructors who was on maternity leave during my senior year. I was happy she was able to attend the dinner and present the gift to me. The gift turned out to be a gift box of "spaghetti." The "spaghetti" was actually some old messages that I had typed on my Canon Communicator. I thought the spaghetti box and the way it was presented were very humorous. Some of my old messages were really some of my classwork. I was surprised that she had saved all or most of my old messages all those years.

During my final 2 years of high school, I took all general education classes. Sometimes I went back to the orthopedic handicap (O.H.) department and completed my classwork on the typewriter. Most of the time I took my classwork home, including my regular homework assignments, and completed them on my own typewriter. I think math was the hardest subject to do on a typewriter since the work had to be lined up, and all work had to be shown on paper. Also, I wasn't very good at math to begin with, let alone having to do it on a regular electric typewriter. Boy, it was very difficult!

Sometimes when I began doing my math homework during my study period in the O.H. department, I asked for an explanation of a math concept I didn't understand. The instructor for my study period would look at the problem carefully. When she couldn't figure out the difficult concept, she would ask another instructor to help me figure it out! Most of the time, I was able to do all the assigned problems on my own. Luckily, I had good math instructors who would explain the concepts in class.

When I was selling candy bars for one of my school clubs for a fundraiser, my math instructor became one of my best customers. He always knew when I was selling since I usually had a box of candy bars in my chair next to me. He would often buy three or four bars a week without me having to ask him. He had a sweet tooth for chocolate just like me. "Aren't you selling candy anymore?" he sometimes asked me when he did not see a box of candy next to me.

Throughout my high school years, I continued to experiment with various AAC devices. However, none of them worked for me. They were either too simple, had a strange-sounding voice, or were too big.

I needed a new Canon Communicator once I began attending college at CSULA. My first device was well used. During my first couple of years at college, I used it to do all my exams. Luckily, the exams were almost all multiple choice and true/false! After completing the exam, a test proctor would transfer my responses from the long strip of paper onto a Scantron answer form. Then, the proctor would put the exam, Scantron, and the strip of paper in an envelope and seal it. I would take the exam packet to the department office for my instructor to grade.

During my college years, I would type short notes on my typewriter at home. These notes consisted of what I needed to communicate to my instructors, advisor, or tutors. I found typing short notes on my typewriter at home would be much easier and faster than typing it on my Canon Communicator. Of course, I used my device when I needed something immediately or when I had a question in class.

I was often asked to present and demonstrate my device at CSULA and to explain my device and communication methods to students who were striving to be special education instructors. To prepare for my presentation, I usually typed up what I wanted to say about my communication methods and college life on my typewriter at home. At the presentation, I would ask the instructor to relay my prepared speech to the class. Then we would have a question-and-answer session where I would respond to their questions using my device and demonstrate how I used it. They were very interested, or at least they put on a good act! I soon found this procedure worked best for the class and me.

A couple years before I graduated from college, I decided it was time to explore voice output again. I was evaluated for another device that talked for me. I tried several devices. I was kinda talked into the big LightTALKER. Sure, I thought it was cool at first—I had a voice! I took a week-long training session to learn how to use it that summer. Some of the students at the training session performed very well and learned how to put sentences together and make the device talk for them. I envied them! I then spent almost all of my 3-week quarter break from classes trying to learn how to use the device. I saved some commonly used phrases and sentences. I took it to school with the big device right in front of me and my fond Canon Communicator as backup. I programmed some commonly used phrases and sentences and used those only. I simply didn't know how to use it. I felt Minspeak icons were very strange. With Minspeak, I needed to think of the words I wanted to say, the grammatical label for each word, and the icons or pictures that needed to be pressed to access each word—all simultaneously! I just felt nobody thinks about nouns, verbs, adjectives, and pronouns when they are talking, and why should I? Also, it was always in my way, especially when I needed to work on the computer at school. I rarely used it. After college, I stopped using it altogether. If I had to start over, I would have never

> *With Minspeak, I needed to think of the words I wanted to say, the grammatical label for each word, and the icons or pictures that needed to be pressed to access each word—all simultaneously!*

chosen the LightTALKER. I would have chosen something simpler and smaller. The Canon Communicator was small, easy to use, and friendly to me.

A few years after graduation when I was into my job search, my rehab counselor and job developers felt I needed a reliable voice to get through the interview process. I went to the Center for Adaptive Rehabilitation Technology (CART) at Rancho Los Amigos Medical Center to again evaluate the different communication devices they had to offer. Molly Doyle, the speech-language pathologist, asked me about my needs and what I wanted. I told her what happened with the LightTALKER—that it was hard to use, big, and bulgy. I wanted a device that was simple to use, small, and portable. She introduced me to the LightWRITER It was small and easy to use. But I still had my doubts since I didn't want to make the same mistake twice. So, I asked my rehab counselor if I could use it on a trial basis. It didn't take me long, however, to decide this was the right device for me! That summer, I really learned how to use the device—in Cabo San Lucas, a beautiful town on the southern top of the Baja peninsula in Mexico! I am able to save messages, talk on the phone, and express my thoughts. It's great!

That summer, I really learned how to use the device—in Cabo San Lucas, a beautiful town on the southern top of the Baja peninsula in Mexico! I am able to save messages, talk on the phone, and express my thoughts. It's great!

Another way I communicate is by e-mail which is very effective for me, even more effective than using the phone. I check my e-mail almost every night, of course! Using this great medium of communication, I feel everyone is on the same level, whereas in person, the verbal person talks more quickly than the non-verbal AAC user. Of course, sometimes the AAC user can still make his or her point more effectively using an AAC device than a verbal person.

I attended an awareness workshop where the attendees were all high school students. The workshop was about how people should treat people with disabilities no differently from their able-bodied friends: with respect. One of the guest speakers was an augmented speaker who uses a Liberator. I was really blown away by how well he presented his stored presentation. The entire audience was listening intently to his well-written address. After his presentation, he invited questions from the students.

MORE THAN ONE WAY!

Currently, I use my LightWRITER to communicate at work, in meetings, and on the phone. At home, I usually communicate by facial expressions, letter signing, and typing notes on my computer. Usually when people get to know me and my communication methods, they have no trouble understanding me. Of course, some people learn faster than others. Also, e-mail plays a heavy role in my communication methods. There are many people to whom I only e-mail instead of picking up the phone and calling them. I feel e-mail is the most effective way for me to communicate.

Using my LightWRITER, I can only save up to 250 characters under one letter for leaving messages on answering machines or presenting speeches. This is the only drawback with my present device. However, I learned how to get around it and not to be so long-winded when leaving messages!

Regarding daily support, I am able to make phone calls using my LightWRITER and speakerphone. I also have the option of using the Speech-to-Speech relay service from the state of California. I usually rely on my LightWRITER to give directions to the drivers who pick me up from work—that is, those drivers who listen to me.

One evening a driver picked me up after a meeting. I told her, using my device, which exit to get off the freeway to go to my house. Before driving off, she checked the atlas. When we got close to the freeway exit, I pointed to get over to the right lane. She looked at me in the rearview mirror and said, "Hey, stop that! You're scaring me!" I was just trying to tell her where to get off and pointing in that direction. I think she was a little nervous by this time. After she got off at the wrong exit, I pointed to go straight because she was about to turn right. She obeyed hesitantly to my next two commands. After we got on the correct block, I pointed to go straight again. She said, "Okay, okay! Let me look it up. Don't scare me like that!" She then checked the terminal for my house number. I figured the poor driver simply didn't know how to respond to my directions and gestures.

I still use the drivers for transportation to and from work. Even though I don't have a full-time job yet, I think my current device played a major role in landing my quarter-time job at CART, where I was evaluated for my device. Hopefully, my device will play a major role when I find a full-time job.

29

More than an Exception to the Rule

Bob Williams

The silence of speechlessness is never golden.

Bob Williams lives in Silver Spring, Maryland, with his wife, Helen, and daughter, Emily. He is the Deputy Assistant Secretary for Disability, Aging, and Long-Term Care Policy at the U.S. Department of Health and Human Services in Washington, D.C. When Bob is not developing policies and programs that support the health and long-term care needs of children, working-age adults, and older people with disabilities, he enjoys gardening, reading, and vacationing with his family and service dog, Decoy.

When I look over my own life, I am thankful for several things. I am thankful most of all for my parents, for their vision and sense of possibility. I am thankful for my brothers and sisters and the friends I have had throughout my life. And most of all, I am thankful for my beloved, Helen, and the new life and family we are making for ourselves.

Equally critical, I am thankful for one other gift I received early on in life which most people can take for granted: the gift of literacy—of reading and writing, of making sense out of the world and having the reciprocal ability of letting the world make sense out of you and come to respect you for all that you have to offer and contribute. This to me is the true gift and power of literacy in each of our lives.

THAT CRUCIAL FIRST DEVICE

The first piece of so-called assistive technology (AT) that I used was an IBM electric typewriter. I was 7 at the time, and it is significant for one important reason. I learned years later that my teacher, at the time, did not believe I would ever learn to read. In fact, I am convinced that had I not had the typewriter, my teacher's perception would have likely become very much of a self-fulfilling prophesy. I would have become like an estimated 50% of my contemporaries with cerebral palsy who, despite their typical intelligence, now face significant difficulties with reading, writing, and comprehending much of the printed word.

You may ask, "What implications does my first IBM electric typewriter have for access to assistive technology in general, and augmentative communication specifically?" First and foremost, it implies why increasing access to assistive technology is so critical in schools, at home, and indeed, in all other situations. Learning—like living—is not a passive act. It is a very active one, one that requires a great deal of communicative give and take. Once again, had I not had a typewriter, I am not certain that I could have ever convinced my teacher or others that I could learn to read. Ann McDonald, an Australian woman who spent most of her first 20 years on the back ward of an institution, wrote that unless others support individuals with communication disabilities to jump outside of our current means of expression, there is no way we can do so alone. Having a typewriter is one of the things that enabled me to make the jump—not just in convincing others that I could read, but even more critical, in enabling me to see that reading and writing had a real consequence in my life.

As a teenager, I wrote the following poem:

When No One Answers

A child sees me.
Naturally curious,
he looks to his mother,
Why?
Shush, is her answer.
Time passes.
We meet again,
the child and I.
I smile, recalling his curiosity.
This time, he isn't curious, though.
He picks up a stone,
throwing it in my direction and yells,
"Get, you mental."
Where did he get that?
Certainly not from his mother!
Her only answer was, shush.

I wrote that poem in the early 1970s hoping to close the communication gap that loomed so large in many of our lives. Growing up in the 1960s and 1970s, I felt powerless to close that gap or to change much of that dynamic. Indeed, even today, on the subway to work, hearing others comment on my perceived lack of abilities, I feel a similar powerlessness. The powerlessness of silence. The silence which the stereotypes around our disabilities continues to fuel, ruling much more of our lives than we typically acknowledge. We must, though, acknowledge it, and then we need to change it.

The silence of speechlessness is never golden. We all need to communicate and connect with each other—not just in one way, but in as many ways possible. It is a basic human need, a basic human right. And much more than this, it is a basic human power, a human power which I am convinced is within each of our inherent abilities to realize. Such power is taken for granted by most. Perhaps this helps to explain why it also is so easily ignored when someone has an expressive disability. Real and perceived disabilities, of course, do much to mask and marginalize these abilities. But it seems increasingly doubtful that they can completely diminish or extinguish them.

In my own case, for example, many professionals viewed traditional speech therapy as the only approach to enhancing my ability to communicate and connect with others. In as much as speech therapy helped me to use my own voice to break the silence of my young life, I am thankful for it. But in many ways, it also reinforced that silence. It is telling that those who helped me to express myself most were not professionals, but rather my family, my friends, and not the least of all, myself.

BREAKING DOWN AGE-OLD WALLS

Much has changed since I grew up. I doubt, for example, that anyone with my level of speech disability would get 10 years of speech therapy today without someone at least questioning if that person also should have access to an augmentative means of expression. But far too much has also remained the same. For example, what is still not certain is whether the same person will gain access, not just to the device, but to the training and support which he or she will need to communicate effectively. We may have torn down some of the communication barriers that exist; however, much of the brick wall that many people with disabilities must break through remains very much intact.

> Having the power to speak one's heart and mind changes the disability equation dramatically. In fact, it is the only thing I know that can take a sledgehammer to the age-old walls of myths and stereotypes and begin to shatter the silence that looms so large in many people's lives.

Access to assistive technology and other effective means of expression is vital. Having the power to speak one's heart and mind changes the disability equation dramatically. In fact, it is the only thing I know that can take a sledgehammer to the age-old walls of myths and stereotypes and begin to shatter the silence that looms so large in many people's lives. Too many are robbed of this power on a daily basis. They are often denied access to needed communication devices and literacy learning, are deemed incompetent to direct their own lives, and are placed in segregated settings.

Cost is, of course, always given as a major reason why some officials refuse to fund communication devices and other technology. In fact, a top of the line communication device like the one I use can cost around $10,000. If training costs are considered, which many fail to do, costs jump to between $15,000 and $20,000. So, it is an investment of some magnitude. But that purchase is of no greater magnitude than the cost of some wheelchairs, of some surgical procedures, or of teaching a child to speak and write English for 12 years. Moreover, those who argue costs rarely calculate the costs of not providing someone with a communication device and the training and support to use it.

If I could not express myself clearly and accurately, I could not tell my physician and others how I feel or describe the health problems I may be having. Similarly, I could not let others know what I know or what I am capable of learning. Nor could I go to work or vote. Furthermore, if I could not express myself, I would become like the tree in the forest—the one for which it does not matter if it makes a sound when it comes crashing down, because there is no one around to hear it. Unfortunately, there are still a great many silent fallen trees all around us if we stop and look.

> If I could not express myself, I would become like the tree in the forest—the one for which it does not matter if it makes a sound when it comes crashing down, because there is no one around to hear it.

Why are so many people consigned to lead lives of needless dependence and silence? Not because we lack the funds, nor because we lack the federal policy mandates needed to gain access to those funds. Rather, many people lead lives of silence because many others still find it difficult to believe that people with speech disabilities like my own have anything to say or contributions to make.

It is this perception and the stereotypes and prejudices that fuel it that we need to challenge. There must be a radical shift in attitudes and expectations. Fortunately, for some of us, that shift occurred early in life. My family and I both expected me to communicate, and we did whatever it took to make that happen. The same radical shift in expectations and life experiences can and must occur in others' lives, as well.

We have much to learn about assistive technology. About its power! About its potential! And, perhaps most of all, about its dreams deferred: about how much work you and I still have left to do to close the gap between its promise and everyday reality.

The device I use is aptly called a Liberator. However, it was not until I gave the keynote at the National People First Conference in Nashville in 1991 that I realized how truly liberating such assistive technology can be—not just for individuals with disabilities, but in a political sense, for our nation as a whole. I had a room full of 900 people, all chanting in unison, with me and my device:

WE HAVE POWER!
WE HAVE POWER IN OUR HEARTS!
WE HAVE POWER IN OUR VOICES!

It was only then that I came to really understand the deep transformational properties of this thing we call assistive technology!

DREAMS DEFERRED

It was in Nashville a year later, ironically following an assistive technology systems change conference, that I learned an equally critical yet bittersweet lesson about assistive technology—its potential and its dreams deferred. I met a woman, a contemporary of mine named Kathy, who has cerebral palsy and who, at the time, was living in Clover Bottom, an institution in Tennessee.

As soon as Helen and I met her, Kathy pointed to the symbols for, "I want to go," on her communication board. Not wanting to jump to conclusions, we asked staff what she meant by this, and they replied that Kathy wanted out—wanted out of Clover Bottom—forever.

When we first met, I talked to Kathy using my manual communication board, and she took a keen interest in it. Later, as we were leaving, I spoke to her using my Liberator. It was then we learned of her interest in obtaining a similar device. When I told her that the law said she should get what she needs, Kathy cried inconsolably and with good reason.

For Kathy is very much like many others we all know: the greatest crippler she faces is not her disabilities, but others' severe ignorance and profound underestimation of her abilities. Having access to supports, like personal assistance and assistive technology, is critical. In fact, for individuals like Kathy and myself, it's often the only thing that can begin to tear down the walls of myths and stereotypes regarding people with disabilities.

The good news for Kathy is that she moved out of Clover Bottom and into a group home, which, while not perfect, is a beginning. The last I heard, though, Kathy still has not received the communication device nor any of the ongoing support and training she needs to learn how to use it. Like millions of other Americans with significant disabilities, Kathy has a strange attraction to proverbial monkey wrenches, and, what I call, plain inertia. The inertia is not on her own part, but is systems inertia—the lack of urgency and sustained efforts on the rest of our parts.

ACCESS TO AMERICA

You know, we all talk a good game about the power and the potential of assistive technology. And, it is all very true. But I am increasingly seeing, both as an individual and a federal official, that where the real rubber meets the information highway is in transforming that power and potential into everyday realities in peoples lives!

Creating true access to assistive technology means much more than creating access to devices—to hardware and software. Much more significantly, it means building in training; building in ongoing support; and building in opportunities for self-instruction and trouble shooting, both for the individual relying on the device and for their partners or assistants. This is especially true for the kind of technologies on which I rely most, but it is also true for a great many other assistive devices and technology solutions which are being used in school and work situations in particular.

Increasingly, I am relying on this Liberator, not just for communication, but as my principal management tool. With it, I am able to access my computer, e-mail, and the Internet, and, the reason I am able to do this is due to the ongoing support I am able to draw on. One of the best management decisions I made early on was to have a trouble-shooter on technology. On average, he now spends over a third of his time troubleshooting, developing macros, making sure everything is backed up—not just with respect to the Liberator, but, with regard to the LAN and Internet as well. He, in turn, has an entire network, inside and outside of government, backing him up as well. He is there to anticipate problems and solve glitches as soon as they occur because, frankly, I cannot afford slow downs or to be non-productive—not for 5 minutes, a half hour, nor, certainly, an entire day.

> *The challenge that you and I face, therefore, is not to come up with a few more exceptions, but to change the rules of the game entirely.*

What is even more important is that America can no longer afford it either. America can no longer afford to have a few exceptions to the rules, like myself, hanging around. Right now there is really just a relatively small number of us who are exceptions to some extremely important rules—exceptions in that we have had access not simply to assistive technology, but to the training, and, most importantly, to the ongoing support we need to make it work to not just improve our own lives, but to make a critical difference in the lives of our families, communities, and our nation.

The challenge that you and I face, therefore, is not to come up with a few more exceptions, but to change the rules of the game entirely. As President Clinton says, America cannot afford to waste any of its citizens.

What does this mean in practice? It means figuring out the best ways to get ongoing technology training, assistance, and support to individuals. It means educating individuals and their families of their rights under IDEA and the most recent rehabilitation amendments—and making these laws work for people.

It also means a great deal more. It means doing a great deal differently from what we typically have done in the past—reaching out and reaching beyond the traditional ways of thinking about and responding to the challenges and opportunities presented by disability in the coming 21st century. Yet, tens of thousands are still robbed of their free speech and other fundamental rights on a daily basis. As a result, they are denied access to needed communication devices and are not given the opportunity to direct their own lives.

And so we come full circle back to the teacher who gave me that first AAC device, and to his low expectations of my potential. Let me suggest some ways in which we need to foster a shift in expectations and attitudes:

1. We need to articulate and advocate for a presumption which affirms the right and ability of every individual to express him or herself. To be effective, such a presumption needs to be incorporated initially in everyday educational practice and later in law.
2. We need to begin to better articulate the links between communication and community. Community is not simply a place: It is a complete way of life, a complete way of communicating with each other.
3. We must recognize that individuals with expressive disabilities are likely no different than anyone else. That is, we learn to express ourselves based on our needs, abilities, and circumstances.
4. There are no right or wrong ways to express oneself. For well over a century, sign language was held in disrepute. And, as I said, in my own case, professionals of a generation ago were cool to the idea of my using a communication board. In fact, I do not recall anyone ever remotely suggesting that I should use one until well into my teens.

    Things are little different in many places today. This is not to suggest that definite progress is not being made. But it is to suggest that we need to reframe much of the debate. Which leads me to the fifth and, to me, the most important task which we must carry out.
5. AAC advocacy must be reframed as an issue of free expression. By this I am referring to not so much the right but the power of free

expression. Free speech has a very checkered history in our country. Whenever Americans are shown a copy of the Bill of Rights and its First Amendment and asked if others should have these rights, inevitably, large numbers of them say, "No." Why? Is it because most Americans do not value their own individual freedoms? No. I think it is because most have the luxury of taking these freedoms, these sources of personal power and autonomy, completely for granted. Indeed, that is what the American experience ought to be about for all citizens. Unfortunately, people with expressive disabilities, like other marginalized individuals in our nation, cannot afford the luxury of taking these freedoms and powers for granted.

Justice Louis Brandeis once wrote that the solution to bad speech was not less speech, but more speech. He was, of course, writing in a different time and within a much different context. But his message has great urgency for many of us. For too long, the voices of those of us who are perceived to have "bad speech" have been stymied and silenced, not merely by our disabilities, but even more so, by others reactions to them. So, the solution does indeed lie in more speech. In a chorus of voices, some clear, others still struggling. All raised in hope. Insisting to be heard. And, in affirmation.

30

Father Warrior of a CP Warrior

Arthur Honeyman

Father Warrior of a CP Warrior

Just as procreators
since the inception
of all existence
have endeavored
to favorably influence
the fates of their off spring
so too my lion hearted blood
father and soul hero
successfully raised me to be
more than merely a survivor
desperately and ignorantly
clawing my way through life
or stepping over the bones
of the less fortunate
or savagely demeaning others
or pursuing bland security
by inculcating in my spirit
the need to march on in pride
even though he knew that
cerebral palsy would often
render me socially unacceptable
and cause me to drool and spit
and stutter and that barriers
would hinder if not eliminate
my chances of independent life
and it is because of this need
that there was more than once
when i spent days crawling up
steps in search of a place
to live on my own after his death
as well as during his life
and it was dad who taught me
that i must often compromise
and acquiesce to others
if i expect to live a productive
and long and meaningful life
even though i might strongly believe
that my way is a better alternative
and even though acquiescing might
make me seem rather indecisive
in the eyes of those asking me

for an opinion of a course of action
and that my strength of character
as well as my immediate survival
might well depend on my ability
to temper ardent pursuit of purpose
with flexibility of deed
for that is the straightest
course to the stars
he taught me to reach for

31

AAC: Past Lessons and Future Issues

Hank A. Bersani, Jr., and
Melanie Fried-Oken

This book has been a journey to produce, and we hope readers will see it as a journey to read. After such a venture, the question arises, How should we proceed with our understanding of the human process of communication and the implications of disability? The authors are telling us that we need to reframe the issue. We must think about old questions in new ways to achieve new answers. We must think in ways that emphasize their abilities rather than their disabilities. We must value self-determination and cultural relevance, and our clinical practices must be informed by an understanding of the critical role played by public policy in the lives of people with disabilities. The greatest disabilities they face are often not their communication impairments but rather social attitudes, professional stereotypes, and public policies designed to limit the financial impact of entitlement programs. These 27 authors offer alternative (and augmentative) points of view and new insights for making decisions about interactions—in short, a new way to frame the issues of disability and expression in society.

PERSONAL EXPERIENCES
MIRROR THE FIELD'S EXPERIENCES

These personal essays and poems are filled with the wisdom, humor, and insights of individuals as they progressed in their quests for sophisticated expressive communication. The authors discuss different stages in their lives and the effects of communication disabilities and opportunities on their relationships. These same essays chronicle the history of AAC. More often than not, the personal developments the authors report mirror the development of AAC as a field. Personal stories raise many of the same questions that engineers, device developers, educators, parents, and clinicians have raised: How can we improve the power of communication? How can we improve the speed of communication? What is the role of the communication partner in social interactions? It reminds us of the biology adage: Ontogeny recapitulates phylogeny—that the development of the individual retraces the stages of evolution. The student new to AAC will be struck by the similarities between personal histories and the class lecture on the history of AAC. The overriding difference between the history lecture and these essays is the human essence: the insights, the struggles, the pressures, the power, the pathos, and the freedom described in these pages. If you lift your eyes from the pages for a minute you can see two histories unfolding: the personal adventures of the writers and the global adventures of a new clinical field being born.

THE SHIFTING PARADIGM

A decade ago, questions were answered by clinicians and researchers, with volunteer subjects for empirical studies who often did not have disabilities. Today's questions must be asked of and with the people who use AAC—the consumers. This change represents, to resort to an overused phrase, *a paradigm shift*. Kuhn (1962) originally coined the phrase *paradigm shift* to describe radical, sudden changes in the structure of scientific thinking. More recently, Bradley (1994) described a paradigm shift in services to people with disabilities—a radical shift (not a slow evolution) from large, segregated, institution-based, medical model services to small, inclusive community services. This new paradigm is also described as grounded in a commitment to the community and families, with an emphasis on human relationships, person-centered services, choice, and control. These themes are each echoed in the personal perspectives of augmented speakers. Seeing the field of AAC from the point of view of people who use it is indeed revolutionary.

Professional-Centric Point of View

Personal stories offer us a clear distinction between two ways of thinking about AAC—a professional-centric point of view and a consumer-centric point of view. In the professional-centric point of view, AAC is the sum of such dichotomous categories as: developmental versus acquired disabilities; communication assessment versus communication intervention; digital versus synthesized speech; novel production versus prestored content; scanning versus direct access; and dedicated devices versus integrated products. Professionals tend to see the need to increase certain variables of communication (e.g., rate and intelligibility) and to reduce others (e.g., technology abandonment). These variables are discussed as problems of AAC, and the challenge facing professionals is to find ways to solve these problems—to improve speed, increase the information contained in messages, reduce technology abandonment, and evaluate the individual to be able to recommend the best possible combination of hardware, software, and techniques for the individual's constellation of disabilities. All too often, however, in addressing these problems, professionals neglect to consult with those most affected: the people actually using AAC.

Consumer-Centric Point of View

The slogan "nothing about me without me" aptly reflects the paradigm shift in the disabilities field. People with disabilities are wearing buttons and t-shirts and putting bumper stickers on the backs of their wheelchairs with this slogan. The message is clear: People are telling us that if they are to be the subject of an activity, they need to be a part of that activity. They explain that when staff meet to discuss a participant in a program (e.g., a student in school, an adult in a service program), that the individual needs to be at the table and participating in the discussion. Similarly, these advocates assert that even·if they themselves are not being discussed as individuals, that if people with disabilities are being discussed, planned for, and so forth, that they (disability activists) should be at the table as well. Too many professionals seem comfortable discussing people with disabilities in their absence in a way that would not seem reasonable with other groups. Imagine a meeting about the needs of female students with no women in the room, or a discussion about the concerns of African American families with only Caucasians participating in the discussion. Imagine a discussion of the needs and interests of people with communication impairments with only people who are proficient, natural speakers at the table. Balandin and Raghavendra (1999) called for AAC researchers to "consider new paradigms of participatory and emancipatory research," and Bersani (1999) pointed out that consumer-driven research is the next logical step in AAC research. Many people who use AAC are now calling for greater participation in the field (Williams, 1995, 1996), and they are saying to us, "Nothing about me without me!" We hope that this text is a significant step in that direction.

Navigating Your Way Through the Chapters

This text is not broken into the traditional sections and chapters that run parallel to the old way of thinking about AAC. Rather, we have read each of these essays with an eye toward theme development, much as a qualitative researcher or an anthropologist would read field notes. In the matrix, we have identified a set of 18 topics, only a few of which resonate with traditional AAC topics. In general, the topics indicated in the matrix point to the future for AAC. Some of the older topics persist; for example, the history of the field is described with the category "what is AAC?" Other topics have changed a bit. We added "the role of technology" to the old topic of "alternative access." However, the majority of the topics were not decided *a priori* and are new to the field. Just as Oliver Sacks turns to Temple Grandin to speculate about what autism would look like to an anthropologist from Mars (1995), we turn, as anthropologists, to our authors to describe how AAC looks form the point of view of the augmented speaker. Consequently, the matrix includes such topics as "multicultural issues and AAC," "personal care attendants," "employment and AAC," and perhaps most importantly, "self-determination and AAC." These are the topics our authors, the experts, told us were needed to understand their lives.

SELF-DETERMINATION AND SUPPORT

The authors continually stress the importance of making their own decisions, doing things their way, being the ones who decide what happens to them. Their words reflect what Wehmeyer (1998) called *self-determination*. He defined self-determination as "acting as the primary causal agent in one's life and making choices and decisions regarding one's quality of life free from undue external influence or interference." Wehmeyer has indicated that one must function in five domains of self-determination. Self-determination includes choice making, decision making, problem solving, goal setting, and self-evaluation.

As we have shown, good augmentative communication relies on the involvement of the consumer in key decision making. Today we would not recommend an augmentative communication device that was contrary to the wishes of the individual who would be using it.

Finally, self-determination does not mean doing everything all by oneself, and our authors do not say that they do not want support. On the contrary, they tell us that successful AAC, as with self-determination, uses different types and intensities of support. The supports used in augmentative communication range from both high- and low-technology solutions, to training, to equipment (including augmentative communication and environmental control equipment to allow the individual to act upon their choices and wishes), and, in some instances, to people, usually referred to as personal attendants. The provision of personal attendant services (PAS) allows individuals that control over their lives referred to by Wehmeyer by providing them with the opportunity to direct others to do for them what they are unable to do for themselves. Finally, self-determination supports can take the form of money—one is in a better position to make choices, problem solve, and plan for the future if one has control over financial resources.

APPLYING THE CONCEPT OF SUPPORT TO AAC

In other areas surrounding disability, the concept of support has become much more commonplace than in AAC. Centers of Independent Living stress the need for supports, and developmental disability services offer supported employment and supported living options. Many systems offer family supports. Support can have many meanings. It must be individually defined and flexibly applied. In their personal stories, these authors comment on the support they have or want to increase their effectiveness. Based on their essays, we have concluded there are five ways to support AAC: 1) AAC is supported by access to devices and equipment, 2) AAC is supported by training, 3) AAC is supported by direct support staff, 4) AAC is supported by funding, and 5) AAC is supported by peers.

AAC Is Supported by Access to Devices and Equipment

Access to equipment is the most basic type of support. The equipment may be a simple letter board or a complex computer. The type of device may change over time, and more than one device may be needed at any given time. However, although devices are necessary, they are not the only support needed for sufficient AAC.

AAC Is Supported by Training

As Rick Creech has warned (personal communication, October 1, 1999), and as Bob Williams (Chapter 29) comments in his essay, assistive technology without training is not assistive. Training is an essential part of any augmentative communication support.

AAC Is Supported by Direct Support Staff

This kind of support may include the use of an interpreter for unaided approaches. This could range from a sign language interpreter to someone who interprets the extremely dysarthric speech of an individual for others. Some individuals are able to access messages that have been stored in a voice output communication aid (VOCA) but are unable to store those messages themselves. Having an individual type those messages into memory for them and possibly even to organize them for them to facilitate retrieval is a type of support for AAC.

AAC Is Supported by Funding

The purchase of devices, especially high-tech devices, can be expensive. Many times the support necessary for AAC to be successful is financial support to purchase and maintain the needed equipment, to pay for training, and to pay for upgrades to hardware and software.

AAC Is Supported by Peers

Last, but far from least important, the lesson from the essays is that support comes from individual mentors or a peer group. There is no doubt that AAC is more successful when people have a peer group with whom to communicate and from whom to learn. Peg L. Johnson (Chapters 4 and 17) reflects on the success of her group, but several authors lament the fact that they grew up without any such peer support.

We hope that this book provides for many the kind of inspiration that peers and role models provide. The majority of the authors in this book grew up with no role models. They have changed all that for the next generation. They are engineers, poets, researchers, and authors who use AAC to live lives never before imagined for people with such significant impairments. Now, the 5-year-old child who is today exploring a VOCA and her parents who are unsure of what she can be can look at Michael B. Williams and see an active parent and a newsletter publisher; Bob Williams and see a top-ranked federal employee; Gus Estrella and see a multilingual policy analyst; Toby Churchill and see an inventor and entrepreneur; Mike Ward and see a materials physicist; or Janice Staehely and see a disability activist and author.

Today, augmented speakers are not just "patients" or "clients"; they are students, employees, colleagues, housemates, and spouses who receive a number of supports. Some support may be technological; other support is within social services: supported employment, supported living, and educational support. For many, AAC is just one support among many and must be integrated into active lives.

SECOND-GENERATION ISSUES IN AAC

The field of AAC is changing very rapidly. If we assume that the field "formalized" in 1985 around the formation of the International Society for Augmentative and Alternative Communication (ISAAC) and its refereed journal, *Augmentative and Alternative Communication,* then we have more than a decade of experience as a formal field.

In 1985, we focused on some very narrow clinical questions: What is the effect of presentation style on sign language transparency? How learnable are Blissymbols? How should AAC be used in the acute care hospital? and What are the demographics of the "nonspeaking population"? These are important topics, to be sure. Today, however, we need to take the next step and refine the initial questions that we asked about AAC systems design, service delivery, and implementation. We are moving on to new questions that can only be asked with input for augmented speakers: What are the social impacts of various communication styles? What is the impact of a clinician's recommendation on an individual's decision making?

How does AAC fit into the broader disabilities rights movement? and What are the social and political implications of "finding one's own voice"?

Individuals using AAC tell us that they are committed to being a part of their families and their communities and that AAC is a tool to facilitate that participation. They tell us of the importance of inter-personal relationships and being able to participate fully in such relationships. They tell us that decisions need to be made one individual at a time—in person-centered approaches. Finally, they tell us that the ultimate goal of communication is personal choice and control.

Now that AAC is established, and a good generation old, we are ready to consider these second-generation issues, issues that in the early days seemed less important and less obvious. The future is about technology; rights, choice, and voice; a new knowledge base; changing our focus; personnel preparation; public policy; and empowerment.

The Future Is About Technology

Texts from the mid-1990s make no mention of popular, user-friendly, and effective devices, the current software, and the current social and political issues. In the last 5 years of the 20th century, the availability and quality of voice output has improved dramatically. People who made a decision a decade ago to abandon or refuse a VOCA may well want to reconsider their decision. Technological gains are not without a cost, however. Although technology can offer more support to more people than ever before, it is also true that technological development creates problems as well. Often, one of the major problems is deciding whether to stay with an older and possibly inferior system that is working versus going through the trauma of upgrading to new technology, a change that is costly in terms of both time and money, given re-tooling, down time, and de-bugging, in addition to the more overt cost of the purchase price. Several of these essays describe individual struggles with decisions regarding upgrading to new equipment versus sticking it out with tried and true approaches. These essays also raise the issues of telecommunication and access to a full world of communication partners from one's home or work computer station. Computers now are smaller, faster, lighter, higher quality, more affordable (still expensive, but more affordable), more mainstream, and more consumer friendly. Commercial technology is more common: Everyone has assistive technology—everyone uses cell phones, palm pilots, and so forth. Although using technology to communicate will be less stigmatizing in the future, we need to work to ensure that technology promotes rather than precludes personal interaction.

The Future Is About Rights, Choice, and Voice

Self-advocacy, the disability rights movement, and a growing awareness of the large number of people with disabilities, including disability in communication, has radically changed our thinking. Our
language has changed. We no longer speak of clients or patients who
are disabled or handicapped. Instead, we focus on the person, with
and without disabilities, supports, or augmentation. We refer to
augmented and natural speakers who all use some form of communication assistance. We discuss the right to be included in school,
work, and leisure activities, from both a social perspective as well as
a policy or legislative perspective. Augmented speakers recount inci-
dences in which choice was not possible and give examples of how
new voices and access to a voice made a difference for them.

The Future Is About a New Knowledge Base

In the past, research has been professionally driven, not participatory driven. It has been designed to answer questions and solve problems posed by professionals. Our need in the future is to promote a
participatory knowledge base that reflects the concerns of augmented speakers on a par with the concerns of clinicians.

The Future Is About Changing Our Focus

These authors are telling us that we need to focus more on their abilities rather than their disabilities. They are demanding that professionals consider issues associated with AAC in ways that value self-
determination and cultural relevance, and that are informed by an
understanding of the critical role played by public policy in the lives
of people with disabilities.

The Future Is About Personnel Preparation

We must train the next generation of professionals to have the same
level of understanding of ideas of Johnson (Chapters 4 and 17) and
Rakhman (Chapter 8) as they now have of those of Beukelman and
Mirenda (1998). They will need to be as conversant in self-determination as they are in alternative access. Training programs must acknowledge changes in the philosophy of the field that include the
switch from a readiness model to a support model, from a professional-centric system to a consumer-centric system in response to
growing pressure for consumer participation, self-determination,
and even consumer control.

The Future Is About Public Policy

Identifying the "best" device for someone is nothing if we cannot also
understand and help shape public policy around what is and is not

worth purchasing. These personal stories make it clear that the kind of services that people receive, the supports and equipment they get, even their income, are driven by public policy. The limitations of what AAC can accomplish are political and economic rather than personal. With the availability of expensive electronic devices, the question is which device, at what cost, and who will pay for it. Authorization is now an important piece of the puzzle. With the political will and more money, many more people could have access to AAC. The limitation is the value placed on them as individuals and on their thoughts.

The Future Is About Empowerment

Communication is power; technology is power; self-determination is power. The next generation of people with severe communication impairments will follow the lead of these authors; they will not sheepishly follow therapists' orders. They will tell us what they want and need and fire us if we are nonresponsive. They will use current and new technologies in ways that differ from our best clinical judgement. They will be active partners in our research, and they will drive public policy. Finally, they will use their technology to say and do things which we did not recommend and in ways which we did not approve. And the next generation of professionals will see that as good news, which is an exciting prospect indeed!

REFERENCES

Balandin, S., & Raghavendra, P. (1999). Challenging oppression: Augmented communicators' involvement in AAC research. In F. Loncke, J. Clibbens, L. Lloyd, & H. Arvidson (Eds.), *Augmentative and alternative communication: New directions in research and practice* (pp. 262–277). London: Whurr.

Bersani, Jr., H.A. (1999). Nothing about me without me: A proposal for participatory action research in AAC. In F. Loncke, J. Clibbens, L. Lloyd, & H. Arvidson (Eds.), *Augmentative and alternative communication: New directions in research and practice* (pp. 278–289). London: Whurr.

Bradley, V.J. (1994) Evolution of a new service paradigm. In V.J. Bradley, J.W. Ashbaugh, & B.C. Blaney (Eds.), *Creating individual supports for people with developmental disabilities* (pp. 11–32). Baltimore: Paul H. Brookes Publishing Co.

Beukelman, D.R., & Mirenda, P. (1998). *Augmentative and alternative communication: Management of severe communication disorders in children and adults* (2nd ed.). Baltimore: Paul H. Brookes Publishing Co.

Kuhn, T.S. (1962). *The structure of scientific revolutions.* Chicago: University of Chicago Press.

Sacks, O. (1995). *An anthropologist on Mars: Seven paradoxical tales.* New York: Alfred A. Knopf.

Wehmeyer, M. (1998). Self-determination and individuals with significant disabilities: Examining meanings and misinterpretations. *The Journal of The Association for Persons with Severe Handicaps, 23*(1), 1–16.

CPSIA information can be obtained
at www.ICGtesting.com
Printed in the USA
LVHW050814070719
623350LV00012B/471